OLD MAIN

OLD MAIN

Small Colleges in Twenty-First Century America

Samuel Schuman

The Johns Hopkins University Press

BALTIMORE & LONDON

© 2005 The Johns Hopkins University Press
All rights reserved. Published 2005
Printed in the United States of America on acid-free paper
9 8 7 6 5 4 3 2 1

The Johns Hopkins University Press
2715 North Charles Street
Baltimore, Maryland 21218-4363
www.press.jhu.edu

Library of Congress Cataloging-in-Publication Data

Schuman, Samuel, 1942–
  Old Main : small colleges in twenty-first century America /
Samuel Schuman.
      p. cm.
  Includes bibliographical references and index.
  ISBN 0-8018-8092-0 (hardcover : alk. paper)
    1. Small colleges—United States. 2. Small colleges—United
States—History. I. Title.
  LB2328.3.S35 2005
  378.1′542—dc22   2004022998

A catalog record for this book is available from the British Library.

Title page illustration: Columbia College, South Carolina, 1930.
Used with permission.

Contents

OLD MAIN

1 | Introduction

> Approaching New Albion College from the east, the writer gained the crest
> of a hill crowned with blazing oak and gaudy maple and, upon glimpsing
> the distant campus through the trees, stopped the team so as to impress
> the agreeable vista on his memory, for against Nature's dying ostentation,
> New Albion unfolds a seemly tableau of such simple unaffected grandeur
> as to appear imagined, an apparition of Academe in the desolate forest,
> with its trim and handsome cottages, the well-laid walks and prome-
> nades, the orderly plantings of ornamental trees, and, bestriding all, the
> majestic spire of Main itself like an upraised finger calling all to stand in
> hushed wonder at what Providence had wrought.
>
> GARRISON KEILLOR, *Lake Wobegon Days*

On a substantial number of small college campuses in the United
States today, there is a venerable building, usually brick, often Victorian,
which is known as "Old Main." It often houses one or several offices of the
administration. The common institutional story is that when the campus
began it had but one building, and this was it. On many campuses today
that building is the college emblem, frequently depicted on the college's
logo, the cover of its view book, in snowy splendor on the presidential
Christmas card, or in similar conspicuous spots.

But it is my thesis that small colleges were, for most of U.S. history, the
"main" thread of our nation's higher education system, the defining core
of postsecondary opportunities for young men and women and their families. That centrality has been lost. Indeed, with only about 4 to 10 percent
of college students today enrolled in small colleges, these often venerable
and valuable institutions are also vulnerable: they are in some real danger
of being so peripheralized as to be irrelevant.[1] I believe this is a serious
threat not just to the small colleges themselves but to the network of
American colleges and universities of which they are a part. If we extract
the old, main thread from the fabric of our higher learning system, we will
have lost something irreplaceable. It is doubtful that the entire skein
would unravel, but I deeply believe it would be tragically poorer and depressingly duller.

Moreover, small colleges might well be the canaries in the mine of our postsecondary system. Their small size means that they respond more quickly and more visibly to the winds of change; as institutions, they have less weight and inertia than large universities. The challenges that small colleges face, and the happier opportunities before them, may presage those that all higher education will meet in the coming years.

Yet I have found a deep and pervasive worry about the future viability of the nation's small colleges throughout the higher education community, especially at the colleges themselves. That worry is tempered by the recognition that for more than two decades educational Jeremiahs have been predicting the demise of all or most small colleges, and yet the great majority of these institutions, the fragile as well as the secure, have shown tenacity and vigor and confounded the prophets of doom by surviving.[2]

This book is an admittedly partisan effort to describe the pasts and presents of our country's small colleges—the well-known, wealthy, and prestigious, the invisible and impoverished, and those in between—with their enormous variety of missions, histories, inhabitants, and resources. I will point with pride to their many virtues and with honesty to their failings, and I will make the case for the importance of their futures.

Bluntly, it is *not* my thesis that small colleges are "better" than large universities. It is my contention that they are different in kind, as well as volume, and that for some undergraduates (and I was one such) they are the best educational option. Oak trees are not better than maples or birches, but a healthy forest contains multiple plants. Some are better for making hardwood furniture, and some are better for making a canoe. Alas, some college students and professors try to build a canoe from the bark of an oak.

This book does not seek to be an exercise in historicism or, worse, nostalgia. The small colleges of the nineteenth and twentieth centuries were fascinating and valuable places, but they will not and should not persist as charming and irrelevant antiques in the new millennium. We need to rediscover the qualities at the center of our institutions which will remain of value to the twenty-first century and to reinvent our colleges to serve students in a new world.

In chapter 3 I discuss what I mean by *small college* and what was meant by that phrase at other times. For the purposes of this study the term means institutions that award primarily baccalaureate, four-year degrees and have between five hundred and three thousand full-time students.

In these next pages I will describe

—*why* this book was written: my sense of the need for such an utterance;

—*how* it was written: my methodology in writing it;

—for *whom* it was written: the audience I envision; and

—more on *what* it is I am writing about.

Why? Small Colleges and the Little House

One of the most enduring storybooks of my childhood, along with *Little Toot* and *The Little Engine That Could,* was the tale of *The Little House* in the city.[3] These are all stories of little guys surrounded by big things who come out okay by virtue of pluck, perseverance, hard work, and innate value.

This yarn is an obvious allegory with which to preface my discussion of small colleges in the United States. The children's book by Virginia Lee Burton (for those too young to recall it) begins with a perky little house: chimney puffing bucolic little clouds of clean smoke, yard well manicured, handsomely sited in an attractive country lot. Soon, however, the peace and privacy of the little house is threatened as other homes, of comparable size and character, develop around it. The suburban phase. Things begin to get really rough, however, as the neighborhood is increasingly given over to taller and larger buildings, closer and closer to the little house. At the crisis of the narrative the house cowers in the midst of the industrial and residential skyscraper development of what is clearly a major metropolitan area. Its sun is gone, its yard reduced to rubble, its happy existence now overshadowed by gigantic buildings, leaving the little house lost in the big city, a tiny relic of an archaic past. This story ends happily through the somewhat deus ex machina plot mechanism of moving the little house out of the big city and back into the country, where it once again fits into its surroundings. It is not so clear that small colleges in twenty-first-century America are heading for an equally happy ending.

The point of this childish prelude is clear. It was not the little house that changed but its neighborhood. The little house was a fine little house, but suddenly it found itself surrounded by gigantic new structures that took away its place in the sun. The little house didn't do anything wrong. It just stayed the way it was, while the whole world around it was transformed. Indeed, the owners may have done extensive internal remodeling and kept the place quite up-to-date (revised the curriculum, incorporated the latest technology, that sort of thing).[4] Nor, of course, is there anything wrong with office blocks and apartment houses and factories—at least there were very few folks who thought there was anything wrong with them in the postwar America in which I grew up having this charming tale read to me. The problem was not inherent in either type of structure: it derived from the competition over limited turf between entities that were created to do very different things and hence took very different shapes and made incompatible demands on the space they occupied together.

The crisis faced by small undergraduate colleges in the United States today is not with these colleges and programs; it is that huge new enterprises that have shot to the sky all around them now threaten to displace them. And these new places all have their own powerful claims to legitimacy and valid service to the commonwealth.

Prior to the Civil War and the founding of the Johns Hopkins University in the final quarter of the nineteenth century, *college* in the United States meant small, usually private and parochial, undergraduate liberal arts colleges. A mere century and a quarter later—not much time at all in the historical sweep of things or in the lives of colleges (or even, we sometimes suspect, in the calendar of decision making at small colleges)—institutions that focus upon the baccalaureate four years are surrounded by a daunting variety of huge, new structures:

—the major flagship public research universities, such as the land-grant universities

—several venerable and distinguished private research universities

—regional comprehensive universities, often with five-figure student populations, a smattering of graduate programs, and free-standing "colleges" of education or business as well as of arts and sciences

—a huge network of largely public two-year vocational institutes and community colleges

—an exploding for-profit postsecondary industry, often involving some deep commitment to distance learning and electronic instructional technology, such as the University of Phoenix

—corporate postsecondary options ranging from short training courses to virtual collegiate experiences under the aegis of, say, hamburger chains (We live in the era of the McBaccalaureate!)

The four-year, small college experience was for roughly half our national life the definitive collegiate experience. By the dawn of the twenty-first century this experience seemed perilously close to disappearing. We're still here, but the skyscrapers of higher learning that surround us increasingly block our sky. The largest collegiate institution in the country is the Community College of the Air Force, currently enrolling 378,000 students.[5]

Two options are not available to today's small colleges. We cannot roll back the clock and return to those bucolic days of a century ago when we were the only folks in town. Nor, with the redefinition of "in town" caused by the electronic revolution and universal air travel and the interstate highway system, can we pack up and move back to a Jeffersonian rural isolation that at least let the little house be itself again. One option, of course, is to try to become skyscrapers ourselves, and, in fact, most of the large group of institutions known as regional comprehensives began their lives as four-year colleges, often teachers' colleges, and have evolved into expanded institutions, with a university structure and graduate curriculum. And, as Breneman demonstrated, many small liberal arts colleges have adopted a survival strategy of attempting to grow through the addition or substitution of preprofessional options and programs of adult and continuing education (see the discussion of the College of New Rochelle which follows for a dramatic example).[6]

Some believe, however, that we may need something else—a different kind of zoning, perhaps, which lets the various mega-institutions have their space but reaffirms the value of ours, too. Some believe that the missions that animate small undergraduate colleges in the United States are anything but outdated or peripheral in this new millennium. Some believe that the humane scale, integrated educational experiences, and intimate communities of smaller colleges can be the optimal setting for many students to cultivate wisdom and learn the value of reflection. For many, small colleges can be the very best places for stimulating creative and critical thinking. Some believe that lifelong learning can mean, in addition to older people coming back to school, teaching all undergraduates the methodological habits of self-instruction which make lifelong learners not just of those who come back to our colleges but also of those who graduate from them and that small colleges make a powerful contribution to such a transformative education. Some of us, in short, believe that the small campus undergraduate experience is not just valuable but rightfully claims its place as the core collegiate unit, the sun around which the rest of the educational planets, even the giants, revolve. As Wellesley president Diana Chapman Walsh notes, even today when students speak of postsecondary education, they say, "I'm going to *college*," and it is small institutions that remain in the American consciousness as a kind of repository of the idea of "college."[7]

Surely it is obvious that I approach this topic from a position that could never be mistaken for that of a dispassionate observer. Since the day I set off for Grinnell College in 1960, I have found my personal and professional home in small liberal arts colleges. I write from the perspective of a partisan, one who can, I hope, be objective about the blemishes as well as the beauties of small colleges but one who is deeply and irrevocably devoted to them.

Virginia Lee Burton's book did not mean to decry hotels or factories or office towers or even to say that the little house was a better structure than those sorts of buildings. What the book claimed, and what I believe, is that only one of these many important and imposing sorts of places is built as a home for humans. Our undergraduate colleges offer places of a sort and scale in which our students can come to know themselves and one another, in which students and teachers live in humane proximity, with enough shelter to be safe and enough space to be free. This is a neighborhood American higher education can't afford to lose.

How? Methodology

This book is an unapologetic combination of induction and deduction, of research and editorial. As part of my research, I read most of the relevant major published studies on postsecondary education and reviewed about 150 doctoral dissertations. I also examined a number of more particularized publications and materials (college catalogs, self-studies, admissions materials, histories, Web sites, and the like).

Perhaps the first lesson one learns from this research is how little these two sorts of printed materials seem to have to do with one another. Many of the general studies of higher education pay scant attention to particular institutions but deal with sweeping statistics (e.g., the number of degrees granted annually in 1850 and 1950). That broad picture is important, especially in contextualizing small colleges, but it tends to leave the reader hungry, as one might be after reading the menu but never tasting the actual victuals. Conversely, writing about individual colleges rarely seeks to link the institutions to the historical or ideological context that gives broad meaning to their development, struggles, commonalities, and idiosyncrasies. While this odd bifurcation is by no means universal, I suspect it is not unfamiliar to anyone who has read widely about colleges and universities. I hope I have made some contribution to moving these two perspectives closer to each other, in a way that helps give depth and texture to both the general and the particular.

A second lesson one rapidly assimilates in reading in this area is the difficulty, indeed the impossibility, of making accurate predictions about colleges and universities over a period even as brief as a decade. It is sobering to read one study after another, from the 1960s and 1970s for instance, written by well-informed, serious, thoughtful scholars who have their facts right and who view their contemporary scenes with discernment and wisdom but who are dead wrong about the next decade. One encounters thoughtful assurances that small colleges, especially those not blessed with an elite national reputation, will surely disappear—which they did not. One reads that historically African American institutions will either lose their black identity and merge into a homogenized universal American collegiate system or disappear—which they have not. One discovers that single-sex institutions or strongly sectarian ones will, perforce, soon lose their uniqueness—many have not (although the number of single-sex institutions, especially men's colleges, has declined). One learns that all liberal arts colleges, or at least all but the national elite, will have to give over their curricula to vocational subjects, or perish—which they have not. The list is depressingly long. The moral is bracingly obvious: American higher education, especially its small colleges, is unpredictable, elusive, and unexpectedly resilient. If, knowing the embarrassingly poor record of predictions for our colleges and universities by observers more informed and more thoughtful than this writer, I have still occasionally ventured to hazard a forecast, it is only a confirmation that fools rush in where angels *have* tread . . . on a landmine.

The final lesson to be gleaned from extensive reading in this area is to respect one's predecessors. From the wise erudition of David Riesman and Christopher Jencks to the thoroughness of A. M. Cohen to the passion of Derek Bok and David Breneman to the straightforward responsibility of Ernest Boyer to the moral sensitivity of Parker Palmer or Robert Putnam to the reasoned wisdom of Eva T. H. Brann, anyone who writes about colleges at the dawn of the twenty-first century is treading on a pathway that has been walked before by giants. It is a journey as pleasurable as it is daunting.

I have supplemented bibliographic research with fieldwork. I visited a small, carefully selected group of colleges and made a pest of myself during those visits, asking irritating questions that, with astonishing grace, dozens of students, faculty, staff, and others have answered. The colleges I visited are these, listed from West to East:

—George Fox University, Newburg, Oregon

—Westmont College, Santa Barbara, California

—Southwestern University, Georgetown, Texas

—Grinnell College, Grinnell, Iowa

—Minneapolis College of Art and Design, Minneapolis, Minnesota

—The University of Wisconsin–Superior, Superior, Wisconsin

—Centenary College, Shreveport, Louisiana

—Warren Wilson College, Asheville, North Carolina

—Morehouse College, Atlanta, Georgia

—The College of New Rochelle, New Rochelle, New York

—Colby-Sawyer College, New London, New Hampshire

—Wellesley College, Wellesley, Massachusetts

A brief narrative and quantitative portrait of these dozen institutions is appended (see app. B).

Of course, no group of 12—or 112—colleges can honestly catch the diverse range of the nation's smaller institutions. But this group was selected to provide a varied sampling. It includes institutions from both coasts and north to Lake Superior and south to the Gulf of Mexico. Some of these colleges enroll fewer than 1,000 students, some from 1,000 to 2,000, and others between 2,000 and 3,000. The list includes coed as well as single-sex institutions. I visited some well-known and prestigious schools and others that labor in relative obscurity, some that possess ample fiscal resources and some that are undoubtedly poor. There are public and private colleges here as well as sharply focused liberal arts institutions, others with a much broader emphasis, and some with an entirely different, professional mission. Some of these colleges were founded in the nineteenth century, others as recently as the second half of the twentieth. All four tiers of the Carnegie National Liberal Arts College classification are represented, as are institutions ranked as regional comprehensive bachelor's and regional comprehensive master's schools. Some of these colleges were once religious but are no longer, some still are, and some never were. Several evolved from very different sorts of institutions (e.g., academies or junior colleges and former single-sex institutions now coed), while others have held a remarkably consistent focus.

At each school I endeavored, usually with success, to meet with

—the president/chancellor

—the chief academic officer

—other members of the senior leadership group

—some faculty

—some students

—a member or members of the governing body (e.g., regents, visitors, and trustees)

At these very diverse dozen institutions, then, I spoke to approximately two hundred individuals.

To each of these individuals and groups I asked roughly the same group of questions (see app. A), with some sensible variation by group (e.g., I did not ask trustees why they decided to come to work at the college; I did not ask students why they decided to serve as voluntary leadership for it; and so on). The level of candor and insight of the responses was gratifying and often happily astonishing. I am very thankful to each of the presidents of these fascinating and valuable schools for their hospitality and openness. And the hundreds of students, faculty, and staff who have patiently shared with me their reactions to my queries and their assessments of their home institutions have a real share of any insight this book may contain. Especially helpful has been a group of astonishingly competent and underpraised professionals, the assistants in the offices of the presidents, who actually made all this happen with grace and graciousness. Not the least of the assistants is mine, Carrie Grussing.

I also perused a fulsome package of materials provided by each institution and diligently clicked through countless relevant links on their respective home pages.

Finally, I have shamelessly badgered close friends and distant colleagues about almost everything I have considered in the following pages.

Many conversations, formal and casual, have had a significant impact on my conclusions and my writing. In particular, Jerry Gaff of the American Association of Colleges and Universities (AAC&U), Richard Ekman of the Council of Independent Colleges (CIC), Rew Godow of the College of Charleston, Anne Ponder of Colby-Sawyer College, and Richie Zweigenhaft of Guilford College have been patient and wise consultants, readers, and guides.

In sum, my analytic methodology was this: I began with some of my own partially formed thoughts and opinions about small colleges in twenty-first-century America. Extensive reading shaped these personal convictions into focused, test-worthy theses—for example, that small colleges work successfully to cultivate campus-wide communities and that small institutions seek to offer students an integrated educational experience that combines the curricular, cocurricular, and extracurricular dimensions of college life. Finally, I tested those theses by conducting over 230 interviews on twelve carefully selected small college campuses.

I hope this volume will answer some questions about small colleges, but it is also my aspiration to raise some important questions for others to continue to pursue. In addition to being a work of academic research, this book is also a polemic, an effort of advocacy. I write from a position *within* my subject, not as an objective outsider. I was an undergraduate at a small midwestern liberal arts college, taught at smaller institutions (and a few large ones), and served as the chief academic officer of a small southern college for a decade and as the chief executive at two public liberal arts colleges. I have served as a consultant at a couple dozen small colleges, met my wife at one, and sent our children to others as students and teachers. From my first day as a callow first-year student until today, small colleges have been my vocational and spiritual homes. I therefore make no claims of detached objectivity. My overt goal is to articulate the best case for the kind of collegiate institutions to which I am devoted. In the pages that follow, I make an effort to find and identify what I think is best about such places and to argue for their value and continuing importance. Worthwhile writing comes with conviction and takes a position: I believe it is much better to recognize overtly one's perspective than to try to erase it.

At the same time, I have tried to be both clear-eyed and candid about the weaknesses and failings of these schools. Indeed, it could be argued that only an "insider" at a small college can have a comprehensive and persuasive grasp of such institutions at their worst. As a student, faculty member, and administrator, I have certainly seen colleges behaving in petty, inhumane, self-referential, and counterproductive ways. Once or twice, or even more, I have behaved that way myself in such settings. Small colleges can be exclusive (in the worst sense) without being good, intolerant while priding themselves on being open, and too often come to see geographical and cultural isolation as an unmixed blessing. What to sentimental outsiders may seem nostalgic and quaint, from up close is all too often timid academic conservatism, closed-mindedness, and fear of the larger academic (and social, business, political, and cultural) world. My hope is that, if I am close enough to the small college cosmos to embrace it fervently, I am also close enough to see and describe accurately its many blemishes.

For good or ill, however, I need to be clear that in addition to basing my argument in the pages that follow upon evidence, I also base it on conviction, aspiration, and experience. I hope that I have been straightforward about which mode I am in, although I am aware that sometimes I am in both. In any event the reader is cautioned to remember that I am an unabashed partisan of that which I describe on these pages, and that affiliation surely colors both what I say and how I say it.

For Whom?

My hope, of course, is that that several groups of readers will find this book interesting and useful. First are those who are about to or recently have come to a small college, as teachers, leaders, staff, or students. Because the cultures of small colleges tend to be self-contained and because our communities are, in fact, small, we are tempted to assume that everyone knows as much about us as we do ourselves. One of the most common sights on a small college campus in autumn is that of an absolutely baffled new member of the college community plaintively searching for someplace called "HFA" or "ARH" or the "ASC" or even the "cow palace." (These are, respectively, the "Humanities / Fine Arts Building," "Alumni Recitation Hall"—still so-called at one college a half-century since students were required to do "recitation"—the "academic skills center," and a small auditorium on my home campus that was used as a venue for judging cattle forty-five years ago, when the predecessor institution was an agricultural high school, and is now used for introductory psychology courses.) The abbreviation that everyone assumes a newcomer will know, and which, realistically, no newcomer could be expected to know or guess, is an emblem of the frequently too-casual orientation small colleges offer to neophytes. While each institution needs to introduce itself to new members individually, there is, I hope, some value in this study as a kind of generic introduction. I would hope this volume might have utility as part of a formal faculty-staff orientation program at small colleges or as an informal resource for those about to begin a career there. All too often, we expect new hires, in faculty or administrative positions, to "hit the ground running" but fail to tell them what ground they will hit. Then we watch with horror as they take us at our word and run right into a tree or off a cliff. *Old Main* offers a road map to decrease the chances of such a painful start.

With this audience in mind, I have included as an epilogue pragmatic advice to small college newcomers, specifically new teachers. In this, my model is Ernest Boyer's *College: The Undergraduate Experience in America*,[8] which has as its epilogue a guide to parents and prospective students to assist in the college selection process. In both instances the conclusionary piece recapitulates much of the abstract and reflective material that precedes it, reformulated to offer concrete advice.

Similarly, I hope this book might be a good resource in programs such as the "Preparing Future Faculty" work of the American Association of Colleges and Universities and similar endeavors on other graduate campuses which mentor graduate students considering embarking on teaching careers at institutions large and small. Since these graduate students are, by definition, currently embedded in institutions large enough to house Ph.D. programs, there is a particularly strong need to balance introductions to the research university with some equivalent scrutiny and study of the small college.

Because this book approaches U.S. higher education from the perspective of the small college, I believe it will help round out the bibliography of works on the contemporary collegiate scene for students and researchers in the field of education studies, especially higher education studies. In particular, it is significant that my focus is on size, more than curriculum. Although *Old Main* is largely about institutions that call themselves, in some form or another, "liberal arts colleges," I am keenly interested in institutions that maintain their small size but do not exclusively offer a tightly defined and structured traditional liberal education. While this is not a study that includes attention to two-year institutions or proprietary vocational institutes (e.g., schools of fashion merchandising or aeronautics), my perspective is significantly different than, say, that of David Breneman, who focuses rigorously on liberal learning.[9] In addition to studying traditional, focused liberal arts colleges, such as Centenary or Morehouse, this book also features institutions such as Colby-Sawyer College, which explicitly seeks to link liberal learning with career preparation, or Westmont College, which defines its identity as a religious institution as well as one committed to liberal learning, or the Minneapolis College of Art and Design, a preprofessional art college with a solid but modest general education component. I believe that this shift of focus, from liberal arts curriculum to institutional size, offers a different point of view of particular institutions and the national context within which they exist. As Virginia Smith and Alison Bernstein argue persuasively, there is a strong "relationship of an institution's *size* to its educational effectiveness."[10]

Further, many of the definitive studies of small colleges and of liberal learning in the concluding quarter of the twentieth century seem dated. It is not that the basic conclusions of thoughtful observers such as Boyer, Riesman, and Breneman are no longer valid. But some of the cases and data on which those conclusions were based have been overtaken by "time's winged chariot." For example, many of the experimental institutions studied by Riesman and others in the 1970s and 1980s have changed beyond recognition or, alas, disappeared altogether.[11] Winter, McClelland, and Stewart's *A New Case for the Liberal Arts,* now over two decades in print, is no longer convincingly "new."[12] This study should help to reanimate and update earlier work and engender more research and empirical studies of small college processes and trends.

I write as well for those administrators, teachers, and pupils who already work and study at small colleges, sense that they are part of something valuable and vital in the national postsecondary matrix, but seek the language and evidence to support that feeling. I do think small colleges need advocates and defenders and that these representatives need to be more articulate and more informed than they have been. The same rationale would apply to engaged alumni of small colleges.

Guidance counselors and parents of prospective college students should find this book a helpful introduction to one large class of American institutions, focusing mostly upon their assets but not neglecting their liabilities. Two additional groups that have been suggested as potential readers of this book are trustees of small colleges (especially those who do not have a background that includes prior experience at such places) and education policy analysts and policy makers.

Finally, it is my aspiration that this work will be of interest and value to that most elusive of creatures, the general reader. Because the institutions studied in *Old Main* are idiosyncratic and unique, they are interesting. Each tells a different story, exhibits a different culture, and appeals to different people. In their quirks and infinite variety their histories and characters are intrinsically fascinating and entertaining. More significantly, however, small colleges have been important to our nation, they continue to be, and will remain so in the future. Thoughtful citizens, including those who are not professional students or practitioners of higher learning, need to know something about these colleges. The history, contributions, challenges, and virtues of these institutions merit serious contemplation for everyone interested in the future and culture of our country.

What? The Size Variable

Vague language and conception often muddle both formal research and casual discussions of small colleges. Because a certain constellation of institutional attributes tend to occur together, I believe that some measurable (and measured) effects of the college experience have been at least partially attributed incorrectly to institutional "type" rather than "size." The three characteristics "small," "liberal arts," and "private" are commonly, but not accurately, conjoined. Size, curricular focus, and charter status are not the same things, nor are they mutually controlling factors. Thus, not all liberal learning takes place in small institutions, nor are all public institutions large and private ones small. Institutions may manifest one, two, or all three of these characteristics, but much research seems to presume their inevitable concatenation.

For example, the Carnegie Foundation survey of undergraduates asked students to agree or disagree with the statement "On the whole, I trust the faculty here to look out for students' interests."[13] The responses were analyzed in terms of public and private institutions, then broken down thus, giving the percentage of students who had agreed with the statement:

Research universities	71%
Doctorate-granting universities	72%
Comprehensive colleges	75%
Liberal arts colleges	88%

But it is worth asking if student-faculty trust is actually connected to a liberal arts curriculum or to other factors that might be commonly but not inevitably connected to colleges that focus on the liberal arts. This list of institutional type with its ascending scale of student trust of faculty ranks institutions by the level of their most advanced programs. But it is also a list that surely descends in institutional size and shows a marked correlation between collegiate smallness and student trust in the faculty.

Similarly, Winter, McClelland, and Stewart report research that shows "students at private colleges are more satisfied with faculty contact and quality than are other students . . . [and] private college students become more verbally aggressive in class."[14] It is not likely that faculty contact and classroom participation are really influenced by whether the sources of institutional operating funding are public dollars or private tuition nor by whether or not students can afford private institutions. More likely, this result is actually a consequence of the fact that public institutions are, on average, larger than private ones, with less student-faculty contact and fewer give-and-take discussion classes.

Fortunately, we do not have to depend on belief or intuition: it is possible to investigate in a careful, quantitative manner some of the effects of the size variable, vis-à-vis the "public/private" and "liberal arts" factors. Institutional research at small, *public* liberal arts colleges shows very high scores on similar questions over a range of issues similar to those noted in the Winter, McClelland, and Stewart research and the Carnegie survey. Moreover, the results for small *public* liberal arts colleges do not show any significant variation from those at small *private* liberal arts colleges. In the 2002 National Survey of Student Engagement, for example, students at *public* liberal arts colleges were more likely, as seniors, to report that they had "made a class presentation" than either the entire all-college sample or all public and private combined baccalaureate–liberal arts college students.[15] They rated their satisfaction with learning relationships with faculty at 5.76 on a 7-point scale, compared with a national average of 5.55.

Similar results were found in a long-range study of student satisfaction at the four campuses of the University of Minnesota (UM). The two small campuses in the university system, a liberal arts campus at Morris and a polytechnic/vocational campus in Crookston, scored higher on questions probing students' perceptions of the quality of the teaching faculty they encountered, active learning, quality of feedback from professors, and faculty availability than students on either of the two larger campuses (Duluth, a "comprehensive college," and Twin Cities, a "research university"). Yet the two larger campuses have a significantly greater proportion of liberal arts departments and student majors than does UM-Crookston, which focuses upon technical, vocational subjects. A series of questions about perceived quality of advising also showed the two small campuses scored well ahead of the undergraduate opinion on the two larger ones. Thus, in this carefully controlled, longitudinal study, the variable that seems to account for student perception of quality of teaching and advising is smallness, not liberal arts.[16]

It seems both intuitively obvious and statistically demonstrable that the relationship among the three institutional characteristics I have been examining is not a simple matter and has perhaps been oversimplified. Although it is common to link small size, private control, and liberal arts mission, there is no necessary tie between any of these institutional descriptors. As Howard Bowen points out, "Because most small colleges specialize in liberal education . . . it is difficult to sort out the separate effects of small size and dedication to liberal learning."[17] As noted earlier, it is also the case that since the 1970s many former liberal arts colleges have shifted to primarily offering preprofessional majors. So, many institutions fall outside of this pattern, including several among the research sample of colleges examined in this study. (Some of those schools are small and private but do not define their mission primarily as "liberal arts"; one is small and emphasizes liberal learning but is in the public sector.) Each of the three dimensions can produce different patterns of institutional character and student experience, independently and together.

I belabor this point because it is central to what follows. Smallness is significant, as is curricular emphasis and the public or private oversight status of a college or university. Further research examining and evaluating the complex relationship between these variables would be valuable in clarifying the precise effects controlled by each.

Whither? What Lies Ahead

The chapters that follow offer

—a survey of the history of American higher education from the somewhat unusual vantage point of the evolution of small colleges;

—a view of some of the ways in which small institutions are distinctive, even among themselves;

—an overview of the students, faculty, and staff who live, study, and work at small colleges;

—a discussion of their shared characteristics and the values they bring to the fabric of the nation's postsecondary scene, particularly in the two areas I am calling "community" and "integrity";

—some examples of how small colleges and large universities are trying to learn from one another;

—thoughts about how the values of small colleges are connected to other aspects of contemporary American life; and

—a series of concrete observations and suggestions about life within a small college.

Following each chapter the reader will find a true short story of a person whose life is intertwined with small colleges. My goal here is transparent: to link the abstractions at the national and institutional level with the concrete and human. Indeed, such an endeavor seems to me an emblem of what small colleges actually *do*—deal with real people, one at a time. In the case of this, the first chapter, and the last, I focus upon students in small colleges. Following this chapter, I describe the college career of a bright and assertive young woman from a tiny town in the rural upper Midwest who was a first-generation college-goer. The personal attention she received there and the chances to try her wings in a remarkable variety of curricular and cocurricular activities are a testimony to the best that small colleges can do for their students.

It is reasonable to anticipate that, ten or twenty-five or fifty years from now, this volume will strike the occasional curious or accidental reader as a quaintly outdated picture of a world that has continued to evolve. To that mid-twenty-first-century reader the struggles and challenges depicted here will be yesterday's news, the unrealized aspirations of today may have become commonplace accomplishments, and new dreams and fears will have supplanted those I have sought to delineate in these pages. I hope so.

A Lawyer from Plummer

Lorie Skjerven Gildea came to the University of Minnesota, Morris (UMM), in 1979 from Plummer, Minnesota, population of about three hundred, located a little over 100 miles north of Morris, which in turn is located about 160 miles northwest of Minneapolis, deep in rural, agricultural west central Minnesota.

Lorie's parents were hardworking and modestly successful. Her mother, with a gift for numbers, worked as a bookkeeper in a local discount department store. Her father ran a small gas station and supplied petroleum products to local farmers. Lorie and her older sister, who began college a year before her, were the first in their family to go on from high school to postsecondary education.

Ever since she could remember, Lorie had wanted to be a lawyer, and her high school counselor and other advisors encouraged her to get a fine liberal education as a first step along that career path. So, she applied to and was accepted at UMM, a public liberal arts college, where she became a political science major. Coming from a family of modest means, she was attracted in part to UMM because of the access afforded by low tuition at a public liberal arts college and by a handsome scholarship.

Although she developed into an excellent collegiate academic achiever, Lorie was hardly a single-minded grind. In addition to her classroom labors, she was a very active member of the band. As her career progressed, she decided to put some of her political science theory into local practice, so she became active in student government and eventually ran for and won the important leadership post of president of the Morris Campus Student Association. Her academic record at UMM was exceptional. Completing her undergraduate career with a perfect 4.0 grade point average, she won one of the college's major student academic prizes. At graduation she received another important award for overall contributions to campus life.

As her undergraduate days drew to a close, in 1983, Lorie's academic advisor, a venerable political scientist, encouraged her to set her professional school goals high and to apply to some of the nation's top law schools. This seemed a little immodest for someone from Plummer, Minnesota, graduating from UMM, but turned out to be good advice. She was accepted at Georgetown

University Law School, where she had a very successful career, graduating magna cum laude.

With her splendid academic history this small college alum could have gone just about anywhere to practice law and could have made heaps of money, some of which she would have given back to her alma mater. Instead, like most UMM graduates, she came back to Minnesota. And she decided to pursue a career in law in the public sector. Today she works as one of several lawyers in the general counsel's office of the University of Minnesota, on the Twin Cities campus. She is a leading litigator, taking a principal role in some of the dismayingly large number of UM legal matters dealing with intercollegiate athletics in the Twin Cities.

Today, reflecting back on her undergraduate experience, Lorie Gildea says:

I grew up in a town of approximately three hundred people (no stoplights and no street signs), and there were thirty-three students in my high school graduating class. Even though I grew up in a small place, I was a teenager with big dreams. Attending a small college allowed me to realize those dreams. At a small college I was able to participate in things that were important to me from the very beginning, and to assume leadership roles when I was ready. I was exposed to new ideas, taught to think and to take risks, while in an environment that made me feel safe and unique. I never felt like I was just one more number in a long line of numbers. I felt valued, and I felt relevant. In short, the day I decided to attend a small college was one of the best days of my life.

2 | Go West, Young Man

The role played by quiet fanaticism is often not perceived
in the history of colleges.

BURTON R. CLARKE, *The Distinctive College*

Where do the nation's small colleges come from? The history of higher education in the United States has been told often and well and does not need lengthy reiteration. Like all historical stories, however, it makes a significant difference who is speaking to whom and to what purpose. What one sees depends both on what is there and the lens through which one peers. Looking at the evolution of American postsecondary learning from the perspective of contemporary small colleges tells us much about those colleges today and provides an unconventional view of the development of higher learning in the nation over the last three and a half centuries. As Oakley suggests, to understand the ethos of colleges it is necessary to grasp "the dense particularities of their specific individual histories."[1] It is not possible to comprehend the vast range of contemporary higher education in this country, and the place of small colleges within that rich mosaic, without historical perspective. Today's colleges are embedded in their own stories and within the fabric of the development of the complex system and culture of contemporary postsecondary opportunities in our country.

In the following pages I draw on many of the institutions from my site visits as illustrations, not so much because these colleges were particularly important in the history of higher education in the United States but because they exemplify aspects of that story. So, for example, the development of the University of Wisconsin–Superior is neither unique nor remarkable, but it is an almost perfect example of the evolution of a public normal college into a small campus within a large, overarching state system of colleges and universities. (The college began as early as 1893 as Superior Normal School; was renamed Superior State Teachers College in 1926, the same year it awarded its first baccalaureate degrees; and became part of the University of Wisconsin system, with its current name, in

1971.) None of the colleges in my sample began in the colonial period, and none were founded after World War II. Still, there is over a century between the formal founding of Centenary in 1825 and of Westmont in 1937. Moreover, many of these institutions have changed remarkably over the years, including the second half of the twentieth century (see tables 2.1 and 2.2). A good place to start is by noting that in the beginning *all* the na-

Table 2.1 Founding Dates

College	Official Date First, then Year of Current Location/Name/Mission	
Centenary	1825	1908
Colby-Sawyer	1837	1989
Southwestern	1840	1875
Grinnell	1846	1858
Morehouse	1867	1897
Wellesley	1870	
Minneapolis College of Art and Design	1886	
George Fox	1891	1949
University of Wisconsin–Superior	1893	1971
Warren Wilson	1894	1966
College of New Rochelle	1904	
Westmont	1937	1945

1625 to 1800   1825   1850   1875   1900   1925   1950   1975   2000

Civil War   World War II

Table 2.2 The Shaping of American Higher Education

Year	National Population	No. Enrolled Students	No. Faculty	No. Institutions	No. Degrees Earned
1700	250,000	150	5	2	15
1790	3,929,214	1,050	141	11	240
1870	39,818,449	63,000	5,553	250	14,080
1945	139,924,000	1,677,080	150,000	1,768	157,349
1975	215,465,000	11,185,000	628,080	2,747	1,665,553
1995	262,755,000	14,262,000	915,000	3,706	2,246,300

Source: Adapted from Arthur M. Cohen, *The Shaping of American Higher Education: Emergence and Growth of the Contemporary System* (San Francisco: Jossey-Bass, 1998).

tion's colleges were "small colleges," and that condition persisted for over half the current life of the United States.

Colonial Colleges, 1636–1776

Nine currently surviving institutions of higher learning were founded in the United States before the Revolutionary War. Most were begun under a mixture of public and sectarian sponsorship; all have grown into complex, multi-college universities. Harvard was chartered, generically, as a "school or college" in what was then Newtown, Massachusetts, on 28 October 1636. It granted its first degrees in 1642 and did not reach the level of one hundred graduates until after the Civil War. Harvard was followed by William and Mary (1693), Yale (1701), Princeton (1746), Columbia (1754), the University of Pennsylvania (1755), Brown (1765), Rutgers (1766), and Dartmouth (1769). At the conclusion of the colonial era, there were no more than 135 collegiate faculty members (usually then called "tutors") in the United States, teaching about one thousand students—the size of *one* small college today.[2] All of these students and all of their teachers were male, and all were white.

Given the nation's infancy, it is not surprising that this is a relatively short, albeit distinguished, list of schools and that all the institutions on it are geographically proximate. While there are certainly substantial differences between, say, Dartmouth and Columbia, it is not difficult to perceive a certain fraternal resemblance between the contemporary versions of these early institutions. They retain strong undergraduate programs, for example, with substantial strength in the liberal arts. All offer a number of prestigious professional degrees. All are highly selective in admissions and certainly have national name recognition.

All nine institutions today could reasonably be described as "mid-sized universities." The smallest, Dartmouth, has about 5,000 students; the largest, Pennsylvania, about 22,500. This is quite a range, but, compared to the difference between, say, Bluffton College of Ohio and Ohio State University, where the latter is nearly one hundred times larger than the former, it is not that dramatic.[3] Although all began as very small schools, not one of the colonial colleges has remained a small, undergraduate institution, nor have any of them expanded into mega-universities.

Colonial college curricula were mandated for every pupil; elective student choice was not a possibility until after the Civil War. Studies in religion and in the classics predominated. According to one description of the early Harvard curriculum: "Aristotelian logic and physics, arithmetic, geometry, astronomy, grammar, rhetoric, dialectic, etymology, syntax and prosodia [sic] were taught for the purpose of disciplining the mind. Upperclassmen studied Greek and Hebrew grammar and there were occasional lectures in history and natural science. Students were expected to declaim once a month and great stress was placed on study of the Bible. For a degree the student had to present evidence of his ability to read the Scriptures in Latin."[4] In its first year Harvard offered twelve subjects, all taken by every student and all taught by Harvard's president, Henry Dunster. This narrow, universal core "general education" curriculum was characteristic of all the colonial colleges.[5]

Looking forward to the evolution of today's small colleges, these founding institutions are important in that they defined a pattern for American higher education which was, from its earliest days, distinct from its European antecedents and out of which grew all our contemporary institutions. Most of the colonial colleges, for example, had a religious affiliation (some changed that affiliation more than once in the intervening centuries; some lost it; some still have it today). So do most of today's small colleges. Most had the education of clerics as an important part of their early mission but not as their entire function. Higher education in the colonies, and subsequently in the United States, was never seen as the exclusive domain of the religious denominations. From the earliest days our colleges and universities were seen as playing a civic role in addition to a religious one, with some corresponding degree of public control in partnership with sectarian oversight. As Richard Hofstadter and Wilson Smith point out, the founders of Harvard and the colonial colleges "did not distinguish sharply between secular and theological learning," and Harvard was simultaneously and seamlessly a Puritan creation and a legal civic institution created by an act of the General Court.[6] Indeed, it was precisely the distinction between public and private collegiate sponsorship that was to be contested almost a half-century after the Revolution in the Dartmouth College case.

In the next era of higher educational history in the United States many issues—the role of religion in higher learning, the relationship between public and private control, the education of women, and the role of colleges on the expanding westward frontier—would move to the forefront of national debate, just as the foundations of many of today's small colleges were first being built.

From the Revolution to the Civil War, 1776–1860

While the first century and a quarter of our history produced fewer than 10 surviving institutions of higher learning, the next ninety years were a time of prolific college creation. Depending on exactly how one counts such a moving target (e.g., how one accounts for merged institutions or those that physically moved), about 180 colleges in the United States when the Civil War began still exist today. Many more came and went, some overnight, some surviving for decades: "The colleges tended to be exceedingly weak—underfunded, too small to support a broad curriculum, too poor to pay their staffs more than a subsistence wage, and in many cases, too marginal even to survive."[7] One source suggests that the mortality rate of colleges, universities, seminaries, institutes, and all degree-granting institutions during this period may have been as high as 81 percent.[8] As the frontier moved westward, many new communities quickly established collegiate institutes, many the unrealistic enterprise of a single energetic individual and others that continue today as distinguished and venerated colleges.

Of 212 colleges identified by Breneman as "true" liberal arts institutions, almost half (103) began before 1860.[9] The list of surviving small colleges founded during this period begins with Washington College, Washington and Lee, Hampden-Sydney, Transylvania, Dickinson, St. John's (Maryland), the College of Charleston, and Franklin and Marshall, all of which were created in the 1780s. It ends with 44 such institutions founded in the 1850s, including Cornell College, Haverford, the University of the South, and Vassar. Within my group of sample colleges, four were founded after the colonial period and before the Civil War: Centenary College (1825), Colby-Sawyer College (1837), Southwestern University (1840), and Grinnell College (1846). Not one of these institutions originally had its current name, however, and three of the four were in different locations.

The years preceding the Civil War were obviously key in creating the identity of today's small American colleges. It is risky to generalize about one hundred institutions created over nearly as many years, but some common characteristics are clearly discernible.

Most of the institutions founded during this period were sectarian in sponsorship, and most of them were Protestant. Presbyterian institutions dominate, followed by Methodist schools (later in the period, after a shift in the Wesleyan movement led to the conviction that an educated clergy was not necessarily one lacking religious fervor and enthusiasm). Baptists, Congregationalists, Friends, Episcopalians, Lutherans, and Brethren also established colleges. There were fourteen Catholic institutions in the United States before the Civil War. As during the colonial period, most of these sectarian institutions trained ministers, and educated others as well. One of the strongest impulses leading to the creation of colleges in the period between the Revolution and the Civil War was the emphasis on evangelism of the "Second Great Awakening" of mid-nineteenth-century American Protestantism. Unlike the Calvinists of the colonial period, who emphasized humankind's "utter incapacity to overcome this [sinful] nature without the direct action of the grace of God," mid-nineteenth-century evangelists focused on human deeds and the importance of virtuous actions.[10] They thought colleges a promising venue for inculcating such behaviors, a belief still deeply held in some quarters today.

The majority of colleges founded in this period were in one sense or another "frontier" institutions. That is, the pattern of college creation tended to move westward as American enterprise expanded away from the Northern Atlantic seaboard. While some institutions (e.g., Vassar and Seton

Hall) were created in the older, more populous and settled regions of the country, it is during this era that colleges were created in the Carolinas, Alabama, Illinois, Louisiana, Missouri, Wisconsin, Iowa, Minnesota, Kansas, Texas, and California. Americans were putting down roots in the western territories, and colleges were one of the first and most important roots they thought about. "The American college was typically a frontier institution," says Tewksbury, citing Absalom Peters's "Discourse before the Society for the Promotion of Collegiate and Theological Education in the West" of 1851: "Our country is to be a land of colleges."[11]

As frontier institutions, these early Protestant colleges were far from stable. For example, Centenary College began its life as "the College of Louisiana" in 1825 in Jackson, Louisiana. Later the Methodist Conference of Mississippi and Louisiana created another school, in 1839, called "Centenary College" in honor of the centenary of Wesley's foundation of the first Methodist Society. In 1845 the two schools merged, in Jackson, operating under the charter of the elder. Then, in 1908, the Jackson campus never having completely recovered from the ravages of the Civil War, the college moved to its present location in Shreveport.[12] Similarly, Grinnell College was founded in 1846 as "Iowa College" in the city of Davenport. In 1558 it moved to the town of Grinnell, well over one hundred miles to the west, and changed its name to recognize J. B. Grinnell, the institution's first significant benefactor. (It was Josiah B. Grinnell to whom Horace Greeley had said, famously, "Go west, young man.")[13]

Like Centenary, many of today's small colleges represent consolidations of two or more earlier institutions. Today's Southwestern University in Texas represents the coming together of four "root colleges": Rutersville College (1840); Wesleyan College (1844), which combined with San Augustine University in 1847 as the private University of Eastern Texas; McKenzie Institute (1839); and Chappell Hill [sic] Male and Female College, which in 1854 was taken over by the Methodists and named Soule University. Finally, in 1873 the four institutions were combined as a single Methodist college in the current location in Georgetown and called "Texas University." Two years later the name was changed to Southwestern University, and it was only at this point that "the name Texas University was relinquished to the state."[14]

One pivotal moment in this story occurred in 1816, when the legislature of New Hampshire attempted to wrest Dartmouth College from private control. The United States Supreme Court's ultimate decision in the

Dartmouth College Case upheld the legitimacy of the charters of private institutions and encouraged the continued foundation and proliferation of small, sectarian, private colleges. It is difficult to imagine the changed landscape of American higher education, particularly in regards to the nation's small private colleges, had the decision gone the other way. Arguing the case, Daniel Webster uttered his famous peroration: "It is, Sir, as I have said, a small college. And yet there are those who love it."

By 1825 Harvard, the nation's oldest college, now nearing the end of its second century, had grown to 234 undergraduates and 407 students altogether, counting 118 medical students. The cost of instruction was fifty-five dollars per year.

Other important developments filled these ninety years as well, including important steps in the collegiate education of American women and minorities, many of which began in institutions that continue today as small colleges. Daring experiments in collegiate coeducation were taking place during the first half of the nineteenth century. In 1837 Oberlin College matriculated four women into the regular collegiate course, and in 1841 three of them became the first female baccalaureate degree recipients in the United States. By the Civil War Oberlin was joined in coeducation by two other Ohio private colleges, Antioch and Hillsdale (since moved to Michigan), and the universities of Iowa and Utah in the public sector.[15] Meanwhile, educational reformers, male and female, founded female academies and seminaries, the precursors to women's colleges. Some of them—for example, Salem Academy in North Carolina and Mount Holyoke Female Seminary (founded by the idiosyncratic and powerful Mary Lyon)—later matured into colleges.[16] And the first women's colleges, as such, were founded. Wesleyan College in Georgia was chartered in 1836 as "Georgia Female College," Mary Sharp College (which closed before the start of the twentieth century) was opened in 1851, and Elmira in New York was begun in 1855. The first of the prestigious "seven sisters" was Vassar College, founded in 1865 by Matthew Vassar. Vassar's first class included 353 women, who paid $350 tuition and began their studies on 26 September 1865. Research suggests that women's colleges continue to be perceived as measurably more supportive of female college students than coed institutions.[17]

The first African American to receive a "regular" degree from an American college was probably Alexander Lucius Twilight, who graduated from Middlebury College in 1823. Twilight became a teacher in Vermont; he was also a Presbyterian preacher. He was later elected to the state legislature, and there is today a building named for Twilight at the University of Vermont.[18] In 1825 two more African Americans were awarded A.B. degrees: John Brown Russwurm from Bowdoin and Edward Jones from Amherst. (The first African American Ph.D. holder in the United States was Alexander Boucher, who finished his graduate work at Yale in 1876.) By 1835 Oberlin College, again a leader, described itself as seeking students "irrespective of color." The nation's first "historically black institutions"—Cheyney College, Lincoln University, Wilberforce College, and Howard—were created between 1830 and the 1860s. A substantial proportion of institutions created for students of color have remained small in size, although their impact upon American life has been great.

The other huge social leap forward in higher education at the conclusion of this era and the beginning of the next was the Morrill Land Grant Act. The Morrill Act, giving states land (hence, the name "land grant") to use to fund public collegiate instruction, had been proposed throughout the 1850s and finally was passed in 1862. The act made its grants to each state for "the endowment, support and maintenance of at least one college where the leading object shall be, without excluding other scientific and classical studies . . . to teach such branches of learning as are related to agriculture and the mechanic arts . . . in order to promote the liberal and practical education of the industrial classes in the several pursuits and professions in life."

Some of its proceeds were used to create new state universities, but some also passed to already existing schools, which then became their state's land grant universities and were immeasurably strengthened as a result. Depending on which portion of the mid-South from which one hails, the first state university was either Georgia or North Carolina: both trace their origins to the 1780s. More typically, the University of Michigan was founded in 1817, the University of Iowa in 1847. Minnesota was founded in 1851 (preceding the creation of the State of Minnesota). It is remarkable to recall that the Morrill Act, which is arguably the single most important governmental action in the development of American higher education, came at a moment when the United States was in the midst of the Civil War. The Morrill Act is important in the story of small colleges because it set in motion a movement toward large, comprehensive public institutions, which have since become the dominant sector of our higher education system at least in terms of the number of students served.

Two other, closely related innovations in American higher education occurred during this period. One was the creation of the Normal School movement, beginning with Horace Mann and the Normal School at Lexington, Massachusetts, in 1839. By 1875 there were at least seventy normal schools receiving some state support.[19] Initially, these teacher-training institutes were modest: "Admission to the normal school required only an elementary education. The course of study lasted one or two years . . . Overriding the curriculum was a concern for the development of moral character."[20] (The phrase *normal school* is derived from the French *école normale*, which was a school established as a kind of model for other teacher-training institutions.)

In a pattern we will see duplicated in later years, some institutions that today are colleges trace their founding to precollege institutes and academies created in the period before the Civil War. Colby-Sawyer College thus began as the New London Academy in 1837 but did not award baccalaureate degrees for nearly a century and a half.

During the late eighteenth and early nineteenth centuries, new subjects, including modern languages and scientific and technical subjects, were added to the curriculum, although not without resistance. In general, Yale was the foremost defender of the older curriculum, articulating a position of balanced curricular conservatism in the influential "Yale Report" of 1828.[21]

In the period between the Revolutionary and Civil wars a substantial number of lasting, high-quality small colleges were founded, the seeds of the state university system were planted by the Morrill Act, normal schools were invented, and higher education opened for women and students of color. At the end of this era, circa 1865, *all* American higher education was carried out in small colleges: "Higher education in the United States at the time of the Civil War was carried on by very small colleges. With the majority of colleges less than two hundred strong, Harvard, Yale, Virginia, and Michigan were the giants of the day with five and six hundred students at the end of the eighteen-sixties."[22]

From the Civil War to World War II, 1865–1944

The second half of the nineteenth century and the first of the twentieth was a time of major innovations and explosive growth, and often almost equally explosive contraction, for higher education. As in the period just before the Civil War, scores of colleges were founded, often by dynamic and ambitious churchmen on the expanding frontier. Some of these colleges survived and continue today as small institutions, including the majority in my sample. Many more did not live longer than their founders. Perusing the histories of American small colleges, it sometimes seems that each Protestant denomination felt obliged to found a college in every frontier region to which it moved. "Between 1870 and 1944 the number of colleges quintupled, and enrollments increased by several *thousand* percent."[23] Colleges were founded at the beginning of this era (e.g., Morehouse in 1867 and Wellesley in 1870) and at its end (e.g., Westmont, which began in 1937 in Los Angeles as the Bible Missionary Institute).

Building upon the base of the Morrill Act of 1862, sixty-five land grant institutions also were created, including separate and unequal agricultural and mechanical colleges for students of color in the South. Provision was made for these historically black universities by a second Morrill Act of 1890, which stipulated "that in any State in which there has been one college established in pursuance of the act of July second, eighteen hundred and sixty-two, and also in which an educational institution of like character has been established, or may be hereafter established, and is now aided by such State from its own revenue, for the education of colored students in agriculture and the mechanic arts."

Other institutions created for African Americans date their creation to this period as well. Morehouse College, for example, was created first as Augusta Institute in the basement of Springfield Baptist Church in Augusta, Georgia (the oldest independent African American church in the United States), in 1867. Morehouse moved to Atlanta in 1879, became a college rather than a seminary in 1897 as Atlanta Baptist College, and took its new name early in the twentieth century under the presidency of Dr. John Hope, the college's first African American president.

In another development of this period, normal schools became teachers' colleges that became state colleges, which began to be aggregated into the sometimes baffling and variegated state systems of higher education we see today. For example, today's University of Wisconsin–Superior began in 1893, when the state's legislators established Superior Normal School. The school's first class, which graduated in 1897, included twelve men and women who completed either the "full course" or the "elementary course" and became pioneer teachers. Some of the normal schools developed into junior colleges (e.g., Saint Joseph Junior College in Missouri), others into small baccalaureate institutions (e.g., the University of

North Carolina–Asheville), and a great many evolved over time into state teachers' colleges then state colleges, which are today regional comprehensive institutions, typically offering bachelor's and master's courses of study. Now some of these institutions are no longer "small colleges"; they are by any measure very large universities (e.g., Northern Illinois University with more than twenty-two thousand students). According to the Carnegie Commission, in the United States today there are more schools offering the master's degree as their highest option (611) than there are doctoral (261) or baccalaureate (606) institutions.

College education for women showed strong growth at this time. Wellesley College was founded by Henry Fowle Durant in 1870; the College of New Rochelle, the first women's college in New York, was founded by the Order of Saint Ursula in 1904. Similarly, Colby-Sawyer College, which had been created as a coeducational pre-college academy as early as 1837, became a junior college for women in 1928. (In 1943 it began baccalaureate programs and in 1989 returned to coeducation.) The major swing toward coeducation took place between the end of the Civil War and World War I.[24] By 1880 nearly half of U.S. colleges admitted women. (It is worth recalling that the nation's women were not admitted to the national polling place until 1920.)

Another development was the invention of the junior college, beginning perhaps with the suggestion by the president of Baylor University in 1894 that his institution and some of the smaller Baptist institutions in Texas enter into a formal compact whereby the small colleges would provide the first two years of instruction, and Baylor would accept their graduates to complete their baccalaureate educations.[25] Some earlier institutions had featured two-year programs, but junior colleges, which implied articulation with "senior" ones, were new. As one study notes, "The junior college is a product of the twentieth century but the idea for it was germinated earlier [by those who] advocated what has been termed the 'bifurcated university'—a university in which work of the freshman and sophomore years would be turned over to the secondary schools."[26] Today two- year colleges, including community colleges, technical and/or vocational institutions, and associate's degree–granting junior colleges, add up to more institutions than bachelor's-, master's-, and Ph.D.-granting institutions combined (1,669).[27] Some institutions founded as junior colleges have become four-year small colleges. Warren Wilson college began its life during this period as the Asheville Farm School for boys (1894) but early in the twentieth century added a junior college division and, just prior to World War II, merged with the Dorlan-Bell School of Hot Springs, North Carolina, a women's school, thus becoming a coeducational two-year school, only to become a baccalaureate institution in 1966.

This period also saw the beginnings of serious efforts to educate American Indians in the European tradition, an effort that ultimately led to today's tribal colleges, all of which fall into the "small college" category. Indian education also led to some non-Indian colleges: a few contemporary institutions, such as Fort Lewis College (Colorado) and the University of Minnesota, Morris, began their lives as boarding elementary schools for Native Americans.

Yet, despite these innovations, small, traditional, sectarian liberal arts baccalaureate colleges remained at the core of the American higher education establishment from the Civil War to World War II. David Breneman estimates that at the turn of the twentieth century two-thirds of all American college students were enrolled in such institutions.[28] By 1987, he calculates, that figure had declined to 4.4 percent. It was during this period that two of our oldest, pre–Civil War sample institutions, Centenary and Southwestern, moved to their current locations and took their current names.

A crucial instructional development during the years immediately after the Civil War was the introduction of the elective system into the college curriculum. Although there had been an occasional experiment earlier, it was largely the leadership of President Charles William Eliot of Harvard (who assumed that position in 1869) which led to curricular choice becoming a permanent aspect of collegiate education. Not for the first nor for the last time, Yale and Harvard found themselves disagreeing: the chief opponent of the elective system was Yale president Noah Porter, who affirmed in 1871, "The [elective] plan involves the certain evil of breaking into the common life of the class and the college as well as of unprofitable expenditure and insuperable complexity."[29] One wonders what President Porter might think of today's catalog and budget at Yale. In a related development it was in 1877 that, for the first time, the concept of the "major" was used in connection to college curricular choice.[30]

Two additional important curricular developments took place in a period of renewed interest in general education during the first decades of the twentieth century. First, in 1909 the notion of "distribution" requirements was introduced by President Lowell at Harvard. Distribution requirements were seen as a mechanism for allowing students choice but within a prescribed structure. Second, the "survey" course was invented; the pioneering course at Amherst entitled "Social and Economic Institutions," for example, was first offered in 1914.[31]

These years were also a period of consolidation for the nation's small colleges. As we have seen, Southwestern University in Texas first opened its doors in Georgetown in 1873 but traces its origins to four small, marginal Methodist colleges created in the 1840s and 1850s. Similarly, George Fox University (launched by Quaker missionaries as Pacific College with fifteen students in Newburg, Oregon, in 1891) dates its origin from this era. At the end of the Civil War there existed between 150 and 200 institutions that would today be recognized as small baccalaureate colleges. At the start of World War II that number had tripled.

College enrollments of all types grew dramatically during the years prior to World War II, as the number and size of institutions expanded. By the end of the 1920s there were over a million Americans in colleges of one sort or another. Within twenty years, from 1920 to 1940, the number of American junior colleges grew from 52 to 456, and during that same period the number of teachers' colleges expanded from 45 to nearly 200.[32]

A significant development in kind, rather than size, occurred with the foundation of Cornell University in 1869 and, even more dramatically, Johns Hopkins University in 1876. The first institution to elevate graduate education to a position of primacy, Hopkins was, famously, founded on the Germanic model. Although various options for "professional" training had existed for many years, this moment represents perhaps the first real challenge to the baccalaureate degree as the credential of a thoroughly educated individual. At the end of the Civil War there were about two hundred graduate students in the nation; by 1930 nearly fifty thousand were enrolled.[33] The growth of graduate programs represents the first alternative to the notion that a baccalaureate-granting institution offers a "complete," much less "final" or "terminal," college education. Tangentially, the period between the Civil War and World War II also saw the founding of many specialized and professional collegiate institutions: the Minneapolis College of Art and Design, for example, began in 1886.

The evolution of the American version of the research university had two additional important, and closely related, consequences. It enhanced the professionalization of the faculty, who now became "professors" rather than "tutors," and it was crucial to the development of the modern academic "department." Jencks and Riesman see the 1880s and 1890s as the decades in which "knowledge was broken up into its present departmental categories ('physics,' 'biology,' 'history,' 'philosophy,' and so forth), with the department emerging as the basic unit of academic administration."[34] Not coincidentally, the American Association of University Professors (AAUP) was founded in 1915 and twenty-five years later issued its statement of principle, which articulated standards for tenure which still have currency in the twenty-first century.

The history of my own discipline, English literature, and the development of English departments, journals, and professional organizations such as the Modern Language Association (MLA) provide a typical illustration. As Gerald Graff points out in *Professing Literature: An Institutional History,* literature has been studied since ancient times and was an important part of the curriculum of colleges in the United States from the colonial era onward. But there were not formal academic literary studies in the United States or elsewhere "until the formation of language and literature departments in the last quarter of the nineteenth century."[35] That formation, in turn, was "part of the larger process of professionalization" which entered U.S. higher education around the time of the foundation of Johns Hopkins and the introduction of graduate study, beginning in 1876.[36] Graff points out that the first time Harvard University's catalog grouped courses by department was 1872. As Richard Ohmann and others have pointed out, in the United States English departments have often spent much of their resources and energy teaching things other than English literature, an "amalgamation of partly contradictory tasks and interests that made up our field."[37] Most often, English literature departments have justified, and still do justify, their staffing and funding with colleges and universities by virtue of having laid claim to the teaching of writing and composition. Especially in small colleges, it is rare for faculty in English to teach exclusively either literature or writing courses.

Ohmann, too, links growing faculty professionalism, the origination of graduate education, and the strengthening of academic departments. He notes that in the late 1970s there were well over 150,000 people teaching humanities in American universities, as compared to a few thousand in 1871, and "the first Ph.D. in English to be given by an American university was awarded in 1875 . . . in 1871 there were no graduate students in English in this country; now there are 15,000."[38]

The most obvious impact of the new research universities on small colleges was the creation of another model of higher learning. Also the strengthening of academic departments and professionalization of the faculty had an impact on the governance of small college communities. With the development of the departmental model, for example, the hiring of new faculty came to be seen as the prerogative of departmental colleagues as much as senior college officials. Similarly, decisions relating to contract renewal, promotion, and tenure were increasingly assigned to disciplinary colleagues.

Taken together, the evolutionary developments within American higher education from the Civil War to World War II can be seen as a key transition from earlier European and colonial models to colleges and universities that are structured in a way that is recognizable from a contemporary vantage and which serve most of today's constituencies, albeit in very different proportions. At the beginning of this era small colleges were ubiquitous; at its end they still constituted the core of American higher education, but rival collegiate options had taken hold and were rapidly growing into a position of dominance.

Following this chapter is a brief intermezzo describing the graduation exercises at one of my sample colleges, Centenary, in 1900, almost exactly in the middle of this period. The passion and fervor of this picture tells much about the loyalty and dedication of graduates of small colleges between the Civil War and World War II. While statistics and a grasp of the national picture are essential to understanding these institutions at this time, the partisan particularities of each small school are perhaps even more telling.

World War II to the Present, 1945–2005

Compared to the steady expansion of American higher education in the preceding years, the second half of the twentieth century has been a roller coaster ride. From 1945 to 1975 "more than 600 public institutions were added, 500 of them two-year colleges. In the private sector, 650 new institutions were opened, but half as many closed, for a net gain of 325."[39]

During this same thirty-year period the regional comprehensive state colleges and universities evolved very rapidly from former teachers' colleges, community colleges and the like. By 1975 a third of all the nation's bachelor's degrees were awarded by this sector, which, prior to World War II, had hardly existed. At the same time, small liberal arts colleges (by any definition) declined in number: the Carnegie Foundation considered 719 colleges in this category in 1970, and by 1976 the figure had dropped to 583. David Breneman's study concluded that the number of colleges with a claim to liberal learning fell from roughly six hundred schools to just over two hundred.[40] In 1950 a quarter of all students in American higher education were enrolled in small colleges; by 1975 that proportion was reduced to less than 10 percent.[41] Altogether, by the late 1990s approximately thirty-seven hundred institutions were accredited to give the associate's or bachelor's degree or beyond, and thousands of other postsecondary institutions (e.g., proprietary, electronic, and specialized) were competing for the attention of high school graduates.[42]

With the return of war veterans in the later 1940s and into the early 1950s, whose schooling was supported by the generosity of the GI Bill (passed in 1944), most institutions in the country experienced a rapidly expanding student population, after the scarcity of (particularly male) students during the war years. A few of the least prestigious colleges lost population as public funding enabled students to pick more elite institutions. Temporary housing and classroom space was thrown together to accommodate these vets; indeed, over a half-century later we are seeing the demise of the last surviving Quonset hut collegiate additions of the late 1940s. To the dismay of deans of students across the nation, returning veterans, many of whom had marched across Europe or fought from one jungle-covered Pacific island to the next, were not willing to revert to a passive and subservient adolescent style of life when they came back to campus. From the vantage point of the twenty-first century it seems likely that the days of "in loco parentis" were numbered on the morning the first GI Bill returnee arrived back on campus.

Shortly after the war, another period of interest in general education was both marked and inspired by Harvard University's study of the curriculum called the "Red Book."[43] Officially, the "Report of the Harvard Committee on the Objectives of General Education in a Free Society," the document was sweeping in its perspective and recommendations and only partially successful in reforming general education at Harvard. It recommended that at least six year-long courses be set aside for general education and that all students be required to take a humanities course entitled "Great Texts in Literature" and a general social science offering, "Western Thought and Institutions." It specified introductory courses in the sciences, and recommended other broad and interdisciplinary classes across the curriculum.

After the war, and through the 1950s the United States also enjoyed a time of economic well-being, and in that era of the GI Bill and the Eisenhower aura it seemed that all of the nation's institutions of higher education had nowhere to go but up—up in size, up in budget, up in mission expansion. Colleges built residence halls and classroom buildings as fast as they could. There seemed an unlimited market for young people who wished a career in college teaching, so graduate programs flourished along with undergraduate instruction, and graduate schools and professors developed the habit, still not really broken, of boasting about how large a number of doctorates they could produce. Moreover, the startling launch of the Russian *Sputnik* space satellite guaranteed a boost, in prestige and in funding, for higher learning in general and especially for the sciences in American colleges and universities.

College costs in this era escalated more rapidly than family income. According to the National Center for Educational Statistics, tuition, room and board at all accredited two- and four-year, public and private institutions averaged about 15 percent of family income in 1976; by 1999 it was 21 percent, a significant jump, and one that was met largely by debt, loan, and increased student financial aid.

Also in the 1950s and 1960s, racial integration at long last came to all of the nation's universities, sometimes peacefully and uneventfully, sometimes accompanied with raucous rancor, as when the governors of Alabama and Mississippi defied court orders to admit African American students to the flagship universities in their states. Private colleges also moved, some smoothly, some with controversy and confrontation, toward racial integration. A similar step for women's rights at the nation's colleges occurred with the passage of Title IX of the Education Amendments of 1972, an action that continues to have dramatic and often controversial repercussions, especially in athletics.

Although contemporary popular culture has sanitized and romanticized the 1960s, it was in reality a difficult time on many of America's college campuses. The civil rights movement radicalized young people and taught them effective means to challenge previously unquestioned authority, on and off campus. Increasing African American populations in student bodies intensified, rather than deadened, demands for better treatment. The expansion of an unpopular war in Southeast Asia exacerbated these tensions, and campus after campus exploded in protest and conflict as the decade neared its conclusion. At the same time, the phenomenal expansion of the college student population was slowing, and for the first time in memory, there were more potential college teachers than there were jobs to be had teaching college. Finally, college campuses were shocked when students were slain at Kent State University and Jackson State University: Student protest had evolved into riot and armed warfare, with real bullets killing real kids outside what most Americans still thought of as the gracious and bucolic halls of ivy.

An important and apparently lasting legacy of American colleges of the 1960s is the atmosphere of open educational experimentation which had consequences large and small throughout higher education. At all but a handful of conservative colleges, curricula expanded to include topics and areas that had hitherto been off-limits. Early in the decade, when resources still seemed abundant and the winds of change were starting to gust, several very interesting and important collegiate experiments were launched. Some of the handful of public liberal arts colleges that are now a fixture on the U.S. educational scene were founded during this period. And some of these, and other small colleges reinventing themselves or newly created, offered the most dramatic alternative educational philosophies and styles the nation had seen (e.g., Evergreen State University, Simon's Rock, and New College). Other older, more traditional institutions initiated curricular revisions and experiments alternately lauded and decried, which had the overall effect of enriching the texture of the educational tapestry of the nation.

One important curricular legacy of the 1960s was the establishment of the Freshman Seminar, a course that has recently been revived on a number of very large university campuses (e.g., Washington State University, the University of Wisconsin–Madison, and the University of Texas) as a mechanism for promoting small classes, closer interactions between students and teachers, and similar "small college" opportunities and values (see chap. 7 for a fuller discussion).

During the second half of the twentieth century many formerly small colleges grew into small universities. Many, but not all, of these are the former teachers' colleges that are today regional comprehensive / master's degree institutions. Others, such as Elon, Hamline, Ithaca, Simmons, Pacific Lutheran, Belmont, and Rollins, are now members of the consortium of "Associated New American Colleges," which describes itself as "comprehensive colleges and universities . . . [which] possess trademark features of both larger research universities (e.g., a diversity of undergradu ate, graduate, and professional programs serving residential, commuter and older adult students) and smaller liberal arts colleges (e.g., a highly personalized residential campus environment with small classes)."[44] To some commentators such an evolution was a rather cynical effort to follow the money: "The temptation, then, is to change the college's mission to get in on the funding."[45]

It was not only experiments on the political and cultural Left which flourished during the midcentury period. This was also the time when several new small colleges with deep Christian commitments, such as Westmont College in Santa Barbara, were launched. This was, perhaps, both a consequence of a revival of interest in evangelical Christianity and a reaction to the perception that many colleges had drifted to the Left, politically, and had simultaneously moved away from a strong program of direct ethical guidance of students.

Other small institutions changed their mission and character dramatically during this period. For example, the College of New Rochelle had been established as a Catholic women's college in 1904 but added a graduate school in 1969, a school of nursing in 1976, and a "School of New Resources" for adult learners in 1972. Colby-Sawyer College added baccalaureate programs in 1975 and admitted men beginning in 1989. In 1971 the University of Wisconsin–Superior became part of the University of Wisconsin system. And in 1966 Warren Wilson became a four-year college.

At the end of the twentieth century college students had moved away from the brink of revolution. And their institutions for the most part had also stepped back from the patterns of authoritarianism that had fanned the flames of student protest. But life at the nation's colleges, large and small, urban and rural, liberal and professional, would never be the same. The World War II "baby boomer generation" had reached college age during the 1960s, and now these young people were looking for teaching jobs, just as these jobs were in decline. And, as that demographic peak leveled out, colleges were forced to compete ever more rigorously to recruit students to fill their first-year classes. One outcome of this increased pressure was the rapid expansion of continuing education programs and other offerings outside the traditional curriculum or beyond the traditional student population or both.

Meanwhile, institutions found themselves ensnared in a continually escalating pattern of ever higher expectations (in information technology, outcomes assessment, regional economic development, workforce preparation, and the like). They were coping, for example, with exploding technological needs and costs, at a time of declining enrollment (and, hence, tuition revenue) and, in the public sector institutions, ever-lessening shares of pinched state budgets. By the turn of the new century it was difficult to find much viable evidence of the ebullience of the postwar period and impossible to find a college or university, from Harvard or Stanford to the tiniest and least prestigious sectarian junior college, which would proclaim itself financially comfortable.

Even in these comparatively lean times significant progressive social change has occurred. If women and people of color still often seem to be treated as less than equals, in education as throughout the culture, the progress of both in the last half-century is both breathtaking and gratifying. Gay, lesbian, and bisexual students, faculty, staff, and curricular issues have gone from being unmentionable to being unremarkable. White students attend historically black colleges and vice versa; women now tend to be the majority at most undergraduate institutions, and female and minority faculty are no longer a curiosity. State systems of higher education, while universally acknowledged as imperfect, seem more "systematic" than they were a quarter-century ago. And perhaps the most important development, and one of the least recognized, of the final years of the twentieth century is that, quietly but pervasively, postsecondary education has become the universal standard in the United States. At the beginning of the twentieth century nearly all Americans had some schooling. At the century's midpoint most graduated from high school. At its end a postsecondary option existed for virtually every high school graduate, be it a conventional college or university, a two-year institution, distance education or a proprietary school, or a postsecondary educational experience within a corporate setting. Today over 65 percent of high school graduates matriculate directly to a formal postsecondary educational setting. Of those who do go on to college and university, about 4 to 10 percent choose small colleges.[46]

For most Americans, as the new century begins, high school is not the end of the educational career. We are today the first nation in the world to be entering an era of universal higher learning. If we do not yet know exactly what this means or how we need to handle it, it is nonetheless a dramatic and significant moment not just in the history of American higher education but in the history of human development.

This historical sketch suggests the pattern in which today's small colleges have developed. The story is a dramatic one, with its fits and starts, long-lived developments, and quick flops. Not surprisingly, the small collegiate institutions that arise from this evolution exhibit today a substantial range of characteristics that set them apart not just from other sorts of schools but from one another. In chapter 3 we will look carefully at the many ways in which smaller colleges are different from one another before turning in later chapters to those characteristics that they share and which constitute their unique and important contribution to the nation's rich panoply of postsecondary opportunities.

Graduation at Centenary College, 1900

The following passage is from *A Burning Touch and a Flaming Fire,* a history of Centenary College of Louisiana written by William Hamilton Nelson in 1931 (Nashville: Methodist Publishing House, 368–71). This passage describes the graduation exercises at Centenary in 1900. Reflecting on the historical development of small colleges, it seems appropriate to consider a personal narrative, which catches wonderfully the flavor of small, church-related colleges at the turn of the twentieth century. And, as noted in chapter 2, there was a prodigious growth in just such colleges in the years between the end of the Civil War and the dawn of the new century, when the commencement ceremonies here so joyously and effusively described took place.

In 1900 Bishop Warren A. Candler preached the commencement sermon, and how well do I remember it . . . And how that man did preach that morning, and no little twenty-minutes-for-lunch sermon, either. He preached for an hour and thirty minutes, and I recall that one of the biggest businessmen of Jackson, a Presbyterian elder, cried like a child at some of the sublime and pathetic passages. I noticed all over the congregation men and women were weeping. Professors in a church college in those days were not too highbrow to shed tears—even in public; and some of the boys who liked to be considered hard-boiled had developed a first-class case of the snuffles and their eyes were red. And there were others; in fact, I was doing a little crying myself. And what philosophy there was in that sermon; deep, ponderous truths were brought from the recesses of the storied chambers of God; epigrams and aphorisms bristled all along the road, and the wit was scintillating in its brightness; and the humor—it was rare. When we were not weeping or openmouthed in astonishment at the rich wisdom we were laughing, heartily—and healthily. But above all there was a deep, spiritual note running like a motif throughout all of this magnificent sermon, and this spiritual tone was one loud, clear trumpet call to service, which made me want to go out and proclaim to the world that I, also, was not ashamed of the gospel of Christ, and I was glad I was going to preach the gospel. . . .

Commencement at Centenary in those days was an occasion. It is hard for me to believe that any other school in the world approximated it. How the boys did dress up, a new necktie every day! and in all the colors of the rainbow. And the girls dressed, too, in those days. It was summer time, and they wore white dresses which made them look more like angels than ever; and the restrictions were off to some extent, and you could actually walk across the campus with a girl and not get a demerit, only we never walked across the campus with a girl—we floated and we knew something about what Paul meant when he said he was caught up to the seventh heaven. And the meals! Groaning tables and youthful digestion to take care of everything. How glorious is youth, and how we simply reveled in the speakers from Prep to senior, as thick as monthly installments, but we enjoyed them, only they were too short and not enough of them. In the good old days back in the seventies some of the commencement exercises would last six hours, but they were short in 1900—they never went over three hours. And then, when the time came to leave, when all the boys had pulled out, and you had all their autographs in your little album, and you were alone on the campus, it was like going to a funeral to go to the train, for you certainly did hate to leave a place that made you so happy. . . .

There are some things the world may willingly, even gladly, let die. The age is full of superfluities, and the cosmos is cluttered with things irrelevant, but the world could not get along without the Christian college. It is not only heresy to believe that the world does not need the Christian college, but it is disloyalty to Christ and his Church. And of all the colleges I know of Centenary College is the one college in my estimation that deserves to live. Not only the State of Louisiana, but the Church and the nation would be infinitely poorer without the marvelous contribution she has made throughout the hundred and six years of history; and her unique, magnificent contribution to the spiritual life of the future is needed as much as ever.

3 | Colleges of Character

A University is, according to the usual designation, an Alma Mater, knowing her children one by one.

CARDINAL JOHN HENRY NEWMAN

It could be said of higher education and its institutions, as Tolstoy said of families in the opening sentence of *Anna Karenina* (1878), that all large universities are like one another; every small college is small in its own way. This is, of course, as much a simplification of higher education as was the Russian novelist's overgeneralization about happy and unhappy families.[1] Small institutions, by virtue of their very smallness, tend to be distinctive. Their size compels a kind of programmatic selectivity less necessary in larger places.

Before we can discuss what small colleges have in common, their collective strengths and weaknesses today, and their prospects for the future, we need to take a careful look at just how different they are from one another. Some of these differences are obvious—for example, single-sex institutions or institutions that were historically single-sex compared to coeducational schools. Others are a bit more subtle. In this chapter I examine some of the areas of distinction and individuality (hence, the use of *character* in the chapter title) which seem definitive: size, mission or emphasis, residentiality, and extracurricular activities including athletics, finances, locale, calendar, curriculum, religiosity, age, governance and administration, and prestige. Teasing out the complex pattern of threads of distinctiveness in small colleges turns out to be a kind of Linnaean exercise in institutional taxonomy. By looking at the range of diversity among small colleges, we can define the boundaries within which they operate and learn much about their missions, characteristics, cultures, and populations.

Size

There is a considerable range of what is called "small" when it comes to colleges at the turn of the twenty-first century. Even among the group of representative institutions selected for this study, there is a dramatic variation in size. Colby-Sawyer College has roughly doubled in size over the past decade to a student population of about 900 in 2002; Morehouse has over 3,000; the College of New Rochelle has 475 students in its traditional, residential, liberal arts core, the School of Arts and Sciences, but nearly 7,000 in its complete range of multi-campus programs. Warren Wilson College and the Minneapolis College of Art and Design both have student counts in the 600s. Morehouse proclaims with some pride on its Web site that it is the nation's largest liberal arts college for men; some students at Colby-Sawyer express worry about the college's goal to grow to 1,000, and some students at Warren Wilson are equally distressed that the enrollment there now exceeds 500 students.

The borders of what might be said to constitute a small college can expand considerably beyond even this wide range. Deep Springs College, isolated in the eastern desert of south-central California was recently profiled in the *Christian Science Monitor* and the *Chronicle of Higher Education*. The former entitled its story "Twenty Six Renaissance Men," accurately describing the size of the entire student body.[2] The College of Charleston, a charter member of the Council of Public Liberal Arts Colleges, describes itself as a place where "the faculty and administration take pride in knowing each student by name."[3] There are more than eleven thousand students at the college, over 4,230 percent more than at Deep Springs.[4]

Obviously, what is meant by "small" when it comes to colleges is not very precise. Different observers have different criteria, some objective, some highly subjective. For example, one college president defines a small college as one where there is a reasonable likelihood that every member of the faculty would know virtually every other member of the faculty—presumably a number at or below roughly 150. Others, students particularly, see a kind of psychological barrier at the point beyond which not all students know all other students, at least by sight. One writer, with undisguised strong opinions, affirmed in 1996, "Most good colleges are 1,000 to 2,000."[5]

A look at the literature dealing with small colleges reveals that what is meant by that term has evolved in the past half-century. Around 1950 books about small colleges concentrated on schools of approximately one thousand students or fewer (see, e.g., Alfred T. Hill's *The Small College Meets the Challenge* and Lewis Mayhew's *The Smaller Liberal Arts College*).[6] Today the literature commonly includes in this designation institutions two or three times as large (e.g., most of the articles in *Distinctively American: The Residential Liberal Arts College*, ed. S. Koblik and S. R. Graubard).[7]

A doctoral dissertation written as recently as 1982 recommended as a strategy for survival of small colleges "increasing enrollment to about 1,000 students."[8] Although there are obviously some economies of scale possible, even within smaller institutions, I found no evidence, either in the contemporary literature or in my site visits, that colleges of, say, two thousand or three thousand students are financially healthier than those of five hundred to one thousand. Overall today's small colleges are larger than yesterday's.

For the purposes of this volume, a small college is defined as one enrolling between five hundred and three thousand students—an obviously arbitrary but probably reasonable set of limits. My assumption is that with five hundred students there is a realistic possibility of offering a curriculum that includes most of the major areas traditionally associated with liberal learning—some foreign languages, some history, a choice of laboratory sciences, literature, and the like. When student population rises above three thousand, it seems common for a "college" to proclaim itself a "university" and for different schools or colleges to develop (e.g., a college of business), and it becomes less common for, say, a faculty member in geology to have as her closest colleagues and friends on campus professors of French literature, economics, and special education. Certainly, this is not a "digital," on-off decision that draws a firm boundary line between one school of 2,999 and another of 3,001. Some students of higher education would set a lower limit—2,000 or 2,500—for the maximum size that could be considered small. Other individuals and institutions seem quite comfortable using that description for institutions of 4,000 or 5,000. According to the National Center for Educational Statistics (NCES), in the fall of 2001 there were 902 public and private, baccalaureate or above, institutions enrolling between 750 and 3,000 students.[9]

Emphasis

There is a fairly common assumption that all small colleges are liberal arts colleges and, as a corollary, that all liberal arts colleges are small. (In chapter 1 I discussed the often-confused designations *small, liberal arts,* and *private,* citing Bowen on the difficulty of separating these elements.)[10] The second proposition seems closer to being accurate than the first, although institutions such as the College of Charleston and Miami University of Ohio raise doubts. And, of course, the College of Liberal Arts or College of

Arts and Sciences is often the largest single unit within very large universities, sometimes topping out at over ten thousand students.

Liberal arts college is an even harder phrase to define than *small college*. David Breneman, in his important study *Liberal Arts Colleges: Thriving, Surviving, or Endangered?* tries to identify this type of institution using some fairly generous but rather classical criteria:[11] for a school to qualify as a "liberal arts" college for Breneman, at least 40 percent of the student body must graduate with a major in a traditional liberal arts discipline. From among some 600 institutions classed as "Baccalaureate" by the Carnegie Commission, Breneman's filter produces 212 colleges he is willing to denominate "liberal arts colleges." He notes that, if he drew the line at a slightly more rigorous, but by no means irrational, level and determined that no more than 25 percent of the college's majors could fall into vocational as opposed to liberal studies, his list would consist of fewer than 90 institutions. (Breneman's liberal arts colleges are all private institutions—even the most outstanding small, focused, public liberal arts institutions escaped his attention.) The 2000 revision of the Carnegie Commission Classification of American Colleges and Universities has a class of "Baccalaureate" institutions, with three subgroups, one of which is "Baccalaureate–Liberal Arts," which includes 228 institutions, and another "Baccalaureate-General" with 331. The third class consists of the 57 "Baccalaureate-Associate" colleges, institutions that give 90 percent or more of their degrees at the two-year level but award some baccalaureate degrees. There are also over 600 institutions classified as "Master's degree" institutions, some of which would identify themselves, and be identified in the public mind, as liberal arts colleges—for example, Hood College, Bentley College, Marist College, Augsburg College, and Simpson College.[12] It seems reasonable to estimate that there are about 300 small colleges that can be accurately described as focused or (in a most unfortunate locution) "pure" liberal arts colleges at the dawn of the twenty-first century. Conversely, using the National Center for Educational Statistics' figure of roughly 900 small colleges noted at the conclusion of the previous section, there must then be about 600 small colleges that are something other than strictly liberal arts in their emphases and missions.

One large group of American institutions chooses to emphasize liberal arts as part of a dual-focus mission statement. Several schools, such as Colby-Sawyer College in New Hampshire, present themselves as combin-

ing vocational preparation with liberal learning: "A Colby-Sawyer education combines the values of liberal studies in the traditional arts and sciences with those of professional preparation. The Liberal Education Program fosters the development of skills and competencies and the
acquisition of knowledge that is believed to be essential for all students to
acquire. Through a variety of major programs, students develop the
knowledge and abilities that are required in the profession of their choice
. . . preparing students to define and pursue their personal, educational,
and career goals."[13] This is a sharp contrast to Breneman's more traditional concept of liberal learning as articulated, for example, in the far
more Cardinal Newmanesque statement of "pure" liberal learning offered
in the Grinnell College catalog of 2001–2: "Grinnell College is committed
to liberal education in the arts and sciences. Seeing knowledge as an end
to be pursued for its own sake and acknowledging the sense of achievement and the pleasure that comes with learning, Grinnell wants students
to experience the confidence that proceeds from thinking clearly, logically,
and imaginatively . . . [Grinnell's students] possess the ability to plan and
direct their own lives: they realize that their eventual careers may not even
exist today. The College holds that the mind attuned to being flexible,
adaptable, and unprejudiced is the mind that can most readily pursue
more than one career."[14] In contrast, a senior administrator at the University of Wisconsin–Superior described his institution as having a "mini-
land-grant" mission and compared it, explicitly (and with no prompting
from the interviewer), with what he called the "pure liberal arts mission of
schools like Grinnell."[15]

Another large and significant group of small colleges defines their dual
mission as combining liberal learning and religious education. Westmont
College in Santa Barbara proclaims: "Westmont is a liberal arts college,
and classically so. Our single, overriding objective is to launch our students into a lifetime of flourishing, so that they might become the people
God created them to be. We prepare our students for life—the whole of it
—enabling them to follow God's call into any career, any avenue of service
. . . What do we hope for our students? Simply this: that they would follow
Christ, becoming like him in character and affections, loving God and
neighbor with heart, mind, and soul and strength, and responding to his
call in their lives to be faithful stewards of all that God has given to them
. . . to understand Westmont is to understand its motto—Christ Preemi-
nent in All Things." In its "Philosophy of Education" the first two items of

Westmont's mission are "liberal arts" and "Christian," affirming, "It is this Christian faith that the college seeks to integrate fully into its life as a liberal arts institution."[16] Similarly, George Fox University proclaims as the first of its institutional objectives: "Teach all truth as God's truth, integrating all fields of learning around the person and work of Jesus Christ, bringing the divine revelations through sense, reason, and intuition to the confirming test of Scripture."[17] The mission of this university is "to demonstrate the meaning of Jesus Christ by offering a caring educational community in which each individual may achieve the highest intellectual and personal growth, and by participating responsibly in our world's concerns." The character of the religious mission at William Jewell College in Missouri is discussed at some length in Chad J. Jolly's dissertation, "The Relationship between 'Official' and 'Operative' Identities of a Private Liberal Arts College."[18] Likewise, Yeshiva University in New York City requires all students to follow parallel tracks in liberal studies and Jewish studies: "Undergraduate programs for men (Wilf campus) and for women (Midtown campus) combine rigorous programs in the arts and sciences (and in some instances business) with extensive offerings in Jewish studies. The philosophy behind these programs is called Torah Umadda (Torah and Western learning). The goal is to convey both wisdom and knowledge, to imbue in students a system of values that can help guide their personal, professional, and communal lives long after they graduate."[19]

A related, but different, sort of small college mission is the liberal arts institution with a very distinct, idiosyncratic special area of particular emphasis. Northland College in Ashland, Wisconsin, for example, has a very strong, overarching emphasis on liberal arts and environmental studies. The College of the Atlantic in Bar Harbor, Maine, has a similar ecological focus, with a strong maritime component. The University of Minnesota, Crookston, describes itself as a "polytechnic" college, combining the liberal arts with computer-based technological learning and careers. Warren Wilson College's mission is threefold: liberal learning in the classroom, the work program, and community service. Both the national and private military academies—West Point and the Citadel, Annapolis and Maine Maritime Academy, the Air Force Academy and Virginia Military Institute—seek to combine liberal learning with an overt, strong emphasis on military training.

An interesting group of small colleges are those focusing on "work" as an area of particular emphasis. Although there are several variations and gradations in this cluster, it seems to me that there are three sorts of "work colleges." First, there are a handful of institutions where students perform a significant part of the physical labor involved in keeping the campus operating. They join, in effect, the college's workforce. Among the schools of this sort are Warren Wilson College, Berea College, Deep Springs College, and Blackburn College. Second, in some institutions (Berea and Berry College in Georgia) students work on or adjacent to campus, not necessarily to do essential campus labor but to help the campus pay for itself by running auxiliary moneymaking enterprises. Students at Cumberland College in Kentucky help operate a profit-making inn, as do those up the road at Berea. Students at the Brigham Young University–Hawaii campus staff the Polynesian Cultural Center, one of the largest tourist attractions on the Islands, the profits of which help to support the students and the college. The third sort of work college is the Antioch model, in which all students, on a formalized basis, work off campus, as an explicit element in their educational programs.[20] Universally required internships and work experiences have become ubiquitous and popular in the past decade, as institutions have struggled to make the case for career preparation as an intrinsic element of the collegiate experience. Colby-Sawyer College, for example, boasts that 94 percent of its students complete an internship within the area of their majors during their college years.

An increasing number of colleges are building service into their programs. In some cases service is voluntary; in others it is mandated. At some colleges service is purely an extracurricular opportunity, but at others it is part of a service learning program in which the service programs are deeply linked to classroom experiences—for example, students in a first-year writing course who donate time to a local nursing home then write essays about their experiences there.

Finally, there are a considerable number of small, four-year baccalaureate institutions that make no pretension to liberal education and are explicitly devoted to some other purpose. Minneapolis College of Art and Design's mission is to prepare students for careers or further study in art. Embry-Riddle Aeronautical University has a general education component but offers majors only in aeronautical studies. The Savannah College of Art and Design offers baccalaureate work leading only to the B.F.A. and B.Arch. (architecture) degrees. The Ringling School of Art and Design in Florida is similar, as is the Rhode Island School of Design. Saint Joseph Seminary College "provides the undergraduate preparation required for graduate study of theology" by the Benedictine Monks of St. Joseph Abbey, in Louisiana.[21] The Research College of Nursing in Kansas City is self-evident in its mission. Dyke College in Cleveland offers all business programs, and Capital College in Maryland offers only engineering. Many of the smaller self-described "Bible colleges" (e.g., Columbia Bible College in South Carolina, Puget Sound Christian College, and Southeastern College of the Assemblies of God) confine themselves exclusively to Bible studies or preparing students for religious careers.

Residentiality and Extracurricular Life

Small colleges range from being entirely residential in student population to entirely nonresidential. Even among the small group visited for this study, there is a remarkable range. The University of Wisconsin–Superior houses approximately 20 percent of its undergraduate students in college residence halls on campus; at Southwestern University 83 percent of students live in college residence halls.

In turn, residentiality seems to be correlated to the range and the participation of students in cocurricular and extracurricular activities and events. "The residential liberal arts college, by virtue of its small size, residential nature and linkage of educational ends and means, promotes student participation in the ongoing civic life of its community."[22] Institutions with a lower rate of resident students, such as UW–Superior, frequently express concerns that the general level of campus participation in academic, cultural, and recreational events is disappointing. Conversely, resident students, especially at small colleges in small towns, tend to rely on the out-of-classroom college events calendar for a substantial share of their noninstructional life.

One frequently cited reason that this issue is important to small college leaders is the widely reported finding that college success and persistence to graduation is linked with student involvement in the life of the campus beyond the classroom. "Other factors held constant, the stronger the individual's level of social and academic integration, the greater his or her subsequent commitment to the institution and to the goal of college graduation."[23] Both logic and empirical data suggest strongly that students who sing in the choir, act in plays, participate in varsity sports, are active in student government, take leadership posts in student organizations, and make similar commitments to their colleges are students who flourish and graduate; conversely, students who fail to establish any such meaningful connections with the extra-instructional life of the college tend not to persist in their studies. According to the 1984 findings of the Study Group on the Conditions of Excellence in American Higher Education, "Perhaps the most important [condition] for improving the undergraduate educa- tion is student involvement . . . the more time and effort students invest in the learning process and the more intensely they engage in their own edu- cation, the greater will be their growth and achievement, their satisfaction with their educational experiences, and their persistence in college and the more likely they are to continue their learning."[24] (*Involvement* here is defined as "the investment of psychological and physical energy in some kind of activity, whether it is specific, such as organizing a blood drive or singing in the choir, or more general, such as attending a concert or occa- sionally using the campus recreation facilities.") Such involvement is of- ten the hallmark of smaller institutions, as Alexander Astin and Calvin Lee note: "The typical small college is characterized by a more friendly atmos- phere, close contacts between faculty and students, a stronger identifica- tion with the institution, and a feeling on the part of the students that they matter as individuals."[25]

Rephrased somewhat negatively, Ernest Pascarella and Patrick Teren- zini find that "attending a large institution [compared to a small one] tends to inhibit a student's level of social involvement (extracurricular activities, interaction with faculty, and the like) during college, and social involve- ment is a nontrivial determinant of such outcomes as educational attain- ment and self-concept."[26] Similarly, Astin reports that "almost all student involvement in campus life is decreased by attending a large rather than a small institution. Students at large institutions are less likely to interact with faculty, to get involved in campus government, to participate in ath- letics, to become involved in honors programs, and to be verbally aggres- sive in their classrooms."[27] Astin notes the disharmony between the major findings of his study (that smallness promotes involvement, which creates student success) and the contrary trend toward more and ever larger insti- tutions.

Obviously, different small colleges tend to emphasize different co- and extracurricular emphases. Thus, one (e.g., Saint Olaf College) will have an outstanding choral music program; another (e.g., Guilford College) will offer a rich array of international service opportunities; and yet another (e.g., Saint Andrews Presbyterian College) a very popular equestrian pro- gram and a bagpipe band.

Certainly, the most visible extracurricular activity across the postsecondary scene is intercollegiate athletics, and here, again, there is a tremendous variation among small institutions. It is hard to imagine a university with thirty thousand students without an NCAA Division I athletic program, including some highly visible (and expensive) sports such as football, men's and women's basketball, volleyball, and baseball. Conversely, small colleges manifest just about every imaginable permutation in the realm of athletics.

Some small colleges mount full-fledged NCAA Division I athletics programs including football—for example, Centenary College affirms it is the smallest Division I school in the nation; Elon University, Gardner-Webb College, and Davidson College are three other examples, all within North Carolina. While such affiliation is frequently a significant financial stretch, in terms of the proportion of the institutional budget allocated for competitive intercollegiate athletics, for some colleges it is seen as a worthwhile investment in student recruiting, regional visibility, alumni and donor enthusiasm, and the like. (According to the NCAA, the national average athletic operating expenses for Division I schools with football was a bit over $7 million in 1999.)[28] Many other small colleges also compete in NCAA Division II. The average annual expenditure in athletics of Division II members nationally is about $2 million for institutions with football, $1.5 million for those without. Division II permits athletics scholarships and, nationally, the average institution offered about 47 (compared to just over 150 in Division I). Hillsdale College, Saint Josephs College (Indiana), and Mercy College all are small college members of Division II. Many—probably most—small colleges are members of NCAA Division III, which does not allow athletic aid and, on average, costs about $800,000 per year to sustain. Even within Division III, however, there are substantial variations between schools like St. John's College (Minnesota), a perennial national powerhouse in football, and Colby-Sawyer or the University of Wisconsin–Superior, which do not sponsor football. A fourth affiliation possibility for small colleges is the National Association of Intercollegiate Athletics (NAIA), which falls somewhere between NCAA Division II and III; scholarships are permitted, but expenses and commitment are a bit lower than Division II. Albertson, Malone, and Virginia Intermont colleges are illustrative NAIA affiliates. A fifth option is the National Christian Collegiate Athletic Association conference (e.g., Moody Bible Institute, Northwestern College [Minnesota], and Mid-America Bible College), some but not all members of which also have an NCAA affiliation. The U.S. Collegiate Athletic Association (USCAA) serves schools of under a thousand students (e.g., Warren Wilson College). Finally a few small schools are unaffiliated and either improvise some sort of non-conference intercollegiate schedule in some sports on an ad hoc basis or do not play.[29] At Minneapolis College of Art and Design there flourishes an athletic program that consists solely of a few intramural sports (e.g., a campus coed baseball team).

Financial Profile

Perhaps the only thing small colleges have in common when it comes to finances is that none thinks of itself as rich. Still, there are certainly small institutions with dramatically deeper pools of resources than others.

Astin and Lee's study *The Invisible Colleges,* profiled small, relatively unselective institutions, a group of about five hundred schools which they believed to be about half of all private institutions in the nation. They concluded that, "with respect to financial resources, the invisible colleges are in a dismal position."[30] On the other hand, the most affluent private liberal arts colleges—for example, Wellesley and Grinnell in this study—are, on a per-student basis, among the wealthiest in the nation.[31]

Books much longer than this have been written about college finances, and there are scores of indices and measures that have been designed to describe them.[32] Most of these are useful, at least in some context (e.g., it is probably useful to know what an institution is spending on building and landscape maintenance in relationship to FTE student population compared to similar institutions when that institution is considering whether or not to hire an additional groundskeeper). Other measures strike some observers as pernicious. These would include such tactics as measuring the cost of generating student credit hours as a means of ascertaining faculty "productivity" and using that data to compare departments within institutions or to make comparisons across institutions. Such measures offer the opportunity, frequently taken, to see colleges as mechanisms for producing credit hours as opposed to, say, wisdom. A look at a few key financial indicators, however, will indicate clearly the dramatic differences in the resource bases of small colleges.

One important fiscal measure is faculty salaries (and compensation), which have a direct bearing on the recruitment and retention of teachers. It is true that few enter the teaching profession for motives of pecuniary avarice and certainly not at small colleges. Although faculty salaries have inched much closer to those of other learned professions during the past few decades, they are still significantly lower than those of doctors or lawyers or other professionals with whom professors often compare themselves. Few faculty members will take a job simply because it pays more than another, and few will change institutions simply for a small salary boost. Still, competing offers of twenty-five thousand and forty-five thousand dollars per year to fill a new assistant professor slot are not going to produce many who opt for the first position, unless some other factors are wildly favoring it. One small institution has regularly done "exit interviews" on faculty members who leave tenured or tenure-track positions of their own volition (i.e., not on the basis of negative personnel reviews or other external compulsions). It found that over a several-year period no faculty members who chose to leave gave as the primary reason a higher salary at the institution to which they were going. Rather, reasons such as spousal employment or education situations, research opportunities, and geographical desirability were given as the primary rationale for career relocation. But in roughly 90 percent of the cases the faculty member *was* moving up perceptibly in the pay scale as part of the move.

Faculty salary disparity can be relatively dramatic, even among neighboring institutions. Consider the two New England colleges among the focus institutions in this study, Colby-Sawyer and Wellesley. Both have a women's college tradition, and both occupy handsome, leafy collegiate-looking campuses. They are a short (two-hour) drive apart. True, there are differences in the cost of living: Colby-Sawyer is in a more rural small city than suburban Wellesley, but New London, New Hampshire, is a thriving, prosperous town, which is drawing an increasingly affluent retirement and commuter population—it is a very long way from the fictional Egypt, Maine. According to the American Association of University Professors (AAUP) faculty salary data for 2001–2, the average salary for a full professor at Colby-Sawyer was $57,600 per year; at Wellesley it was $104,300. The overall average for all professorial ranks was $89,500 at Wellesley and $44,700 at Colby-Sawyer. The salary-benefit figures for average compensation at all ranks showed the Massachusetts institution at $110,400 and the New Hampshire college at $57,200. But Colby-Sawyer is not a particularly penurious institution: the lowest salaries in New Hampshire at a level IIB (baccalaureate) college were at New England College, at $38,500.

Nor was Wellesley the richest school in Massachusetts: two other AAUP-IIB schools were higher (Babson and Amherst colleges) and Williams, Boston College, and Mount Holyoke were virtually the same.

A second key indicator of fiscal strength is endowment. Historically, funding from endowment has been much more important for colleges in the private sector than public institutions, but this distinction is diminishing in importance in an era of shrinking legislative financial support for public higher education. A large endowment is desirable as a kind of fiscal insurance policy—money in the bank, so to speak. More important, colleges "harvest" annual income from their endowments, at rates that typically vary from about 4 to 6 percent (often calculated on a rolling multi-year average, to even out bumps and dips in the market). So, every million dollars of endowment generates roughly fifty thousand dollars of operating funding every year, in perpetuity. That means, in a kind of Platonic fiscal world, that a college that had an annual operating budget of twenty-five million dollars could, mathematically, operate forever with no income whatsoever from grants, legislature, philanthropy, or tuition if it had an endowment of five hundred million dollars. Actually, some of the colleges in my sample do have endowments in this range—but, not surprisingly, they tend to be schools whose annual operating budgets handsomely exceed twenty-five million dollars.

Thus, Grinnell's endowment in the fall of 2002 was valued at $1.14 billion. The college's budget is about $61 million annually; its tuition, room, and board fee is (for 2002) a bit over $26,000. The college harvests 4.5 percent of a rolling average of its endowment value as annual income, about $50 million at this point, but spends some of this endowment income on special projects (e.g., building the collection for a new art museum a few years ago as well as facilities expansions and improvements), leaving about $30 million for annual operations (just a bit under half the cost of operation). The college's other sources of income are tuition and fees ($17.2 million), gifts and grants ($4.8 million), and auxiliary enterprises such as dining, phone, and bookstore (about $8.7 million). Wellesley's endowment in fiscal year 2001 was also just over $1.1 billion. By way of contrast Colby-Sawyer's endowment as of 30 June 2002 was $17 million; that of the University of Wisconsin–Superior was $7 million; and my own institution, in the public sector, had an endowment valued at about $6.5 million. It is clearly the case that faculty and administration at Grinnell recognize that their institution is comparatively wealthy, while those at Superior know that they are not. Nonetheless, counterintuitive though it is, I consistently found as much or more concern about finances at the rich schools than at the poorer ones. Faculty at Grinnell worry, a great deal, about whether or not they will have enough money to do what they want in the instructional program with students. Those at Colby-Sawyer know they will not and, consequently, tend not to fret about it as much. As one member of the Colby-Sawyer faculty said, "We are experts at 'plan B.' " The intermezzo that follows this chapter, an interview with the president of the University of Maine–Farmington, is a good illustration of a college CEO at an institution that is not wealthy. Dr. Theo Kalikow is obviously aware and concerned about budgetary constraints, but, equally obviously, she is not obsessed by them and believes that those fiscal challenges will not prevent her college from achieving its mission.

Perhaps the most important fiscal measure is the amount of money institutions spend in annual operating costs per FTE student. These costs include salaries and benefits, supplies, equipment, and other ongoing operating items such as computer replacements, phone lines, and paper. It does not necessarily follow that the more a college spends per FTE pupil, the higher the quality of instruction. Since a very large percentage of any college's budget is spent on salaries (frequently about 60–70 percent), it could be that a college with an aging, and therefore relatively highly paid, senior faculty might have a higher cost per FTE student than one with a younger, cheaper, but not necessarily inferior corps of teachers. Still, it seems a self-evident principle that overall the more money an institution has to spend on personnel and operations, per student, the greater likelihood that the student will have a productive and positive learning experience. A former professional wrestler who served a term as the Independence Party governor of the State of Minnesota complained that education was a financial black hole. If it is true that more money equates to a better learning experience for students, then Governor Jesse Ventura was, in fact, correct, at least to a point. (That "point" seems more an abstract theoretical limit than one any institution I know has ever decided it has actually reached.) Educational enterprises *can* spend virtually every dollar they can acquire, and, although some schools surely waste money, in most cases every additional dollar will buy at least a slightly improved education: more and better technology, more and better facilities, more and better teachers, smaller classes, lighter teaching loads—all things money really can buy.

Good economic times tend to be good for both the private and the public sectors (e.g., the late 1990s) and vice versa. Thus, private small colleges and those in the public sector tend to prosper and to suffer at about the same times and to about the same degree. Often state budgets tend to lag a bit behind the private sector, so that public colleges may feel economic declines a bit later than private institutions but then harvest the rewards of budgetary renewal a bit later as well.

At one end of the spectrum a private college among my sample institutions has an annual operating budget for 2002–3 of about $61 million, for thirteen hundred students, generating an expenditure of just under $47,000 per FTE student per year. A public institution within the group serves slightly more than twenty-two hundred FTE students with an operating budget, for the same year, of just under $39 million, generating an FTE expenditure of $17,825. This seems a very remarkable range.[33]

Prestige

In *Achieving Educational Excellence: A Critical Assessment of Priorities and Practices in Higher Education,* Alexander Astin remarks that "most of the 3,000 institutions [in American higher education] are organized into a highly refined status hierarchy."[34] The prospective college student, for example, picks up a reputable college guide such as Cass and Birnbaum and notes that "Williams College is one of the most prestigious liberal arts colleges in the country."[35] The very widely consulted *U.S. News and World Report* annual ranking of colleges and universities uses "peer assessment" as its top indicator, a somewhat circular process, since colleges will receive top rankings because people think they are excellent, and people will think colleges are excellent because they receive top rankings. "Prestige" may be one of those things everyone recognizes but which is hard to define. Obviously, it involves both visibility and an aura of excellence. Prestige is important to colleges because it attracts potential students of excellence, engages donors, impresses foundations and corporations, helps recruit outstanding faculty and staff, among other things. Those of us with egalitarian impulses may be discomforted by the fact that small colleges range from the highest prestige to near-complete "invisibility." But this variable is a real and an important one.

A convincing case can be made that the opposite of prestige when it comes to colleges and universities is not some abstract and parallel term such as *disrepute* or *undistinguishedness* but more concrete descriptors such as *impoverished* or *invisible*. In a 1972 report to the Carnegie Commission on Higher Education, Alexander Astin and Calvin Lee investigated 494 "invisible colleges." They found that those institutions represented 21.5 percent of all American institutions and enrolled close to a half-million students. And, as noted earlier, they concluded that in fiscal matters these colleges are in a dismal position.[36]

Astin notes that often what we think of as the "best" colleges are not able to demonstrate convincingly that they do a better job of educating students than other, less prestigious places. He suggests the merit of a "talent development approach," which asks how far a college moves students from their entry to graduation: a "value-added" assessment. He notes that traditionally we make judgments regarding what colleges are best based on reputation (e.g., the sorts of average SAT scores entering students present) and resources (e.g., the size of the endowment).

Astin's talent development approach is an excellent tool for assessment, but it has done little to alter the prestige hierarchy for which he proposed it as a substitute. Clearly, he is correct that certain reputational and resource factors tend to impart prestige to colleges. I would add some other variables—age and place, for example.

All things being equal, older colleges will naturally have greater prestige than newer ones of comparable quality. They will have had more time to become known, will have graduated more celebrities and leaders, will tend to occupy a more handsome and historic campus, and, because they have been involved in fund-raising for a longer time, will likely have larger endowments.

Similarly, geographic locale can add to or detract from a small college's prestige. Generally, a location in the Northeast will benefit an institution. Thus, for example, students and trustees at Colby-Sawyer College recognize that the institution's New Hampshire home is a strong lure for students who are seeking an "Eastern liberal arts college." Conversely, several groups with whom I spoke at Southwestern University in Georgetown, Texas, noted that, if their college were transplanted to New England, its national visibility and its image would be raised, even if nothing else whatsoever changed.

Astin concludes by observing that research has demonstrated that the best mechanism for developing talent is involvement and that "students attending smaller institutions are usually on more familiar terms both with faculty members and with other students and see both faculty members and students as being more involved in the classroom experience."[37] This suggests that there may be as strong a correlation between size and the development of student talent as between prestige and instructional effectiveness. Nonetheless, prestige is a daily reality, both for the small colleges that possess it and those that seek it.

Place

It certainly can make a difference where a large university is located—one is unlikely to confuse the environment at University of California–Berkeley with that at Columbia University or Ohio State. But it is also the fact that where there is a large university there is also at least a small city. This is emphatically not the case with small colleges, which are located just about everywhere it is possible to be in the United States.

Some small colleges—Macalester in Minneapolis, Barnard in New York, North Park in Chicago, Whittier in greater Los Angeles, Westminster in Salt Lake City—are nestled in the cores of large cities. In some cases these institutions are like little oases in the midst of urban concrete; in others they are indistinguishable from the cityscape that surrounds them. Minneapolis College of Art and Design is contiguous with, and flows into, a major art museum. Other small colleges are located in smaller cities (e.g., Coe in Cedar Rapids, Guilford in Greensboro, Westmont in Santa Barbara, and Centenary in Shreveport) or suburbs (e.g., the College of New Rochelle, National-Lewis College in suburban Chicago, and Wellesley). Many are in small towns—some by accident (if the town did not grow, the college founded there remained small) and some by design (a significant number of small colleges were founded in locales that were deliberately chosen to protect impressionable youth from the wicked lures of the big cities—a spectacular misjudgment of the creative energies of the young). It is not clear to me how many of the small college / small town conjunctions are deliberate and how many are unplanned. This would be an interesting subject for further research and exploration. A few small colleges come near to constituting the entire town in which they find themselves. Kenyon College is a classic example, with most of the businesses and services in Gambier, Ohio, being owned and operated by the college and the population of the town very largely made up of individuals connected to the institution. (The University of the South might be said to claim it constitutes not simply an entire town but a complete kingdom, since it refers to its campus environs as "the Domain.")

Many small colleges that are either in small towns or self-contained are remarkably inaccessible, even in twenty-first-century America. St. Mary's College in Maryland, while not wholly outside the urban orb of Baltimore/Washington, manages to be a healthy half-day drive, mostly on two-lane roads, from the nearest airport, as does the University of Minnesota, Morris, and Truman State University in northeastern Missouri.

Issues of accessibility and isolation can be crucial to small and relatively poorly funded institutions. A small college in or adjacent to a large city will have available for its students the social, cultural, and recreational resources of that city, without much more cost than listing forthcoming events and perhaps helping with transportation and arrangements. If students at a more isolated college want to attend a symphony orchestra, see a touring Broadway play, hear a major political speaker, or, for that matter, go to a rock concert or a nightclub or have a Thai seafood dinner, then the odds are that the college itself will need to provide it. And the development office of the urban college will have close proximity, and therefore perhaps greater access, to a wide range of corporate, individual, and foundation wealth. Such philanthropic opportunities are less contiguous and hence less available two hundred miles away in the midst of struggling agricultural communities.

Small colleges are not only *in* some place; they *are* places themselves. Many smaller institutions conform attractively to the "halls of ivy" image of "what a college should look like." Although few college campuses have been able, or have sought, to retain completely the appearance of a nineteenth-century school, many cling to the core of a cluster of architecturally unified buildings, often red brick, often with a central chapel. Very frequently one of these venerable brick structures is an "Old Main" hall, which was the first building of substance constructed on the campus. Such colleges were commonly constructed in a rectangular pattern, surrounding a handsome green quadrangle or mall. In some cases this inner core is surrounded or mixed with more modern structures—gyms, residence halls, libraries, science buildings. On other campuses the conventions of traditional architectural styles have been zealously preserved. George Fox College is an example of the former, Mary Washington College the latter.

Other campuses, especially those founded and created in their entirety within the past fifty years, have a dramatically different and more modern look. Saint Andrew's Presbyterian College, for example, is constructed entirely of brick and concrete, with most buildings utilizing blocks imprinted with the Celtic cross. The University of North Carolina–Asheville, also built on a brand-new campus in the second half of the twentieth century, has a large, traditional open campus mall surrounded by austere yellow brick modern structures.

And, of course, most small colleges fall somewhere in between: a handful of older buildings interspersed—sometimes tastefully, sometimes seemingly randomly—with modern buildings. Some colleges of this "mixed" sort have tried to follow the model of several of the more elite private universities, Yale especially, and built new buildings in the most contemporary styles of their day, producing a mixture of structures representing many different decades of architectural taste.

Place is, to a greater or lesser extent, a determinant of human experiences and outcomes. It is probably impossible to prove but seems compellingly persuasive that the experience of those who live, work, and learn in a quiet, harmonious, traditional campus, nestled in an attractive, even bucolic, isolated small town, will not be the same as that of those who inhabit a campus of innovative, challenging buildings, set in an exciting and bustling metropolitan area. I would not argue that one or the other experience would be better or worse, but surely they would be different.

Calendar

Small colleges (like large universities) not only find themselves operating in very different sorts of places; they also work within different scheduling contexts. Some small colleges operate on the quarter calendar of the academic year: often three ten-week terms, with the midwinter break separating the first and second quarter (although occasionally with it coming in the midst of the winter term). Some operate on the semester system, most commonly with the semester break occurring at the Christmas / New Year's holiday (there are still a few remnants, however, of the older, inhumane semester calendar, in which students return after midwinter break for a week or so of classes and first term final exams). Some small colleges have a roughly three-week-long January term between semesters; some have a May term between graduation and summer session. Some small colleges don't have a summer session; others have one or two. A few small colleges (e.g., Colorado College and Cornell College) have a "one-course-at-a-time" academic calendar, in which students take, and professors teach, one intensive course for a three- or four-week block, have a short break, then do another course, and so on. Antioch, with its work/study curriculum, divides up the academic calendar to accommodate student time on and off campus throughout the school year. Other small schools have tried various experimental calendars. Carleton, for example, has a first term that ends at Thanksgiving, and then students are gone until Martin Luther King Day in late January, when they begin two more quarters. It seems that smaller institutions have considerable flexibility, both in setting their annual calendars and in periodically altering them. This is perhaps less the case at very large institutions, particularly major research universities, where this sort of movement is both a huge political hassle and a logistical nightmare, with scores of schools, colleges, departments, centers, institutes, hospitals, and legislative mandates to wade through.

Curriculum

The curricular variations within the small college universe are remarkably diverse. Some small institutions offer an entirely prescribed curriculum, in which every single course students take is sequentially required (this, as noted in chap. 2, was the pattern for all American colleges in an earlier era). St. John's campuses in Annapolis and Santa Fe are the best-known schools of this type. At other small colleges virtually nothing within the curriculum is required. "In the Grinnell College curriculum, the only requirements for graduation are completion of a first-year tutorial, 124 credits, and the academic major."[38] Many small colleges have a highly prescriptive general education curricular sequence—for example, all students are required to take a first-year writing class, a laboratory science, a foreign language, and a history course. Many others focus less prescriptively on distribution requirements ("In order to provide students with as much flexibility as possible, Wellesley requires no specific courses except Writing 125. However, to ensure that students gain insight and awareness in areas outside their major fields, the College requires that they elect nine units drawn from eight substantive and skill-based categories"). Likewise, the College of New Rochelle specifies "Liberal Arts Categories" and requires a minimum of three credits in each: Religious Studies, Philosophical Approaches, Social Analysis, Literature and the Arts, Foreign Language, Scientific Inquiry, and a Capstone Seminar. Some colleges phrase their general education requirements in terms of skills (e.g., Westmont's

"Mathematics Proficiency" requirement), others in terms of traditional subject matter areas (e.g., the same college's distribution requirement in "Literature").

A growing number of institutions have a universal first-year seminar— for example, Centenary College's "First Year Experience": "a two course [eight credit hours] sequence that introduces students to the liberal arts in an interdisciplinary context with an emphasis on rhetoric (written and oral communication)." Many have some sort of required core sequence— Colby-Sawyer College, for instance, requires a four-course core sequence with one specified course each in Fine and Performing Arts ("Creative Expression"), Humanities ("Judgment and Belief"), Natural Sciences ("The Process of Discovery"), and Social Sciences ("Social Analysis"). Saint Andrew's Presbyterian College has a core sequence that spans seven semesters and all four years. Many colleges with a religious tradition require all students to take either a specific or a distributional religion course— George Fox, for example, requires both: a six-hour sequence in "Bible and Religion," plus one of three courses in Religion is required of all students, then either a course in "The History and Doctrine of Friends" required of all Quakers or any one of seven electives in "The Bible" for students of other faiths.

Other curricular emphases are nearly as broad as imagination can invent. I have already mentioned, for example, colleges that integrate internships, work experiences, and service learning into the curriculum. Others expect some sort of international experience of virtually all students (the institution formerly known as Beaver College, now Arcadia, has a one-week London seminar for all students; Moravian College requires every student to have an international experience at some point during the undergraduate years; Warren Wilson is seeking to build a nearly universal international experience into all students' careers).

Many colleges with special institutional emphases integrate their concerns, such as environmentalism or technological literacy, into the curriculum. Others pay curricular heed to their unique histories. The College of New Rochelle requires that all students take a course entitled "The Self in Context: Women, College, and Society." My own institution, which enrolls about nineteen hundred students, began its life in another incarnation as an American Indian Boarding School and teaches today two different upper midwestern Indian languages.

Religiosity

Issues of sectarian emphasis have surfaced in several earlier sections of this chapter. Given the religious origins—indeed, often, the origins in religious fervor—of many small colleges, this is not surprising. At the turn of the twenty-first century small colleges in the United States exist in a very wide spectrum of religious emphasis.

At one end of the scale there are a number of small colleges that are overtly nonsectarian in foundation and contemporary manifestation. Today's public liberal arts colleges, such as the University of Wisconsin–Superior, were created as agents of the state. While public small colleges often do provide outlets for religious expression for students, faculty, and staff, participation tends to be wholly at the choice of the individual, and usually those voluntary options cover some spectrum of religious inheritance. Thus, a public college may have Christian and Jewish and Muslim and other student clubs, such as the Intervarsity Christian Fellowship or the Newman Club or Hillel, in an affiliated relationship with the campus. Certainly, public colleges teach courses about religion as an academic discipline, such as history of religion and philosophy of religion. But such public colleges will make no denominational claims, at least officially, on students or employees, and keep clear the constitutional barriers between church and state college. Similarly, a number of small private colleges, such as Reed College in Oregon, were created as secular institutions and have remained so.

At the other pole are small collegiate institutions that are wholly or primarily in the business of educating clergy for a specific denomination. So, for example, Columbia Bible College confers 100 percent of its undergraduate degrees in "theological studies," and Lancaster Bible College, in Pennsylvania, "exists to educate Christian men and women to live according to a biblical world view and to serve through professional Christian ministries." Obviously, the small Christian seminaries that train priests and ministers for various Protestant denominations and Roman Catholic orders define themselves as religious institutions.

Many faculty members at Christian colleges are convinced that they have more academic freedom than their colleagues in nonsectarian institutions. Thus, for example, a group of faculty interviewed at George Fox University vigorously affirmed that, although all institutions have their biases and cultures, at the Christian college those leanings are overt and recognized, thus freeing those at the Christian college to work within boundaries that are no more constrictive but much more explicit and clearly defined than at secular institutions. The student recruitment materials from Westmont College are equally assertive about students there finding more academic freedom than on public or secular campuses:

> Professors and administrators at the world's top colleges and universities hold one concept dear beyond almost any other: the idea of academic freedom. In order to understand the truth and to allow the best ideas to have dominance in society, they say, we must have the freedom to discuss all ideas. To let them rise and fall on their merits. But just try adding a Christian perspective to the discussion in classrooms on secular campuses around the world, and you may find out where the limits to academic freedom lie . . . Why limit yourself? On a Christian college campus such as Westmont, you'll have academic freedom that extends to include all your thoughts, ideas and beliefs on every subject in God's world. Westmont's commitment to academic freedom is obvious, not only in courses that demand your best critical thinking, but also through a wide variety of opportunities and organizations that explore the world of ideas.[39]

Similarly, Mary Ellen Ashcroft, in an article about teaching at Christian liberal arts colleges, says, "The teacher's responsibility is to make the classroom a safe place for students to bring out their beliefs and look at them and argue about them and decide what they hold dear."[40] And, she believes, that is far more the case at a Christian institution than at a state university. Comparing sectarian and secular institutions where she had taught, she states, "I feel much more freedom in the classroom, in my office, in the halls at Bethel than I ever felt at the University of Minnesota." She cites James H. Daughdrill, former president of Rhodes College: "Today, research universities are thoroughly secular and comprise one of the few places in America where openly acknowledged religion is not a life option. Consequently, academic freedom has become a casualty at these institutions."[41] It is also the case that many of the evangelical colleges require an affirmation of religious conviction of all students and/or faculty, a condition some might find restrictive of academic freedom.

Between the nonsectarian public liberal arts colleges and the denominational seminaries, there is a full spectrum of religiosity. Some institutions, such as Westmont and George Fox among my sample institutions, which profess a very strong religious character, offer majors and studies in a wide variety of nonreligious subjects as well as studies in Christian history, theology, the Bible, and the like.

Many colleges retain some elements or vestiges of their religious origins without affirming an overtly sectarian mission. An institution may retain some seats on its board of control for nominees or representatives of a founding denomination (e.g., the Methodist bishop of Iowa has an ex officio seat on the Cornell College Board of Trustees; multiple seats on the board at Southwestern are reserved for officials and nominees of sponsoring Methodist conferences). Some still receive significant or symbolic financial support as a result of historic religious affiliation. Some private small colleges still employ a chaplain, commonly linked to the founding church. Cultural practices of the church may continue to influence life at institutions of religious origin. At Salem College, in Winston-Salem, North Carolina, the traditional Moravian tea ceremony at Christmas time is celebrated. Just a few miles away Guilford College in Greensboro, a Friends' college (but with fewer than 10 percent Quaker students), practices government by consensus at every level, from student organizations and faculty committees to major decisions of the senior administrative leadership and the board of trustees, and all meetings begin in prayerful silence.

Roman Catholic institutions are a special class of religious institutions.[42] Some Catholic schools (e.g., Notre Dame, Villanova, and Georgetown) have achieved university status. Others, particularly very small, poorly funded, single-sex institutions have closed or suffered in recent years (e.g., Mount Senario College in Ladysmith, Wisconsin, and Sacred Heart College in North Carolina). But there remain many small Catholic colleges, coed and single sex, which continue to play a significant role in the U.S. higher education community. These schools (the College of New Rochelle in my focus group; others include places such as Saint Mary's of California, Notre Dame College of Maryland, and Saint Scholastica of Duluth) maintain a strong, overt Catholic emphasis, in population, curriculum, and mission. While certainly "religious colleges," these institutions seem on the whole less assertive about their religiosity than the "Bible colleges" and the more fundamentalist Protestant institutions. Perhaps this is because these are generally older institutions and represent a large denomination and may, as a consequence, feel less challenged by other faiths and by secular institutions.

In the 1970s, when I was a young assistant professor at a Methodist-related liberal arts college, I served on a presidential search committee.

Among other questions we put to each finalist was one about the candidate's sense of what the college's religious heritage meant at the end of the twentieth century. The successful candidate, Dr. Phil Secor, gave what struck me then, and now, as a profound response. He said that the greatest virtue of working at a college with a religious heritage is that it gave one a sense of humor about that work. He explained he meant that at such colleges there is always an implicit understanding that no matter how important the daily business of the college—and that work *is* important—there is a recognition of a theological, cosmological perspective from which the challenges, irritations, triumphs, and tragedies of the academic world shrank to nothing more than a grain of sand.

Age

A handful of institutions that would still be universally called "small colleges" today were founded in the late eighteenth century—Washington College (1782), Washington and Lee (1782), Hampden-Sydney (1783), Transylvania (1783), Dickinson (1783), St. John's–Maryland (1784), and Franklin and Marshall (1787) are among the oldest.[43] Most of today's small colleges were first founded in the nineteenth century. Several were founded in the twentieth century, including some in the second half of the twentieth century (e.g., New College [1960], the College of the Atlantic [1969], and Unity College [1969]). It makes a real difference in many aspects of institutional life whether a college is long-lived or, say, less than fifty years old.

Perhaps most obviously, unless the college occupies a campus with a prior history (as, e.g., the Morris campus of the University of Minnesota does), new colleges will have physically new campuses. Of course, older institutions may move to new quarters or thoroughly rebuild a traditional campus so as to eradicate any trace of older structures—for example, Centenary College, as we have seen, or Carthage College, now in Kenosha, Wisconsin, but formerly in three different locations in Illinois. Still, recently founded colleges are most likely to have buildings that were mostly built in a modern style, at about the same time. This can mean that the newer campuses have considerably more up-to-date facilities for, perhaps, laboratory sciences, computing, and libraries. One hidden peril of this inevitable fact, however, is that, for the first twenty years or so, such a campus will have virtually no significant costs for major maintenance and may have made no provision in its budget for such expenses. Then, when the roofs all need renovation at the same time about a quarter-century after the campus was constructed, some major infusions of new money may have to be found, rapidly.

Another age-related fiscal problem that can face colleges less than fifty years old derives from the fact that they lack an alumni base. If a college opened its doors in 1960, its first large group of alumni will reach the age of sixty-five in the year 2007. It is not until a college is about fifty years old that a substantial collection of graduates has reached the age at which significant philanthropy tends to happen. And, since for most of that first fifty years there were neither as many nor as rich alumni, most newer institutions hit their half-century birthdays with relatively underdeveloped alumni and college relations offices.

A somewhat less demonstrable effect of newness on colleges has to do with institutional culture. It has been my observation, and others have confirmed it, that newer colleges, even those that begin with a strong initial impulse toward experimentation and an openness to new educational ideas and methods, tend to grow very conservative in some important respects very quickly. After all, once a new college has "invented itself" during its founding years, those founders and inventors dominate the school for the next several decades. Probably there is no more deeply entrenched conservative than yesterday's innovator who sees her innovations challenged. Seen from the other side, at a Swarthmore or Dickinson, it has been inevitable that during their relatively long histories virtually everything about the institution's curriculum, personnel, and operations has changed before, several times. In contrast, a college that is only twenty or thirty years old has probably not had to change very much at all since its creation. Harvard cannot continue to build its curriculum around Latin literature, but many an institution founded in the 1960s has found it astonishingly hard to move beyond the curricular and pedagogical models that were then considered advanced.

In this context it is fascinating to compare the three small institutions profiled in Burton Clark's *The Distinctive Colleges*. Reed College, created early in the second decade of the twentieth century, and Antioch, which virtually reinvented itself at the same time, both launched very vigorous experimental programs that broke new ground in American higher education in the 1920s and 1930s. By the end of World War II both institutions had grown protective and inflexible about those innovative programs. Swarthmore College, by contrast, had evolved much more steadily into a national leader over a longer period of time and seemed, as a consequence, to remain more comfortable with substantive, steady, and accretive, change.[44]

Governance and Administrative Structures

There are significant differences in the ways small colleges manage themselves and make decisions. Most small institutions have a governing board. In a few cases, especially in the public sector, such as the University of Wisconsin–Superior, it will be a board that has responsibility for all the institutions within a system. Wisconsin has a statewide board of regents with seventeen members which has direct responsibility for all the institutions of the University of Wisconsin system. Typically, too, the system itself has an administrative structure, with a president, vice presidents, and staff, and each campus has its administration. Most private small colleges have an independent governing board that serves only one campus. In some cases a member, or more, may be an official of the church that sponsors the institution. At Southwestern University six different conferences of the Texas Methodist Church are represented on the board by twenty members, and the bishops of these conferences are additional ex officio members. Some small college boards are large: the biggest I encountered among my site visits had forty-eight members at Centenary. Some boards are smaller, with between a dozen and twenty members.

Most boards will have some official alumni representation, and alumni of the institution dominate some of them. Many boards have a member who is a student. Governing boards are commonly divided into working committees in such areas as personnel, educational programs, facilities, and finances. Some meet as infrequently as twice a year; others meet monthly. Most have between four and six annual meetings, often with an executive committee meeting more often.

On-campus administrations are in some ways quite alike, and in other ways each is different. One can count on small colleges to have a chief executive officer, usually a "president" although occasionally a "chancellor" or "provost" (or until very recently at New College in Florida a "warden"). Almost all will have a senior officer in the area of academic affairs, one in student affairs and one in financial affairs. Usually (although not always) the financial affairs officer will be distinct from the chief fund-raising administrator. Beyond having a president, academic dean, dean of students, and finance officer, campus administrations have an infinite variety of structures. For example, in some cases the admissions office (now often called "Enrollment Management" or "Enrollment Services") reports directly to the CEO as a member of the senior administrative team. In others that individual reports to the chief academic officer and sometimes to the chief student affairs person. Similarly, the athletic director is frequently housed in any of those three reporting areas. The campus security office may report to the business office or to student affairs. The bookstore may, or may not, be the responsibility of the academic officer. Some small colleges have deans who report to a provost or academic vice president (e.g., Southwestern University has a dean of the School of Fine Arts), but this is a far more common structure in larger institutions. Others have division chairs (e.g., Colby-Sawyer); most have department chairs, sometimes on a regularly rotating basis and in other cases with virtual life terms.

At some relatively wealthy small colleges, administrative offices can be substantial. The Office of the President at Wellesley has, in addition to the president herself, two "assistant to the president" positions, two "administrative assistants," and a "clerk of the Board of Trustees." The Office of the Dean of the College is supported by two associate deans, two assistant deans, and an "assistant to the dean." At Wellesley each class has a "dean," and there is an administrative assistant for the Office of the Class Deans and a "Coordinator of First-Year Students Office." By contrast, the Colby-Sawyer catalog lists under "Office of the President" the lonely name of only the president herself, and under "Academic Affairs" there are no assistant or associate deans. I have not yet encountered at a small college the increasingly common administrative position at major universities of "chief of staff" (as in "Chief of Staff in the President's or Provost's Office").

Small colleges will, of course, have a full panoply of faculty and community committees—curriculum, library, academic standing, planning, and student services. No two campuses have exactly the same configuration of committee structure. It is a distinctive trait that at most small colleges a majority of faculty members will play a significant role within this committee structure annually. Indeed, I have rarely seen a small campus where the faculty and administration were not lamenting about the burdens of too many committees with too many members, who met too often, for too long. I have also rarely seen a campus that was actually able to make a long-term correction of this condition, although most will periodically undertake, with Panglossian optimism, "committee reform."

Small colleges usually have some sort of all-campus governing assembly. This can range from the restricted "campus senate," in which various constituencies have elected representatives (a much more common model at larger institutions), to more inclusive groups (e.g., all regular faculty plus elected staff and students) to genuine town meeting–type democracies: Warren Wilson College has two governance institutions, a student caucus to which everyone is invited and within which "if you show an interest you can be a voting member," and a staff forum that includes all faculty, staff, and volunteers.[45]

A major strength and defining characteristic of American higher education is its vigorous diversity. This is certainly true of collegiate governance. Just as each of the fifty states seems to have devised a slightly different mechanism for operating its university (or university system or systems), so, too, each small college has been free to evolve mechanisms for decision making and daily management which suit its history, its people, and its mission. Some make decisions rapidly; most make them slowly. Some are authoritarian, some are representative or selective democracies, others cling to a kind of town meeting communitarianism, and a few seem, at least from the outside, anarchic.

Idiosyncrasies

Even this extended discussion of the variations within the small college community does not do justice to the range of possibilities, both theoretical and actual, of these institutions. I have mentioned in passing some unique institutions, genuine one-of-a-kind places that march very much to the beat of their own drummers. This is not the place for an exhaustive catalog of these idiosyncratic colleges, but a few samples offer at the very least a little spice.

—St. John's College, in Annapolis and Santa Fe, has already been cited for its unique great works curriculum, within which everyone reads exactly the same books in the same sequence for the entire college career. The two St. John's also manifest a highly unusual pedagogy, in which faculty members, like students, do not specialize, and all have to teach in fields and disciplines outside the areas in which they did graduate work. Thus, a Ph.D. holder in Renaissance English literature will teach Euclid; a biologist will lead discussions of Marx. And all classes are offered as genuine seminars, with the role of the instructor being less to "instruct" in a conventional sense and more to begin conversations with appropriate queries and keep the discussion on track.

—Evergreen State College is surely the only institution anywhere with an obscene mollusk (the geoduck) as a mascot.

—Gallaudet College, with just over two thousand students in Washington, DC, is the only independent liberal arts college for the deaf.

—Deep Springs College has but twenty-six or so students, none of whom pays any tuition and all of whom work on the college's isolated farm. The first time a student has to slaughter a steer, to provide the college's meat, is a rite of passage. The college has two rules in the area of student affairs: no substance abuse and no leaving campus during an academic term. Deep Springs is, to put it mildly, an intense community.

—Moravian College requires all students to spend time studying abroad.

—At Guilford College all campus decisions, from student government to the board of trustees, are made by consensus, without taking a vote.

—Warren Wilson has a "dean of work."

Several of these institutions demonstrate what Riesman and Grant call "telic" reforms: they seek to redefine the shape of the undergraduate experience after radically redefining its end.[46] Others demonstrate what is termed in Riesman and Grant's conceptual structure "popular reforms," which tend to embrace traditional goals for baccalaureate-level education, but believe there are better ways of achieving those goals than the traditional undergraduate experience.

♦ ♦ ♦

The more one knows the small colleges of the United States, the more variegated and diverse they seem. Just as the small colleges together add an important thread to the rich fabric of all American higher learning, so each small college contributes something unique to the pool of such schools. Ecologists warn against monocultures: a forest with one species of tree or a farm with a single cash crop is not healthy. The rich spectrum of small colleges makes a vital contribution to a vigorous, heterogeneous, diverse community of higher education in the United States and the world.

"Here is God's plenty," said John Dryden of Chaucer's *Canterbury Tales*. Like Chaucer's wondrous panoply of medieval humanity, today's small colleges span a huge variety of people, programs, histories, emphases, cultures, and missions across a broad range of institutional characteristics. Like Chaucer's pilgrims, too, they are embarked on their travels for different, sometimes even contradictory, reasons, yet they are all moving along a common way—the path of undergraduate teaching and learning. Will they be able to keep going? What kind of progress will they make? Why is their journey important to others? Where are they going?

In the next chapter I will take a closer look at these small college pilgrims—faculty members, students, and staff.

Old Main . . . in Maine

Dr. Theodora Kalikow is president of the University of Maine at Farmington. UM-F was founded in 1864 primarily as a teacher-training institution. Today it is a public liberal arts college with a complete range of liberal arts offerings. Among its notable graduates are the Stanley brothers, who created the Stanley Steamer automobile. Elementary education remains the most popular major. The college is a unit of the seven-campus University of Maine system. It enrolls about two thousand students on a handsome New England campus adjacent to the downtown of a rather small city of about nine thousand inhabitants. Farmington itself is a pretty but somewhat isolated community, about a half-hour drive from Augusta, the state capital. Dr. Kalikow became Farmington's president in 1994. Here are her characteristically straightforward (characteristically Mainer) responses to a series of queries I put to her regarding her academic career.

---

1. *Tell us a bit about yourself. —Where did you grow up?*
I grew up in Swampscott, Massachusetts, a little town north of Boston, on the ocean. It was a small town that grew into a suburb when I was growing up in the 1940s and 1950s.

—Had your parents gone to college?
My dad went to MIT, first in his generation to go to college (immigrant parents), and my mother studied briefly at art schools in Boston.

2. *And a bit about your high school experience.*
Swampscott High School, class of 1958. There were about one hundred kids in my class, so four hundred all told. I was pre–baby boom, so the classes were getting larger every year.

—Activities?
High school band—I went to almost every football game from the seventh grade on, when I joined the band. We had a big and good band, and I loved my uniform. Also, I was on the yearbook staff and involved in a few other activities.

—Did you like high school?

Some parts were great—I loved English, Latin, sciences. Lots of times I practiced "creative boredom."

3. *Now college.*

I was an undergraduate at Wellesley College and did graduate work at MIT and Boston University.

—What did you like about college? What did you dislike?

I liked a women's college; Wellesley was great. I liked exploring lots of different subjects. Went to college to study chemistry, ended up thinking that philosophy and history of science were what I really wanted to study more. That's what I did in grad school. However, I liked everything, from theater to Latin to chemistry. I was not a particularly good student in terms of grades because I was doing many things besides classes, and trying to grow up at the same time, but I loved the intellectual stimulation, and I learned a tremendous amount about a wide range of topics.

4. *When did you decide to make a career of academe?*

When I decided to go to grad school to study philosophy / history of science, I just assumed I would teach. And did . . . I taught at University of Exeter, England, 1967–68. Then at the University of Massachusetts–Dartmouth (at that time called Southeastern Massachusetts University, or SMU) from 1968 to 1980. Went from "jr. dogsbody" to full professor with tenure, department chair, faculty union president, etc.

—What subjects did you teach? Comments on teaching?

Philosophy, history of science, logic, etc. I loved teaching and thought I would do it forever. Connecting with students (mostly first-generation immigrants, poor folk) and getting them to see that they were capable and they could do high-level work was very rewarding. Then one day . . . the president of my university called.

5. *Tell us about your career, then, in administration.*

At SMU I was assistant to the president, for a couple of years. I had a great time and discovered what it was like to be able to affect an entire institution. Then I became an ACE Fellow in 1983–84 and spent the year at Brown. Got to see another kind of institution and decided I could be a president. And then I didn't go home. I became dean of the College of Arts and Sciences at the University of Northern Colorado from 1984 to 1987; dean of the college (chief academic officer), Plymouth State College (NH), from 1987 to 1994. Then president here at the University of Maine at Farmington in 1994.

—*Comments on your presidency?*
Lots of fun and learning . . . lots of change making . . . discovered that my preference is for small, focused institutions. I like the feedback at a small public liberal arts college—you can really see you're changing lives. And the mission—*how* lives are changed and in what directions—is very congenial. I think I am trying to re-create the conditions that I found so stimulating about my own college experience. UM-F is the best place you can imagine to work. Great faculty, staff, and students. Great community. There's a synergy here that allows more to get done than you'd ever predict.

—*What do you like most about the job?*
Leading folks to make the changes that they want to make and which work for the good of the institution, the community, the state, etc.

—*What do you find most discomforting?*
Very little monetary support from the state, and the university system, considering the tremendous job we do. Sometimes I get frustrated.

6. *What are your worries about small colleges in the coming decade?*
Money . . . demographics . . . keeping up with the competition . . .

7. *What are your hopes and aspirations for these smaller colleges?*
I hope we keep turning out folks who are ready and willing to take their places in their communities as leaders and engaged citizens. We're living in times where a lot of critical choices will have to be made about the character of our country. We can model what it is like to be part of such a community, and have to do this consciously, tell people that is our job, etc. We also have to transmit the learning of the past . . . But without this community piece, our distinctive American character—what's best about America—may be in danger.

8. *Any thoughts about the distinctive character of being the CEO of a small school?*
I made a conscious effort to pick the kind of small place that would be right for my personality and style. Informal, straightforward, friendly . . . Maine-ish (even though I am "from away"). I picked right . . . and over the years I have gotten the community to reinforce these values in the way we behave towards each other and vis-à-vis the larger world. I don't know if that could have been

done at a larger place. It's a question of living out the values that we are trying to teach. Around here it's first name, pipe up, let us know good ideas, and then do 'em. We may not have much money but we do have a good time and we're proud of what we have achieved.

President Kalikow's concluding sentence surely speaks for most of the nation's small college presidents.

4 | People at Small Colleges

My major prof from sixty years ago passed away six months ago.
He was the most important person in my life other than my father.
CENTENARY COLLEGE GRADUATE of the 1940s

Colleges are about learning and teaching; at their core are students and professors. And also central are the staff and senior administrators who work with them.[1] In this chapter I discuss a cluster of characteristics that specifically pertain to faculty work, to student populations, and to administrative responsibility from the small college perspective. For many who work and study at small schools, institutional affiliation becomes more of an obsession than an avocation. As one middle manager at Southwestern University commented, "Working at a small college is not a job; it is a lifestyle, even a passion."[2]

As elsewhere, I have made an effort to ground this discussion in statistically demonstrable fashion and to support any conclusions with objective fact. Even more than elsewhere, such an effort is going to be frustrating when considering the lives of the students, faculty, and staff who live at small colleges. This is, at least in part, because there is not a lot of direct data that actually focuses upon the variable of size. Nonetheless, some worthwhile inferences can be drawn from available material. A case in point is the National Center for Educational Statistics (NCES), a countrywide collector and transmitter of all sorts of information about education, including virtually all the materials required by the federal government. Most of the NCES data is related to institutional control (e.g., public/private), not size. Other NCES material is presented within the following, more finely separated and therefore more helpful, categories:

—Total—All institutions

—Public research universities

—Private research universities

—Public comprehensive institutions

—Private comprehensive universities

—Liberal arts colleges

—Two-year institutions

While it is the fact that some of the center's "liberal arts colleges" might not qualify in this study as "small colleges," there will be a large overlap, and most of these institutions will be classified as liberal arts colleges.

Yet other NCES-reported statistics are collected in terms of four-year doctoral institutions, four-year nondoctoral institutions, and two-year institutions. In such a scheme small colleges will commonly be among the "four-year nondoctoral" class, but so will very large institutions that grant master's degrees but not doctorates.

Beyond frustrating the diligent researcher, this dearth of statistical information about small colleges, per se, is disturbing. If the continuing well-being of smaller institutions is imperiled, as I have suggested, we need to know more about them than we do. It is difficult to defend the unique contributions of smaller institutions or to decry their weaknesses without more, and more precise, data.

All this said, a careful look at liberal arts colleges and four-year nondoctoral institutions can be helpful, at least in a crude way, in examining such issues as faculty salaries; student drop-out rates; and faculty, student, and staff demographics.

Professors

The workload and work conditions of college teachers in small institutions are multifaceted. I have already (in chap. 3) taken a look at the range of faculty salaries from the perspective of differences between small institutions. At the top end some senior faculty at affluent small colleges come close to a salary base that would earn them a place in the economic upper class. At the other end of the spectrum beginning teachers at relatively poor institutions might be uncomfortably close to the bottom edge of the middle income class. As we shall see later, many colleges and universities have large populations of temporary and part-time faculty. Sometimes the salary scale for such employees does not rise to the level of a living wage— for example, at the bottom of the scale remunerations of $3,000–5,000 per course are not rare, and so it is possible to teach seven or eight courses a year at multiple institutions, for less than $30,000 and no benefits. A national conference on the growing use of adjunct and part-time faculty concluded that, "in comparison to their full-time colleagues, the majority of part-time faculty members teach under emphatically substandard conditions."[3] Indeed, in 1999 the total personal income from teaching of part-time faculty nationally was only $11,533, although the total average family income of part-time teachers was significantly higher.[4]

Not surprisingly, not only do small college compensation levels vary from college to college, but there is substantial variation among salary averages at different sorts of institution. NCES data for 1992–93 on average salaries for full-time instructional staff show this variation (table 4.1).

There is, then, substantial variation between small institutions and very substantial variation as well among different kinds of institutions, with small colleges at the bottom of all four-year and graduate-level institutions and more than ten thousand dollars per year below the average.

But salary is not the only significant, nor perhaps even the most important, aspect of faculty work life. At many small institutions, for example, the formal and informal benefits offered can be a very important part of the compensation package, and here the picture is a happier one. It is not uncommon for small, somewhat paternalistic institutions that may have relatively low salaries to offer fairly generous benefit programs. As is common through higher education, medical and dental insurance, retirement

Table 4.1 Instructional Staff Salaries for 1992–1993

Institution	Salary	No. of Professors
All colleges and universities	$54,968	560,000
Public research institutions	65,162	137,000
Private research institutions	73,848	39,080
Public doctoral	59,453	58,100
Private doctoral	69,663	20,070
Public comprehensive	50,204	83,000
Private comprehensive	49,937	37,500
Liberal arts	43,435	47,600

Source: National Center for Education Statistics, figs. 16 and 44.

contributions, family and medical leave, and similar items can easily equal 30 percent or more of direct salary. At small institutions there are other, less formal benefits, many of which might be items of significant cost at larger places. These include, for example, parking (which is sometimes free and always relatively cheap when compared to major urban institutions); free or inexpensive admission to athletic and cultural events; use of college fitness/gymnasium facilities; and, at some institutions at some times of the year, more free food than anyone would wisely consume.

For many faculty members teaching load is as important as pay. The most common faculty teaching load at small colleges is six to eight courses per year, three or four a semester. At many institutions teaching assignments are higher or lower; I have encountered colleges that ask faculty to teach as many as ten courses during the regular academic year. A very few others—relatively rich institutions—require as few as four courses per year. Most prestigious research universities will have a load of no more than four courses and often whittle that number down appreciably. It is far less common at small colleges for faculty members to secure course relief in exchange for research and similar assignments, although often regular faculty members will chair departments or take on other administrative responsibilities in exchange for a class or two reduction. It is difficult to overemphasize what a large difference there is between teaching two smallish classes in a semester, with possibly 35 or 40 students between them, and at the other extreme five larger classes, with perhaps a total of 150 to 200 pupils. And, of course, even in a small college, a large introductory section of Biology or Psychology may have that many students in a single class. It also makes a difference whether a significant proportion of course work is multiple sections of the same subject matter or each class requires separate preparation.

Although teaching is almost universally the top priority and assignment for small college professors, other expectations also play an important part in faculty work lives. Some institutions have virtually no research and scholarship expectations; others make significant demands in this area. Although exceptions exist, generally it is the wealthier and more prestigious small institutions that have the highest expectations of published scholarship. While some small college scholars and departments are highly productive of serious and substantial research, many small college faculty members engage in little or none. Indeed, I remember being chastised, as a brand new assistant professor at a teaching college, because

I had published an article in a scholarly journal. That feat was taken as evidence that I was not devoting myself wholeheartedly to the classroom. At the other extreme, at one small liberal arts campus of a state university system, the scholarship portfolio of a faculty member being judged for tenure and promotion is formally submitted for evaluation to the Office of the Dean of the Graduate School on the flagship research campus of the university. The NCES has some valuable data regarding the division between teaching and research responsibilities at various sorts of institutions (table 4.2).

It is clear that the widely held conception that faculty members at liberal arts colleges (and, I infer, small colleges) do more teaching and less research than their peers at other four-year institutions is an accurate one, although perhaps not as extreme as some might suspect. Thus, for example, University of Texas chancellor Mark Yudof, a senior administrator looking from the outside at small institutions, sees them as "places where strong teaching is taken seriously and rewarded."[5] Liberal arts college faculty also tend to use more individuated and time-consuming methods in their pedagogy: from the NCES we learn that liberal arts college faculty offer more seminar classes than their colleagues at doctorate-granting institutions (17.5 to 11.5 percent), and they make greater use of essay examinations (65.8 compared to 59.8 percent).[6] Conversely, they do less non-

Table 4.2 The Division between Teaching and Doing Research

Institution	Faculty Time (%)	
	Teaching	Research
All	56.6	15.2
Liberal arts	65.4	8.1
Public research	45.9	25.9
Private research	41.9	29.1

Source: Data are from 1998, NCES figure 47.
Note: Other categories, such as administrative responsibilities, did not show significant variation.

face-to-face teaching: only 5 percent of liberal arts faculty instruct electronically compared to 8 percent at public doctoral universities, 6 percent at private research universities, 9 percent at public comprehensive institutions, 9 percent at private comprehensive institutions, and 12 percent at two-year schools.[7]

Another major responsibility of small college teachers is advising. Many large institutions have advising offices, and undergraduate advising, especially for first- and second-year students, is largely delegated to full-time, professional advisors based in these offices. At most small colleges faculty members advise undergraduates, both in the lower division years before the selection of a major and as upper division departmental majors. Moreover, small college faculty members are very commonly asked to serve as advisors to student groups and clubs. I have seen campuses where there are more such student organizations than there are faculty members to advise them.

Helping with co- and extracurricular activities is one kind of service, which, along with teaching and scholarship, constitutes the third leg of the tripod of faculty work and, hence, assessment for promotion, tenure, and salary increases. This is perhaps the most amorphous assignment, the most varied in definition, and generally the responsibility that is considered the least important. In some cases service means assignments on college committees, and involvement with other campus organizations and projects (e.g., chairing task forces, serving on search committees, and meeting with prospective students and parents). Faculty may be expected to be attentive to alumni, at homecoming, and throughout the year, through mechanisms such as a newsletter mailed to former departmental majors. Sometimes, but not always, "community service"—such as being a member of the local Red Cross board, serving as a Scout leader, chairing the local United Way community fund drive, or serving as a "guest expert" for local media—is seen as important to the college and part of the faculty member's professional dossier for salary and other review considerations. Leadership in appropriate professional organizations is yet another service contribution. Organizing a panel at an annual scholarly meeting or serving as an officer at a local, regional, or national level of an academic society is almost always a valued service opportunity, and many small college professors play an energetic and leading role in such activities.

Another very important part of the faculty task at small colleges can be a role in institutional governance. I suspect that the faculty voice in collegial decision making is a larger one on small campuses than big ones: it is certainly a professional responsibility of a far greater proportion of the teaching faculty. The Carnegie Foundation's national Survey of Faculty of 1984 found that at research universities only 9 percent of the faculty usually participated in faculty senate meetings and 12 percent in campus-wide faculty committee meetings, while at liberal arts colleges that figure for both sorts of governance functions was a much higher 55 percent. The same survey found that 21 percent of the research university faculty responded that "my college is 'very important' to me," while at liberal arts colleges that figure was 44 percent. On the other hand, more faculty at the larger institutions than at liberal arts colleges felt that their academic discipline was "very important" to them.[8] Governance concerns affect a far larger share of the faculty when the faculty is small. Many small institutions have an all-faculty "assembly," "faculty senate," or "community council." In contrast, larger institutions almost always depend on more representative, less all-inclusive groups. Similarly, small colleges have pretty much the same panoply of faculty committees—curriculum committees, faculty search committees, budget advisory committees, athletics oversight groups, library committee, honors committee—as huge institutions. But these assignments will be divided among many fewer eligible members. So, if a big university has 250 committee slots, to be allocated among 2,500 faculty members, a small place may have 100 assignments to be assigned to 110 professors. (Even more daunting, of course, is when there are 110 positions and 100 faculty members to fill them.) Most small college professors can expect to have both departmental duties and at least one all-college committee (or task force, study group, or ad hoc organization) assignment. (The NCES reports that faculty at four-year nondoctoral institutions describe themselves as spending 10.2 percent of their time on "administrative" work.)[9]

Across all institutional types many faculty populations are increasingly made up of part-time teachers, who are replacing full-time, tenurable professors. According to the American Association of University Professors (AAUP), the exact figure is 43 percent. According to the American Council on Education (ACE), it is 49 percent.[10] This trend is discernible throughout U.S. higher education, at small undergraduate colleges, large research universities, and, especially, two-year institutions. In 1998, 43.9 percent of faculty at private liberal arts colleges were part-time, up from 36.9 percent in 1992.[11] And it is generally a trend that is lamented by faculty members:

"AAUP believes that excessive use of, and inadequate compensation and professional support for, part-time and non-tenure-track faculty exploits these colleagues and undermines academic freedom, academic quality and professional standards."[12] Often, the rationale for an increasingly part-time professorate is purely fiscal: as noted earlier, part-timers are paid less, and they are often hired without benefits. Moreover, in times of financial stress part-time faculty members offer an institution a kind of flexibility in its workforce which tenured and tenure-track teachers do not afford. A common concern expressed about part-time teachers is that they do not participate fully in the extra-classroom life of the college—advising, service, governance, and such. Sometimes this is true. When it is, this phenomenon serves to heighten the workload burdens of the remaining "regular" faculty members. Some believe that the quality of instruction provided by less-than-full-time faculty members is inferior, although I have never seen compelling evidence to support this contention. I have observed that students tend not to notice the difference between part-time and full-time teachers, temporary or tenure-track hires. They heed what happens in the classroom and, to a lesser extent, the availability of instructors in their offices outside of class. To most students temporary, part-time instructors are still their "professors."

Sometimes, of course, part-time instructors are retained to teach in areas for which there is not sufficient demand for a full-load professor, especially in smaller colleges, where some departments are small and some important academic fields may be unrepresented—for example, a course or two a year in photography or business law. In these cases there seems universal accord that such additions to the professorial workforce are beneficial. In general, it has been my observation over decades in higher education that, more often than not, two half-time, or three one-third-time faculty members will probably contribute to the overall welfare of the college as much as or more than one full-time professor. Most of the part-time teachers I have met work zealously on behalf of their students, although they frequently get a "bum rap"; they tend to be an exploited underclass of the professorate. Some small colleges have virtually no part-time faculty members, especially institutions that are wealthy or physically isolated (and thus may have no pool of potential part-timers to draw on) or both. Others, especially those with strong programs in areas such as business, music, or art in which local practitioners provide significant instructional opportunities, rely heavily on non-tenure-track teachers.

The lives of faculty members can be influenced by many factors attendant upon the types of small colleges in which they find themselves. Living and working at a small college in a small town can pose challenges in the areas of recreation, culture, social opportunities, and even gastronomy. The time is not distant when it was common for small colleges to require faculty members to dwell in the town where the institution was located, but I doubt that restriction applies to more than a miniscule handful of institutions today. I encountered none in my research or visits for this book.

Faculty members at small colleges are less likely to find professional travel supported at the level their colleagues at large research universities expect. Nor are they going to be as well supported by laboratories, libraries, and research or teaching assistants. At some Christian institutions faculty members will find additional extra-instructional demands and restrictions placed upon them—activities such as public drinking or, in some places, dancing will be frowned upon or even prohibited. Some sectarian institutions make rigorous theological demands regarding profession of belief and liturgical practice upon those they hire.

Of many descriptions of the lives of college teachers, two autobiographical books of the 1990s offer particularly winning perspectives. James Kissane's *Mild Outbursts* describes a career in the English Department of a small college from which the author himself graduated. Kissane focuses upon the development of the curriculum at Grinnell, relationships with students and colleagues, institutional politics, and several decades in the life of the college at which he has spent virtually his entire professional life. James Axtell's *The Pleasures of Academe: A Celebration and Defense of Higher Education* offers a balanced picture of the professorial life in a larger university setting (Johns Hopkins, where Axtell teaches humanities).[13]

College teaching, at a small school or a major university, can be the most rewarding of careers; it is certainly one of the most demanding. There is a very wide range of faculty careers available at small colleges: being a small college professor can mean many different things, just as being a small college student does.

Students

The first, and most important, thing to say about students at small colleges is, demonstrably, overall they are well served there. Howard R. Bowen summarizes the research evidence which supports this assertion: "A considerable body of opinion and some documented research supports the proposition that small colleges, other things being equal, produce more desirable change in students than large institutions . . . many researchers have found evidence that smallness is associated with educational advantage."[14]

Alexander Astin found in multiple studies that smaller institutions produce a range of desirable effects in college students. Astin has measured "value added"—how far colleges move student intellectual and social development between their entrance and their exit—and concludes that smaller institutions have been more effective in creating measurable changes during the four undergraduate years.[15]

A. W. Chickering studied the effects of the size variable on "student development" and concluded that it was a significant factor in producing positive developmental change. He argues that those changes are both in more positive directions and more substantial as size diminishes. The areas of student development upon which Chickering focuses especially include: individual autonomy, awareness of one's social, political and cultural surroundings, aesthetic sensitivity, personality integration, liberality in religious views, tolerance, and less concern for material possessions.[16]

K. A. Feldman and T. M. Newcomb concluded that small size increases the "impact" that colleges have on their student populations. They measured such characteristics as practicality (on which liberal arts students did not fare well), community (friendliness, cohesive group orientation), scholarship (academic environment and an emphasis on achievement), awareness (self-knowledge, creativity, concern about world events), and propriety (politeness, creating a considerate environment). On the latter four characteristics liberal arts college graduates excelled.[17]

C. R. Pace demonstrated that small liberal arts institutions produced measurably higher "educational benefits" than other collegiate types. In another interesting report he includes information from assessments of higher education in California, comparing the University of California, the California state universities and colleges, the community colleges, and private four-year colleges. Measuring the "goals" of faculty, he found that among the private (and thus smaller) institutions the top three goals are academic development, community, and individual/personal development. Those goals ranked fourth, eighth, and fourteenth for the faculty at the University of California.[18]

D. A. Rock and colleagues identified areas of "student achievement," sought to evaluate and measure these areas, and concluded that college size influenced such achievements, with smallness demonstrating a positive outcome.[19]

Two important (but now somewhat dated) studies by Robert H. Knapp, Joseph J. Greenbaum, and H. B. Goodrich demonstrated that small colleges have the greatest success in producing both future scientists and future scholars.[20] Concluding that "nondenominational liberal arts colleges constitute an exceptionally productive group" for training future scholars, Knapp and Greenbaum listed the most productive institutions, nationally, for male scholars (I indicate with an asterisk those in the small college category): Swarthmore,* Reed,* the University of Chicago, Oberlin,* Haverford,* Caltech, Carleton,* Princeton, Antioch,* and Harvard, in that order. For women the list was Nazareth College (MI),* Swarthmore,* Reed,* Grinnell,* Kalamazoo,* Aquinas College,* Monmouth,* Sarah Lawrence,* Hillsdale College,* and Antioch* (i.e., 100 percent).[21] Knapp and Goodrich listed the top twenty institutions in productivity of scientists as: Reed,* Caltech, Kalamazoo,* Earlham,* Oberlin,* the University of Massachusetts, Hope,* DePauw,* Nebraska Wesleyan,* Iowa Wesleyan,* Antioch,* Marietta,* Colorado College,* Cornell College,* Central,* the University of Chicago, Haverford,* Clark,* Johns Hopkins, and Emporia.*[22] In sum, small colleges do have a measurable effect on student performance and outcomes; researchers have measured that effect, and it is positive.

I have already examined what kinds of students go to smaller institutions. Some small colleges have a diverse student population in terms of race, ethnicity, family background, academic preparation, and similar demographic and experiential factors. Rarely will they approach the spectrum of students one might find at a really large university—Texas, Ohio State, Minnesota, and the like. At other smaller colleges the student population is homogeneous, sometimes remarkably so, given the range of the American college-going population at the turn of the twenty-first century. The president of one prestigious and wealthy small liberal arts college (an institution with a need-blind admissions policy that meets 100 percent of need and has a rich tradition of social activism) remarked to me that his college is virtually entirely populated by students of upper-middle-class origins from the suburbs of major metropolitan areas. A Catholic women's college is going to be largely attended by Catholic women (who might be of varied ethnic and social class origins); an evangelical Christian Bible college will be peopled by Christian believers. I was very interested when faculty at Morehouse College made a strong case that their institution—all male, all African American—was a diverse one. They pointed out that Morehouse's students came from a wide variety of socioeconomic levels and from very different parts of the country: an affluent African American male student from Portland, Oregon, is very different from another African American male student whose origins are in Detroit's inner city, and both of them are different from a third student who grew up on a sharecropping farm in small-town Alabama. The lesson, clearly, is that, if one looks closely, the most seemingly homogeneous student population is diverse.

There are several important characteristics that are commonly and sensibly used to describe the student populations of various small colleges. From the most to the least prestigious, colleges fret obsessively about the level of academic preparedness of their students (Boyer found in 1984 that 64 percent of the faculty at all institutions felt that "present academic standards for undergraduate admissions should be 'higher'"; this remains a widely held concern among faculty members).[23] There is at least one sense in which this may not be really as important an issue as it sometimes seems to faculty members. As Alexander Astin has pointed out, the schools that admit the most highly qualified students may well do less with those students once they are on campus than colleges that admit seemingly more weakly qualified students. He argues that colleges that do a good job with relatively poorly prepared students "add more value" to the lives of those students than do elite schools such as Harvard and Princeton.[24] I have found no evidence to suggest that the proportion of poorly prepared students is related to school size. But it probably is the case that dealing with underprepared college students poses a special challenge to small institutions. For example, the cost of funding a remedial or developmental skills center certainly diminishes on a per-student basis as the size of the student body increases.

There are two standard primary measurements by which academic preparation is assessed. The first are the much-maligned college entrance tests, the ACT and SAT. These tests have been criticized for insensitivity to the effect that cultural factors can have on high school students' performance on standardized instruments. Those criticisms are probably not without merit, although in reality the SAT and ACT have never marketed themselves as measurements of raw intelligence. Thus, if a bright high schooler performed poorly on standardized tests because she came from a weak high school and her family did not encourage or reward learning, it is still the case that such a student is probably not well prepared for college. Indeed, the initial rationale for the SAT test was to substitute an objective assessment of academic merit for wealth and family connections in college admissions. There are still many college graduates—the author included—for whom the SAT or ACT was an academic lifesaver. These tests, for all their problems and flaws, have offered generations of "late bloomers" and high school misfits one more chance to prove themselves worthy of a college education. In my sample group of colleges SAT scores range from a combined verbal-mathematical result in the lower 800s to the upper 1200s—a significant variation.

High school records, while less easily compared by the various college-ranking publications and services, are almost universally seen to be a more accurate predictor of college success than standardized tests. Students who have done well in meeting academic challenges in the past are likely to repeat that pattern of success in future instructional endeavors. Unlike the standardized tests, of course, success in one high school is not directly comparable to success in another. Sophisticated college admissions offices will frequently discount transcripts from high schools that are known to be weak and, conversely, upgrade records from strong secondary institutions. Many colleges generate a "predictive index," typically a formula that weighs a prospective student's high school record, adjusted for reputation, perhaps twice as much as her SAT or ACT results.

High school students are unlikely to be as well prepared or as talented in every area of precollege work. Thus, one student may be strong in math and science but be a weak writer. Another may be gifted with words but bad with numbers. Some can read and write and calculate but are verbally inarticulate to the point of serious incapacity in a discussion class or seminar.

Another kind of "academic preparedness" has to do with desire and motivation and is virtually impossible to measure but not at all hard to determine in class. Some institutions have a significant number of students who are at college because someone else wants them to be there or because they seek the credentialing a college degree provides. Russell Kirk, in his vitriolic study of "decadence and renewal in the higher learning," suggests that virtually all college students fall into this unsatisfactory group, especially at larger institutions, which he generically dubs "Behemoth U": "teen-agers who have no proper foundation of school learning and who, often enough, feel understandably an aversion to classrooms, after thirteen years of compulsory attendance . . . masses of young people who have very little notion of why they are there . . . crowds of bored and unqualified 'students' . . . shallowly and permissively schooled and reared, with no strong interests of any sort, sometimes with too much money and too little occupation, bored and lacking in strength of will, egotistic without real self-confidence."[25] I am considerably less convinced that such disinterested young people dominate postsecondary institutions anywhere, large or small, but it is a rare classroom that does not have, lurking in the back rows or corners, some students dozing or checking the condition of their fingernails and obviously enduring, rather than enjoying or participating in, the lecture or discussion. Conversely, I have never been to a collegiate institution, no matter how large or small, prestigious or unknown, where I did not discover many deeply engaged and powerfully motivated young women and men who were, without a doubt, bound for successful and reflective careers in college and in life.

It is a common—and commonsensical—belief that small colleges tend to attract students (or the parents of students) who have somewhat higher needs for institutional attentiveness.[26] Small colleges advertise themselves as caring for individual students, in and out of the classroom, as places where "you can't get lost" or where "you are a name, not a number." It is not illogical for parents and prospective students to assume that such places will be a better fit for young women and men who might need a high level of guidance in academic and personal matters.

Another important cluster of student characteristics relates to student engagement, well documented in the annual National Study of Student Engagement (which I examine in chap. 6). Many studies have demonstrated conclusively that students strongly linked to their institution by activities and organizations outside the classroom are more likely to succeed in college and persist to graduation than are less fully engaged peers. (See, e.g., the exhaustive studies of student "involvement" in Alexander Astin's *What Matters in College: "Four Critical Years" Revisited.*)[27]

The NSSE has provided some general information about students and their academic attitudes, behaviors, and work at baccalaureate–liberal arts colleges, in comparison with the entire sample (table 4.3).

Of course, this is information that presents the smaller colleges in concatenated form, and, as noted in chapter 3, students from one such school

Table 4.3 National Survey of Student Engagement, 2002: Selected Summary Results

Student Engagement	Class	NSSE 2002 Mean	Baccalaureate / Liberal Arts Mean	Effect Size
Academic and Intellectual Experiences (1 = never; 4 = very often)				
Asked questions in class or contributed to class discussions	FY	2.80	3.05	.29*
	SR	3.10	3.31	.25*
Prepared two or more drafts of a paper or assignment before turning it in	FY	2.68	2.64	.04
	SR	2.50	2.45	.05
Mental Activities (1 = very little; 4 = very much)				
Analyzing the basic elements of an idea, experience, or theory such as examining a particular case or situation in depth and considering its components	FY	3.14	3.32	.22*
	SR	3.27	3.40	.17
Synthesizing and organizing ideas, information, or experiences into new, more complex interpretations and relationships	FY	2.85	3.04	.22*
	SR	3.05	3.25	.23*
Making judgments about the value of information, arguments, or methods such as examining how others gathered and interpreted data and assessing the soundness of their conclusions	FY	2.80	2.91	.13
	SR	2.93	3.06	.14
Enriching Educational Experiences (0 = no; 1 = yes)				
Work on a research project with a faculty member outside of course or program requirements	FY	0.51	0.66	.30**
	SR	0.28	0.36	.18
Study abroad	FY	0.56	.079	.46***
	SR	0.20	.037	.44***
Independent study or self-designed major	FY	0.28	0.42	.30**
	SR	0.31	0.44	.27*
Educational and Personal Growth (1 = very little; 4 = very much)				
Acquiring a broad and general education	FY	3.11	3.28	.21*
	SR	3.26	3.52	.32**

(continues)

Table 4.3 (*continued*)

Student Engagement	Class	NSSE 2002 Mean	Baccalaureate / Liberal Arts Mean	Effect Size
Acquiring job or work-related knowledge	FY	2.53	2.50	.02
and skills	SR	3.00	2.83	.18
Writing clearly and effectively	FY	2.87	3.06	.21*
	SR	3.06	3.32	.30**
Thinking critically and analytically	FY	3.12	3.28	.20*
	SR	3.33	3.53	.26*
Contributing to the welfare of your community	FY	2.16	2.29	.13
	SR	2.35	2.54	.19
Institutional Environment **(1 = very little; 4 = very much)**				
Spending significant amounts of time studying	FY	3.13	3.26	.16
and on academic work	SR	3.11	3.28	.21*
Satisfaction **(1= poor; 4 = excellent)**				
How would you evaluate your entire educa-	FY	3.19	3.33	.19
tional experience at this institution?	SR	3.24	3.42	.26*

Note: FY = first year; SR = seniors. "Effect size" measures the significance of the difference between the baccalaureate–liberal arts group and the NSSE mean. Items in which the effect size is particularly noteworthy are indicated by one or more asterisks.

are likely to be different from those from another. Still, the data invite us to draw some interesting conclusions, with important implications. Compared to college students generally, those at the liberal arts colleges (and I guardedly extrapolate to other kinds of small colleges) were more likely to believe they have

—asked questions or contributed to class

—analyzed ideas (they are *less* likely to have memorized facts)

—synthesized and organized ideas

—made judgments about the value of information

—acquired a broad general education (less likely to have acquired job skills)

—learned to write clearly

—learned to think critically and analytically

—learned to work on their own

—gained self-understanding

—contributed to the welfare of their communities

—spent significant time studying

Their evaluations of their overall college experience were substantially higher.

◆ ◆ ◆

Alexander Astin's data, over a substantial period of time and covering a substantial cross-section of students, similarly support the claim that students are more satisfied with the faculty and the educational program at small liberal arts colleges, directly "attributable to the . . . college's small size."[28]

Unlike Athena, students do not spring fully formed into college: they come from families. At some small colleges a substantial majority of students come from families in which at least one parent also went to college. This is particularly true of the upper tier of private liberal arts colleges. CIRP data for freshmen in the fall of 2002 showed the levels of parental education at very selective nonsectarian four-year colleges (table 4.4). There are other small schools, however, where there are more first-generation college-goers than not. These tend to be the small state colleges, less prestigious private colleges, and some of the sectarian institutions.

Similarly, students at some institutions tend to come from family backgrounds of relative affluence, others from distinctly more working-class origins. Here the differences between community colleges and small colleges are probably more striking than the differences within the small college bracket. These data are difficult to acquire, other than anecdotally or on an institution-by-institution basis, and impossible to interpret: students and colleges are reluctant to share this sort of family income information, and, particularly in smaller institutions, a handful of very wealthy or abjectly poor students can have a distorting effect upon average numbers. Anecdotally, as mentioned earlier, the president of one top-tier pri-

Table 4.4 Levels of Parental Education at Selective
Nonsectarian Four-Year Colleges

Educational Level	Father	Mother
Some college	8.2	9.5
College degree	26.4	35.3
Some graduate school	3.6	5.4
Graduate degree	49.9	36.8

Source: Sax, Lindholm, Astin, et al., *The American Freshman: National Norms for Fall 2002* (Los Angeles: Higher Education Research Institute, 2002), 110–111.

vate liberal arts college described the students there as virtually all from the upper middle class or above. At one of the least prestigious colleges in my sample group, a couple of somewhat sarcastic but serious students characterized the typical profile as "rich but not smart enough to get into a well-known eastern college." By contrast, students at the University of Wisconsin–Superior were self-described and described by their teachers and the college's administration as "predominately blue-collar."

Some small colleges draw students nationally. In the sample group Wellesley appears to have the most widely dispersed geographical spread among its student population. Wellesley, in fact, has students from all fifty states and sixty-six foreign countries. Others are regional or even local: 92 percent of the students at the University of Wisconsin–Superior are from Wisconsin or nearby Minnesota.

Related to background is the degree of social and political conscious- ness of various student bodies. For generations, for example, students at Oberlin College have viewed their counterparts at Carleton as ivory tower, disconnected academic elitists, and those from the Minnesota college have tended to see their Ohio peers as undisciplined, unscholarly, unthinking activists. Of course, both stereotypes are dead wrong, but it is true that Oberlin has a long tradition of heeding the social gospel: as I noted earlier, Oberlin was a national leader in undergraduate educational equity for

both women and African Americans and has been at the forefront of collegiate social engagement on issues ranging from gay rights to the Vietnam
War. Carleton, by contrast, has tended to cultivate a somewhat more scholarly, less action-oriented, and more reflective student style. In reality both
institutions draw extremely bright, thinking, and engaged students.

There are certainly other distinctions among student populations at
small colleges, some of which are important. Many small institutions are
racially homogeneous—Bennett and Morehouse have African American
student bodies; tribal colleges are peopled by American Indians; many
small institutions with strong sectarian connections to traditionally white
churches draw few or no students of color. Others have been successful in
building multiracial communities, some harmonious, some discordant,
most a mixture. Wellesley College, as a striking example, reports that 48
percent of its students are white: the majority, obviously, are not.[29] At
George Fox University, by contrast, 91.1 percent of the student body are
white.[30] An issue that has drawn increasing attention at many small colleges has to do with the extent to which diverse student bodies interact internally across racial lines. A commonly expressed concern is that, statistically, an institution may have achieved a multicultural student population
but that students from different races or cultures tend to self-segregate
themselves on campus, sometimes even in the classroom but more commonly in residence units, dining halls, and extracurricular involvements.
Clearly, such a condition of statistical racial diversity and de facto racial
segregation deprives students of much of the value of studying and living
in a genuinely diverse collegiate environment. In chapter 6 I will argue
that such a pattern is less likely to develop at smaller colleges, but it is certainly possible.

Students of nonconforming sexual orientations are welcome in some
college communities, which may have highly visible gay/lesbian/bisexual/
transgendered (GLBT) groups and organizations. At the other extreme
small Christian colleges in small rural communities can be unwelcoming
to students who are not—or do not give all visible signs of being—hetero-
sexual. Some small colleges have a significant population of international
students, many as high as 15 to 20 percent; others may have virtually none.

Students at small colleges, like their professors and like small colleges
themselves, come in many kinds and mixes.

Staff

At Centenary College the student lacrosse club forgot to reserve the Intramural Athletic Field for its practices second semester. When the athletes
arrived at the field at 11:30 P.M. on the Monday evening after classes began
and found the lights off, they called the college's president, at home, and
asked him to come over and turn them on. Such is the life of a college
president at many of the nation's small colleges.

During my visit to Morehouse College in Atlanta a faculty member
kindly offered to take me to lunch in the student cafeteria. I, of course, immediately accepted the offer; we strolled over to the dining hall, and fell
into line with the Morehouse men. In front of me in the serving line was a
large young man who looked to be perhaps a student athlete, neatly
dressed and wearing a baseball cap. As he approached the cook dishing
out the main course, the server looked up, spotted the student athlete, and
said, in a loud, clear voice: "Young man, you take off that cap this minute,
or you don't eat here. Don't you know better than to wear a hat inside?"
The student meekly and without complaint removed the baseball cap, was
served his main course, and went on his way. Clearly, students do not just
learn from their official professors at small colleges.

A phrase such as *college staff* or even *administration and staff* cannot capture the range of responsibilities of those who work at small colleges but
are neither teachers nor students. (The range of small college administrative and governance structures is discussed in chap. 3.) The list includes
groundskeepers, deans, electricians, presidents, maids, cooks, secretaries,
and painters. In this section I will focus somewhat anecdotally upon college chief executives, the staff position I know best. But it is not always college presidents or deans who have the most compelling effects upon students. A member of the senior administrative staff at Southwestern
University remarked that, at that institution of 1,250 students, residence
hall housekeepers get to know student schedules, and, if they find a student in the room when she should be in class, they will ask if something is
wrong and urge the student not to cut classes.[31] Most small colleges have
more nonprofessorial employees than they have classroom teachers. Often, these individuals, ranging from the cook to the college president, have
much to teach the students and to contribute to the culture and well-being
of the institution. It is hard to overemphasize the contributions of vice
presidents and directors, coaches, and other managers. Positions such as

chief admissions officer or chief development officer are of enormous importance in the ongoing health of small colleges, often within tiny or even occasionally one-person shops.

Here I will focus on senior administrators at small colleges, not because they are necessarily more important but because they are more visible than most of their colleagues. Like it or not (and it is my personal experience that most of us do like it), one major role of small college presidents is to articulate and even embody the character, aspirations, and values of the institutions they lead. Small college presidents explain their institutions to the Rotary and Lions clubs in their region; they are quoted in the media. When a parent or community member has a complaint about the college, ranging from student behavior to the failure of the football team, the president will be the one to hear it. When things are going well at the college, the president will get far more of the credit than she or he deserves for its thriving and prosperity. To many who have held the post of small college president, the most important part of the job, and in some ways one of its most rewarding challenges, is to tell the story of the college to those outside and within it in a manner that is persuasive, enthusiastic, and honest.

Of course, no two college presidents are alike, including small college presidents. Some will, by need or inclination, spend more time on external responsibilities; others will focus upon academic leadership. There are inevitably differences as well between chief executives at wealthy and/or elite small schools and those at struggling institutions. There are, however, some inevitable commonalities among all small college presidents and some unavoidable differences between those at small and at large schools.

Some of the literature on higher education suggests a kind of "great man or woman" theory of the small college presidency. It is hard to deny the incredible influence that some strong presidents have had on the evolution of the institutions they serve. For example, B. R. Clark's work on three small colleges that he calls "distinctive" focuses upon the pervasive influence of their presidents at crucial moments in their evolution.[32] He traces the story of Arthur Morgan, who rescued Antioch College from obscurity and perhaps oblivion by creating that institution's work program. Clark maintains that, at Reed, William T. Foster, the founding president, created a program of intellectual enthusiasm and strong self-government. And Frank Aydelotte took over Swarthmore when it was a sleepy Quaker college and turned it into an institution of intellectual and scholarly distinction. Clark contends that these three charismatic presidents at three very different institutions, at different times in their development, were central in initiating change that resulted in unique and flourishing colleges. Similarly, Deborah J. Swiss traces the development of Bowdoin College through the stories of four presidencies, seeing in these presidents the embodiment of college itself.[33]

The great man or woman view of the college presidency is not confined to institutions of great distinction. Gary Bonvillian and Robert Murphy focus on the presidency of Arthur Kirk at Keuka College as a model of sound management practices, which saved that small New York college from deep fiscal troubles.[34] President Kirk himself tells much the same story in his doctoral dissertation.[35] His "case study" institution focused on retrenchment, enrollment, and enhanced morale and concluded that "a strong, competent, yet imperfect management can be a potent force in reversing decline." Helen Lefkowitz Horowitz sees clearly the imprint of their early leaders on some of the paramount women's colleges of the twentieth century.[36]

Other students and commentators on U.S. higher education take a different tack. In P. F. Kluge's study *Alma Mater* Kenyon's president from 1975 to 1995, Dr. Philip Jordan, is depicted as scholarly and bright and very successful but largely reactive and somewhat cynical.[37] As Kluge presents it, Jordan tried to say the right thing at the right time but always with enough of a hint of scholarly irony to suggest that the enterprise in question was, to some extent, a sham. Others who were at Kenyon during those years have a sharply different impression of the college's presidential leadership. To Kluge, clearly, the real Kenyon is to be found in the interactions of students and charismatic professors over time. He suggests that presidents and trustees are at their best when they are least active and visible.

If Kluge's take on collegiate presidential leadership is a bit idiosyncratic or even cranky, to some commentators senior academic administrators are a downright hazard. Roger Kimball links "tenured radicals" on the faculty with compliant administrators in "an unhappy tale of intellectual chicanery, pedagogical dereliction, and moral irresponsibility" in which political partisanship has deformed legitimate academic values.[38] Similarly, Charles Kors and Harvey Silvergate accuse administrators of "betraying liberty" on American campuses through speech codes and censorship. To Kors and Silvergate the principal occupation of senior academic administrators is to make sure there is no trouble "on my watch," as they stand back and let a few radical left-wing faculty deform collegiate education.[39]

It is also painfully clear that there have been college presidents whose styles or senses of institutional mission were not congruent with the genuine character of their institutions. Such presidents have occasionally led colleges down the path of ruin. A number of these cases are cited as negative illustrations in *Legitimacy in the Academic Presidency* by Rita Bornstein.[40]

Especially since the advent of graduate programs in higher education administration, there have been numerous valuable studies of the college presidency and various administrative theories and styles.[41] A few observations about the particularities of small college administrative leadership, especially that of the institutional chief executive—president or chancellor or occasionally provost or "warden"—are in order.

Until well into the twentieth century college presidents tended to be clerical patriarchs. It was the custom at small colleges for the president to teach a required course for students in their final year in "moral or natural philosophy" which offered an explicit link between collegiate studies and an ethical life of productivity and service. Reading the histories of small colleges, it is almost always easy to spot the presidential transition—usually between World War I and World War II—from the patriarchal to the more modern presidency. At Centenary College, for example, Rev. Samuel Sexton served as president from 1921 to 1932. He was an ordained minister who served congregations in Texas until arriving in Shreveport in 1914. In 1917 he joined Centenary's board of trustees as pastor of the city's First Methodist Church and four years later assumed the presidency.[42] Rev. Sexton was succeeded by Dr. Pierce Cline, a member of the Department of History, who held academic degrees from Emory and the University of Chicago and served as president for a decade.

A similar transition occurred at Wellesley in the shift from President Caroline Hazard (who served from 1889 to 1910) and had no college degree to Ellen Fitz Pendleton (1910–36), who held both a bachelor's and master's degree from Wellesley itself.[43]

At Grinnell, when President George A. Gates left in 1900, the faculty championed the candidacy of professor of Greek John H. T. Main. "However, the trustees were still faithful to the tradition that the head of a Christian college be a minister . . . their choice fell upon another prominent churchman who seemed to possess all the desired qualifications: the Rev.

Dan Freeman Bradley."[44] But after a few years President Bradley "realized he was better fitted for the pastorate than for a college presidency," and in 1906 Professor (now Dean) Main ascended to the post. "Dr. Bradley's brief administration marked the end of the ministerial tradition at Grinnell. Henceforth the presidency was to be considered as primarily an educational function, demanding the service of men with a definite training and experience in an academic field."[45]

It is not as clear at the beginning of the twenty-first century as it was a hundred years ago just what the background of small college presidents should be. Many come from a prior position of academic leadership—as dean, provost, or department / division chair—but others come from student affairs or financial affairs administrative apprenticeships. Rita Bornstein's book *Legitimacy in the Academic Presidency* chronicles her evolution from chief development officer to small college president.[46] Some have degrees in traditional academic fields, others in law or higher education administration or business. Some presidents come from outside academe—from business and industry, for example, or from not-for-profit organizations. I would venture the opinion that this diversity of background and preparation is potentially valuable: it keeps the profession and position heterogeneous and lively. It also reflects an important, even dominant, trait of the position itself: at a small college the president does (if not "everything") an awful lot.

In general, college and university presidents have various responsibilities to diverse constituencies. This is especially true at smaller colleges. At times the job feels like the Platte River in Nebraska: a mile wide and six inches deep. Bornstein remarks that "while many large universities have already adapted to having their presidents serve as remote figureheads, largely devoted to external affairs, small colleges still expect and enable their presidents to be involved in all areas of the institution."[47] Thus, any university chief executive will spend time with faculty leaders, trustees, alumni, students, faculty, staff, donors, the community, and political leaders. At the small college, however, dealing with these contacts can rarely be delegated to helpers and subordinates. Moreover, a level of personal accessibility and a constancy of presence is a universal expectation. Small college presidents as much at Wellesley as at Warren Wilson are expected to respond to student e-mails and phone calls; their presence or absence at athletic contests, art gallery openings, and student plays and concerts is keenly observed. It is assumed that they will take the time to write or call in response to alumni compliments or complaints. They will deal with the faculty not in the venue of a representative governance system but as a whole and individually. On the basis of an informal poll of most of the presidents I interviewed for this book, it is clear that at institutions with about 150 or fewer faculty it is the expectation that the president will know each faculty member by name, face, and department. One president among my sample institutions interviews every candidate for every position on her campus, from provost to cook. Most of them personally interview all candidates for tenurable faculty positions, and many know a substantial proportion of the student body.

Although small college presidents are hardly invisible within their campuses or communities, they rarely occupy the positions of high public visibility and political prominence of their peers at major universities. The "trade-off" for a small college president's huge range of obligations and opportunities is the unlikelihood of appearing on a daily basis on the front page of the state's major newspaper or the kind of celebrity recognition and public lifestyle enjoyed, or suffered, by chief officers of the states' land grant universities. The year-end edition of *Newsweek* magazine for 2003 profiled in its "who's next 2004" section Mary Sue Coleman of the University of Michigan (herself the graduate of a small college): it is unlikely that Diana Chapman Walsh at Wellesley, as prominent a small college president as can be found, will find herself in a similar media position.[48]

Because small college presidents are usually expected to be highly visible campus personalities, they are often torn by the tension between off-campus obligations (e.g., fund-raising, cultivating political support, communicating with alumni, and community service) and on-campus expectations (e.g., leading committees or making presentations, presiding over campus assemblies or senates, being available for informal meetings, returning phone calls and e-mails promptly). Most small college presidents feel that they could well spend 100 percent of their time in either venue, and many try to achieve some sort of rational balance that often fails fully to satisfy anyone.

It is amusing to read advertisements for small college senior administrators, especially chief executives, in such venues as the *Chronicle of Higher Education*. Often, the institution makes clear that it is seeking an individual who is an accomplished and continuing scholar, with a solid track record of fund-raising, skills in leading strategic planning, an unimpeachable moral character, a history of community service, the social grace to deal with the widest possible range of constituents, who is an inspiring speaker, has a sense of humor, is comfortable with the college's church connections, and has an ability to delegate effectively. One is reminded of Benedick's description of an ideal bride in *Much Ado about Nothing* (2.3.29–37): "But till all graces be in one woman, one woman shall not come in my grace. Rich she shall be, that's certain; wise, or I'll none; virtuous, or I'll never cheapen her; fair, or I'll never look on her; mild, or come not near me; noble, or not I for an angel; of good discourse, an excellent musician, and her hair shall be of what color it please God." Like Benedick, most search committees refrain from specifying hair color and precious little else. It needs hardly be said that, like spouses, college presidents come with a wide range of talents and inclinations, but, in fact, none possesses them all.

I conclude this sketch with a personal but emblematic anecdote about the expectations of small college presidents. The day before Christmas 2002, deep in the midst of a snowy Minnesota winter college vacation, I was called on the phone at home by a frantic student. It seemed he had just received an impromptu invitation to travel to Germany over the holiday period but had left his passport in his dorm room. It seemed logical to call the college chancellor and ask me to contact campus security and persuade them to let me into his residence hall, reclaim his papers, and overnight-mail them to his home in time for his forthcoming flight. It was; I did.

• • •

In many ways people associated with small colleges are just like those at large universities. Most are curious, bright, eager to do a good job as students, faculty, or staff; a few are bored time servers and are uninspiring. But in many other ways they are a distinctive breed. They have, for example, in most cases deliberately chosen to place themselves in a small college setting, which makes them part of a distinct minority in U.S. higher education. Here I have suggested other characteristics and distinguishing qualities of small college teachers, learners, and workers. In the final assessment, however, the thing that distinguishes small college people most certainly is their relationships with other small college people. At a small college students will get to know the president by name, and vice versa. Housekeepers will send students to class, and cooks will teach them manners. Students will know all or most of their colleagues and learn to live in close proximity with them. Faculty members will interact with colleagues across disciplines, will see senior administrators daily, and will have their morning coffee in a café they share with students and groundskeepers. To many of us who are small college people, this is "the point." Small colleges are human sized, offering the daily opportunity for a range of humane interactions. Small colleges *are,* and are about, people.

In chapters 5 and 6 I will explore two overarching themes of small college distinctiveness, *community* and *integration* (or *integrity*). Both turn out to be more nuanced concepts than might at first appear. But, when understood with appropriate complexity, these two related clusters of characteristics clarify some of the most important qualities small colleges bring to the matrix of American higher education.

Basketball, Rock and Roll, and a Quaker College

Often we think of small college professors as devoted exclusively to teaching and those at large universities strictly as research scholars. In fact, many of the best faculty members at both kinds of institutions do a splendid job in both spheres. Here is a brief picture of a small college faculty member who is a beloved teacher and also a respected, serious scholar.

Richie Zweigenhaft is professor of psychology at Guilford College, a small Quaker liberal arts college in Greensboro, North Carolina. Dr. Zweigenhaft grew up in the suburbs of Washington, DC, in Silver Spring and Bethesda, Maryland. Neither of his parents had graduated from college: his father had taken classes at City College of New York but not completed his studies, and his mother never attended college. Richie graduated from Walter Johnson High School, a public institution in Rockville, Maryland, of some 2,100 students: there were 715 members of his graduating class. He enjoyed high school and did well academically. He recalls himself as a rapid learner and his classmates as bright students. He was something of a student leader, serving as president of his high school class for both the junior and senior years.

Professor Zweigenhaft's older sister attended Mount Holyoke College, and, instead of the traditional round of college visits with his parents, he relied mostly on her recommendations and interests when it came time to pick a college for his own studies. His sister had dated men from Wesleyan University in Connecticut, and she helped arrange a visit to Middletown. Richie spent a weekend there with some friends of his sister and had a great time: today he is still in touch with some of the men he met as a prospective student. After visiting Wesleyan, he went directly by bus to another recruitment visit at Brown University, had a less positive experience—it rained; the people seemed less friendly —and settled on Wesleyan.

When Richie went to Wesleyan, it had about eleven hundred students and was a men's college. He found it an eye-opening experience intellectually and culturally, especially in the diversity of students' interests and backgrounds. Nervous at first about his ability to compete academically with his classmates, he worked hard and built a record of success. Looking back on his undergraduate years today, Dr. Zweigenhaft recalls getting to know faculty members well and having opportunities to do independent studies under them beginning as early as his sophomore year.

Columbia University came after Wesleyan for a master's degree, followed by two years teaching at a community college and earning a doctorate at the University of California–Santa Cruz. When it was time to seek a full-time, permanent position, Dr. Zweigenhaft looked primarily at smaller places, based on his undergraduate experiences at Wesleyan compared to his graduate student years. He landed a job at Guilford College, where he has remained ever since.

Professor Zweigenhaft has stayed at Guilford for several reasons. The small college department that is his home provides amiable and stimulating colleagues. Moreover, it has encouraged him to develop new courses to match his expanding scholarly interests as well as asking him to teach the traditional "bread-and-butter" courses in psychology.

Regarding his success in balancing teaching and productive scholarly research, he notes their synergistic relationship.

I chose to come to Guilford in part because I did not want to be under intense pressure to publish in order to survive. I had enjoyed doing research (though my dissertation experience was not a happy one), but I had observed junior faculty under a great deal of pressure at Wesleyan, Columbia, and Santa Cruz. I was not eager to put myself under such pressure, and I was more confident that I would be a good teacher than a good researcher. Those with whom I interviewed at Guilford made clear that teaching was much more important than research and that one could get tenure and be a highly valued member of the faculty if one were an excellent teacher who did little or no research. Ironically, this was liberating, for I then pursued research interests only because I was interested in doing so, not because I thought that I had to. As a result, I've published far more than I expected. Moreover, my research interests have led me to offer a number of new courses I had not taught before (or contemplated teaching while still in graduate school), courses like "The American Upper Class" and "Class, Race, and Gender." Teaching some of these classes has had an influence on research projects I have done, and the research I have done, in turn, has influenced the nature of the classes.

Also, though I did not realize this when I arrived, the best students at Guilford are quite good, and I have much enjoyed working with advanced students on research projects. This has led to a number of coauthored articles with my students.

To date, Zweigenhaft has authored four books in his field and one monograph and has published some seventy-five scholarly articles. He has written on such subjects as "Jews in the Protestant Elite" and the long-term effects on minority students of attending elite boarding schools.

Another reason Professor Zweigenhaft has happily remained at Guilford is the warm and productive relationship he has enjoyed with his colleagues, especially in psychology but also across departments. He remarks that his colleagues in big schools report they miss such cross-departmental friendships. Indeed, he has on occasion team-taught across departmental lines, such as a course in psychohistory with a member of the history faculty.

The liability of small colleges which has weighed most heavily on this productive faculty member is his college's perennial struggle for resources. Guilford is, Professor Zweigenhaft notes accurately, richer than some small colleges and poorer than others, but it is always struggling to acquire funds to support its aspirations.

How can a full-time teacher, at a teaching college, be so productive a scholar? Dr. Zweigenhaft reports that he works on smaller projects during summer breaks and in odd open moments throughout the day and academic year. He observes that he has had four sabbatical leaves during his career and has published four books, and the books have each been linked to a leave. He also admits that he is well organized in his work and able to say no to assignments that he believes he will not find gratifying.

Richie is far from an academic drudge. He is a regular member of the thrice-weekly noon basketball game, in which faculty members, students, and others from outside the college compete—fiercely. He remarks that occasionally he finds himself playing basketball against students from his own classes. For years he also hosted a popular music show on the college's student radio station but has recently given up his career as a DJ. He does, however, still periodically teach a class in mass media. About that course he remarks that, while many of his colleagues at this small Quaker college begin each class with a moment of silence, he always begins with a moment of rock and roll.

5 | Colleges of Community

I'm an only child, but the day I arrived on the Morehouse campus,
I realized I have three thousand brothers.

MOREHOUSE COLLEGE STUDENT

When a multitude of young men, keen, open-hearted, sympathetic, and
observant, as young men are, come together and freely mix with each
other, they are sure to learn one from another, even if there be no one to
teach them: the conversation of all is a series of lectures to each other . . .
Here then is a real teaching . . . it is a something, and it does a something,
which never will issue from the most strenuous efforts of a set of teachers
with no mutual sympathies and no intercommunication . . . and with no
common principles, who are teaching or questioning a set of youths who
do not know them, and do not know each other, on a large number of subjects, different in kind, and connected by no wide philosophy.

CARDINAL JOHN HENRY NEWMAN, *The Idea of a University*

Small colleges frequently seek to explain and promote themselves
to a public with only a vague understanding—or an antiquated and ro-
mantic notion—of their nature. Potential donors, influential citizens, key
political leaders, and especially prospective students and their families are
important constituents who need to understand the nature of colleges. But
complex institutions cannot be described in a few quick phrases or sound
bites with any degree of accuracy. One of the descriptive phrases utilized
pervasively by small college public relations offices is that these schools
foster "community." A glimpse at the view books designed for admissions
recruiting at my sample colleges reveals this tendency.

—Warren Wilson College: "With more than 800 students [head count]
and an average class size of 15, each person is a significant part of
our *community*" (4; my italics). (As I was working on this chapter, I
read that a fire at Warren Wilson College had destroyed a dormitory.
Fortunately, there were no serious injuries or deaths. One student
responded in the 20 January 2003 *Asheville Citizen-Times,* "Every-

body's been so helpful and nice to us. You see a real sense of *community* out here" [A4; my italics].) At Warren Wilson the dean of student life describes "community" as the "unwritten part of our mission statement."[1]

—Westmont College: "offers students a vibrant *community* for living and learning. Because Westmont is residential and entirely under-graduate, our students quickly find common bonds that transcend their diverse backgrounds and interests—and lead to lifelong friend-ships. Many faculty members live on campus, contributing to an environment in which in-depth interactions take place as a matter of course" (3; my italics).

—Colby-Sawyer College: "Because Colby-Sawyer professors and staff genuinely care about you and your ideas, you can turn to anyone at the college for feedback or advice. These exchanges help create an academic *community* where everyone encourages each individual's personal and academic development" (1; my italics).

—The University of Wisconsin–Superior: "It's a nice mix of people from different states, different lands, different backgrounds, differ-ent religions and different races. They come together to learn with each other and from each other. They share a sense of *community;* a feeling of togetherness with each other" (7; my italics).

This is a random selection. It is difficult to find *any* college that does not mention *community* in its recruitment materials.

Claims of and about community abound in discussions of higher edu-cation. In *Liberating Education* Zelda Gamson reports that one of the six goals of the required core sequence in general education at Saint Joseph's College is "to build a *community* of common seekers after truth."[2] Indeed, one chapter in Gamson's influential book is entitled "Creating a Lively Academic Community." Education writer Loren Pope in *Colleges That Change Lives* sees in small institutions "a familial sense of communal en-terprise that gets students heavily involved in cooperative rather than com-petitive learning."[3] Diana Chapman Walsh, president at Wellesley College, notes that small colleges offer a *community* that is at once intellectually rig-orous and supportive.[4] And Douglas Heath observes that, at Haverford, "'small size' means to the alumni to experience being a member of a *com-munity* . . . the experience of belongingness . . . [to] a small, organically in-tegrated unit of faculty, students, administration and campus."[5]

Research has demonstrated that college size has a measurable effect on community. For example, Alan E. Bayer reports a strong positive correlation (.776) between small institutional size and students' perceptions that the institution shows concern for individual students. He draws on data derived from the Cooperative Institutional Research Program (CIRP), which includes 225 randomly selected colleges and universities. He concludes "an institution's structure—particularly its size—persists as a strong determinant of the institutional environment . . . institutional growth beyond some optimal limit leads to alienation, absence of community and numerous other outcomes which are dysfunctional for all members of the college community."[6]

Similarly, looking at historically black private colleges, Humphrey Doerman and Herman Drewry observe that "small size and the tradition of nurturing that often goes with it can produce close personal support that is particularly valuable for unsophisticated students."[7]

What are the implications for small college communities of the fact that the number of "minority" students at American colleges grew from 16 percent in 1976 to 27 percent in 1997 and continues to increase?[8] Somewhat more precise enrollment figures calculated by ethnicity show a striking (and heartening) trend over a two-decade period (table 5.1).

Table 5.1 Demographic Profiles of Small Colleges in the United States

Group	No. Students		% Change
	1980	2000	
American Indian	83,900	151,200	+80
Asian American	286,400	978,200	+342
Black	1,106,800	1,730,300	+56
Hispanic	471,700	1,461,800	+310
White	9,833,000	10,462,100	+6
Foreign	305,000	528,700	+73

Source: Chronicle of Higher Education, 29 August 2003.

As late as the 1960s, according to the American Association of Colleges and Universities "American Commitments" project, "the nation's system of higher education was *de facto* almost completely racially segregated, basically either all-white or all-black with at best a 1 to 2 percent variation at some major institutions."[9] How does this changing demographic profile change what we mean when we say that small colleges are communities?

Certainly, some of this profession of being a community may be in part unthinking advertising: it is, after all, hard to be against it. But I believe that colleges are generally telling an important truth when they make this assertion, albeit a truth that is a bit more nuanced than view book prose allows. The very typical marketing citations quoted earlier suggest that community is, respectively, small classes, ample opportunities for faculty-student interaction, an attitude of mutual helpfulness, and a feeling of togetherness. What is the complicated set of characteristics at small colleges which lies beneath the view book words? Indeed, do the larger communities of our nation actually continue to exhibit a sense of community as populations grow more varied and polyglot?

In the following sections I will try to answer two questions: what do we really mean when we speak of small colleges as communities, and why is this characteristic so important as to be definitive of the small college experience for many students and teachers?

Focus and Mission

The *Oxford English Dictionary* defines *community* as "life in association with others" and refines that definition by adding, under "certain circumstances . . . of pursuit . . . common to them."[10] This could, of course, refer to a very large group of people with a very large, overriding common pursuit or mission. (Colleges and universities commonly use the word *mission* to describe their overriding pursuit or aim. For the purposes of this discussion, I am assuming that institutional "mission statements" represent an honest, albeit sometimes awkward, statement of that vision.) In 1943, for example, the people of the United States could be said to have been a community working together to win World War II. Similarly, the University of Michigan is striving to serve the state and the nation through a mission of teaching, research, and service.

Generally, however, the smaller the community, the stronger the bonds between its members, and the clearer and more precise the goals toward which it seeks to move. As Gamson observes: "Some small colleges still retain a strong sense of their purposes and can build on this to create a single expression of their educational vision. St. Joseph's Core [the college's universal general education program], Talladega's curriculum based on that of the University of Chicago, and Hampshire's divisional structure are three examples of what small colleges can do. Larger schools cannot be expected to reach fundamental agreement about educational purposes and curriculum."[11]

So, while the entire nation had an overarching purpose of victory during the war years, the daily work of individual Americans toward that large mission was fragmented into thousands of clearer and more exact goals: the workers at an airplane factory strove to exceed last month's production record; families on the home front tended their victory gardens; the men of Easy Company—documented movingly in Stephen Ambrose's book *Band of Brothers*—worked heroically to defeat their German opponents in battle. Similarly, underneath the umbrella tripartite mission (teaching, research, service) of a major research university are dozens of more sharply defined missions, which, together, are expected to accomplish the composite, large, and somewhat vague institutional goals. Thus, the mission of the staff of the freshman writing course is helping undergraduates improve their composition skills; the mission of the student daily newspaper is informing the campus of important local activities and events; the mission of the office of institutional research is providing important information accurately; and the mission of the legislative lobbyist is making the best case for the university to senate committees.

Small colleges, when they function well, are more like the "band of brothers" than like the entire U.S. Armed Forces, with the entire unit working directly on the general mission as well as more specific objectives. As an illustration, the Morehouse College catalog refers to overall collegiate goals in its description of the mission of each academic department. So, as the college as a whole includes in its mission statement the cultivation of disciplined minds in order to inspire graduates to lead lives of leadership and service, specific departments make reference to these objectives:

> In harmony with the mission of the College, the mission of the Department of Chemistry is to develop the ability of students to apply the techniques of sustained and critical analysis to the solution of problems . . .

> The vision of the management education program at Morehouse is service to humanity through excellence in business leadership . . .

All courses in the [English] department are designed to meet the overall mission of the College as stated in this publication. Thus, the department asserts that a properly educated Morehouse student, trained through the medium of English, should read, write, speak, listen, and reason with above-average skills and should understand and appreciate the ways human beings express themselves and their culture through literature and other arts.[12]

Another striking example of total institutional engagement in the overarching collegiate mission took place at Southwestern University. At the end of the 1990s Southwestern was finishing two decades under the presidential leadership of Roy Shilling. The school had changed significantly since 1980, as had most of U.S. higher education. At Southwestern the sense that it was time to revisit and renew institutional mission and goals became an enterprise that involved the entire campus community in a direct, democratic fashion:

In November 1997 and in February 1998, the University suspended classes for two days so that all members of the campus community could explore and define Southwestern's core values and core purpose. Southwestern University's core values were defined as: promoting lifelong learning and a passion for intellectual and personal growth; fostering diverse perspectives; being true to one's self and others; respecting the worth and dignity of persons; and encouraging activism in the pursuit of justice and the common good. Southwestern University's core purpose was defined as: fostering a liberal arts community whose values and actions encourage contributions toward the well being of humanity.[13]

The process led to the development of an "envisioned future" statement for the university to use as a guide in preparing a master plan leading to 2010. This story is of interest not because Southwestern's mission, goals, or purpose are especially noteworthy (although they are not without interest: e.g., there is no mention of research or the expansion of knowledge nor of the institution's religious affiliation or the divine; there is an unusually fully developed mission of service to humanity). What does seem remarkable is that an entire university population, with all its on-campus and several of its major off-campus constituencies, could make the effort to sit down together at one time, in one place, to undertake such a project. Discussions of university values and purposes certainly take place in all colleges and universities. Indeed, continuing accreditation of all institutions of higher education hinges upon such discussions happening. But it would only be possible to carry forward such a conversation among all members of the entire campus population at a relatively small institution. At larger places (and some smaller ones too) this discussion of institutional mission would be conducted in a series of representative committee meetings, brought to a university senate for faculty confirmation, then to a student government assembly for student approval, and presented to a cabinet of senior administrators. Only at a small college could *everyone* sit down together, at one time, to focus on the school's character, purpose, and direction. Such a discussion strengthens the cohesiveness with which an institution can pursue its overarching purpose, across disciplines and across constituencies. And it helps to keep sharp and fresh the focus of a college.

It is certainly not the case that all small colleges have a clear, distinct, and focused sense of mission nor that large institutions lack clarity in their goals and purposes. Many a small college has blurred the clarity of its identity, often under pressure of declining enrollments and/or fiscal strains. A recent issue of the *Chronicle of Higher Education* profiled the demise of a very small midwestern college, in which a series of presidents and trustees reacted to ever shrinking enrollments by initiating program after program aimed at recruiting a few more students. At the end the college seemed to be reinventing itself literally on a semester-by-semester basis, and even those who knew it intimately no longer had any sense of its identity. The *Chronicle* found that the college "never settled in to a specific identity, but kept reinventing itself with the arrival of each new president. In the 1970's, it was known for its music programs, and adopted a slogan in 1977, 'liberal arts with a purpose.' In the 1980's, it reached out to local Native American tribes, and offered courses in their interests. As the college turned to the '90's, it was known almost exclusively for its athletics programs." Even more troubling, once the institution was on the verge of collapse, the president, his critics charged, "was changing his course every week, wanting to try new ideas based on whatever management book he had read over the weekend. But he never followed through."[14] It is certainly possible to be small and unfocused.

Similarly, it is possible to be large and have a clear mission. Massachusetts Institute of Technology, for example, does many things, including teaching introductory humanities subjects to beginning undergraduates, but it has a clear communitarian accord that the university's focus is advancing the frontiers of scientific and technological knowledge. It can also be argued, persuasively, that the breadth and diversity of mission and focus at large institutions such as the University of Michigan or California or Ohio—or at Duke or Vanderbilt or Northwestern—is one of their most stimulating and exciting characteristics. My argument is that the focus of small colleges is a more pointed one, not necessarily a better one.

At most small colleges, then, there is the possibility of a kind of broad-based, near-universal accord focusing on a very tightly defined mission. One example, briefly cited earlier (chap. 3), is the focus at Colby-Sawyer on combining liberal learning with professional preparation. The mission statement of the college was relatively recently revised, with broad, multi-constituent participation, in this case through a series of "community forums." The mission statement affirms that "the College provides programs of study that innovatively integrate liberal arts and sciences with professional preparation." It goes on to reiterate that it "emphasizes the importance of internship and other complementary educational experiences as a component of its academic programs" and "prepares graduates to define and pursue varied personal, educational, and career options." The catalog further clarifies the mission of "innovative integration of the liberal arts and sciences with professional preparation":

> A Colby-Sawyer education combines the values of liberal studies in the traditional arts and sciences with those of professional preparation. The Liberal Education Program fosters the development of skills and competencies and the acquisition of knowledge that is believed to be essential for all students to acquire. Through a variety of major programs, students develop the knowledge and abilities that are required in the profession of their choice. This approach to integrating liberal and professional studies provides the finest foundation for developing student potential and for preparing students to define and pursue their personal, educational, and career goals . . . students confront the challenges and issues that they will eventually encounter in their lives and careers.[15]

Certainly, all colleges and universities recognize that students and their families are hopeful that the undergraduate experience will connect with later vocational opportunities. But few institutions are as straightforward and focused about seeking to make, throughout their programs, this sort of connection between liberal learning and professional preparation. It is interesting to compare Colby-Sawyer's dual mission of liberal learning and vocational preparation with more traditional and monolithic mission statements. For example, Wellesley's 2002–3 catalog asserts only that "the mission of Wellesley College is to provide an excellent liberal arts education for women who will make a difference in the world" (a phrase cited by every individual and group with whom I conversed there). Wellesley goes on to note that "the liberal arts curriculum has changed little since the College was founded. Though the structure of distributions requirements has evolved, the requirement that each student should be acquainted with the main fields of human interest has remained a constant . . . The College is committed to this framework because it emphasizes the essence of education: the ability to speak and write clearly, the knowledge to manage quantitative data with ease, the confidence to approach new material, and the capacity to make critical judgments. These skills are essential—whatever the student chooses to do with her life."[16]

The point is not that Colby-Sawyer's self-definition or Wellesley's is superior to the other but that each institution has been able to refine its statements about its own nature and goals in a precise manner. Communities are, as the *OED* suggests, people living with others to pursue common ends. By virtue of their efforts to build broad consensus among all campus constituents around a tightly focused shared purpose, small colleges are strong communities.

A shared sense of purpose and a focused mission are obviously internal strengths for a collegiate entity. But how does such an internal sense of community serve larger, external purposes? Are small college communities simply inward-looking, isolated, and self-referential units? Or are there ways in which such communities can have a positive impact on contemporary American culture? This question leads us in the direction of learning for civic engagement and the cultivation of social capital.

Bowling Together

Robert Putnam's book *Bowling Alone* was a surprising bestseller of 2000.[17] Putnam describes and laments the withering of what he calls "social capital" in the second half of the twentieth century. His title suggests the shift from bowling in small league teams to performing more individualistic, isolated activities. I think a strong case can be made that the character of small colleges as communities suggests they can be, and in fact are, a potent conservator of social capital.

Putnam defines *social capital* as a network of interpersonal connections through organizations such as politics, clubs, and churches. This web of connections is linked to volunteerism and philanthropy, which Putnam believes are also declining. *Bowling Alone* seeks to explain why this pattern of "generalized reciprocity" weakened in the final third of the twentieth century. Among the causes Putnam investigates are financial anxiety, excessive busyness, the changing roles of women, suburbanization and the commuter lifestyle, and the impact of television. World War II shaped a generation of civic engagement, but that characteristic has diminished with each successive generation—the baby boomers, generations "X" and "Y," and so on. Why, Putnam asks, does this matter? He links social capital to child welfare, education, safe and productive neighborhoods, economic prosperity, health and happiness, and democracy. Putnam concludes with an agenda for social capitalists, suggesting they get involved with youth and schools, workplace issues, urban and metropolitan design, and religion, the arts, culture, and government.

Robert Putnam does not pay much heed to higher education, but colleges and universities merit a place on the agenda of social capitalists. (He does note of high schools, however, that "smaller schools encourage more active involvement in extracurricular activity than big schools—more students [proportionally] in smaller schools have an opportunity to play trombone or left tackle or King Lear. Smaller schools, like smaller towns, generate higher expectations for mutual reciprocity and collective action.")[18] There is a growing body of significant scientific evidence demonstrating that the experience of going to college makes a marked contribution to exactly the sorts of postcollege activities Putnam values. Howard R. Bowen reports that 80 percent of college alumni report that college-going was useful or very useful in developing "leadership."[19] He concludes that "higher education does provide abundant opportunities and incentives for students to develop their leadership potential."[20] Bowen also reviews research on the attitudes of college graduates in regard to "citizenship." He reports that college produces changes between entering and graduating students in several key measures of citizenship. Graduates are significantly more engaged on a range of public issues, including foreign affairs, environmental protection, and racial justice. Bowen and other researchers such as George Gallup and Daniel Yankelovich consistently find that college tends to move students in the direction of political liberalism and away from religious conservatism.[21]

A particularly important set of findings concerns actual involvement in political affairs. Voting habits, for example, are one of the key measures that Putnam uses to demonstrate the loss of social capital. Bowen reports that in one study 69 percent of those whose education ended at graduation from grade school voted in presidential elections, 82 percent of high school graduates did so, and 92 percent of college graduates were voters.[22] Similarly, those who reported a "high degree of involvement in political affairs" included only 23 percent of the grade school group, 32 percent of the high school grads, and 48 percent of the college respondents. Bowen also reports on data from another survey, which found that 62 percent of its sample noncollege graduates were registered to vote, whereas 86 percent of college graduates were.[23] Additionally, he reports that "college education appears to favor community participation and the cultivation of a disposition toward community activities," including volunteerism and service work.

Bowen's data, and those of others he summarizes and reports, suggest these positive results for all college graduates, but he also notes that his research shows that the results are most pronounced at small institutions.[24] The research of David Winter, David McClelland, and Abigale Stewart is more specific and moves us closer to our investigation of small colleges. In their comparison of a liberal arts college ("Ivy College") to a public teachers' university and a two-year community college, they considered a number of post-college activities and characteristics, including the social capital characteristics of membership in volunteer organizations and office holding in these public service groups. They define a cluster of competences and attributes enhanced by attending liberal arts colleges—critical thinking and analysis, self-image, flexibility, achievement motivation, among others. In a longitudinal study they attempt to measure the extent to which the acquisition of these competences had demonstrable effects on the later lives of the students being scrutinized. They found positive correlations between the competence that was called "self-definition" influencing later membership in volunteer organizations and that of "leadership motivation," which predicted office holding in these organizations.[25] Winter, McClelland, and Stewart concluded that their "longitudinal study of the Ivy College class of 1964 has produced some important and encouraging results. These . . . liberal arts competence measures have significant and important relationships to later life outcomes, relationships that seem to be a good deal stronger than those we found for SAT scores and college honors, two of the most popular education-related predictors of academic performance and life outcomes."[26] D. A. Heath also reports a significant correlation between attendance at one small college, Haverford, and maturity and social involvement in later life.[27]

Such findings make clear that colleges and universities are laboratories for building social capital. (In chap. 6 I will discuss ways in which small college communities that have successfully achieved significant diversity gain maximum impact from that demographic variety, by virtue of their small and intimate size.) Robert Putnam's focus is on participation and leadership in political activities, clubs, voluntary organizations, and service groups.

To survey such activities and opportunities at a small college, let us consider Wellesley College. Wellesley has a student population of about 2,285 women. It reports with some pride that it has 160 student organizations, ranging alphabetically from "A La Mode" (a fashion and design club) and *Aeolus* (the literary magazine) to WZLY (the student radio station), Yanualou (a drum and dance ensemble devoted to Haitian and Brazilian rhythms), and Zeta Alpha Society (a literary and social group). These student organizations certainly reflect—indeed, perhaps, magnify—the range of cultures and interests of the larger society that surrounds Wellesley. If the average student organization or club has a leadership cadre of only four individuals (e.g., officers or an executive committee) this means that Wellesley offers 640 opportunities to students each year to fill such a post. If the average student organization has 15 members, there would be more membership opportunities than there are students. In fact, of course, there is considerable overlap, with some women holding membership in multiple organizations. On the other hand, many of these student groups are large: the radio station, for example, has 100 student DJs, 50 interns, and 50 newswomen, which means that almost 10 percent of Wellesley students are members of this group alone.

Student activity clubs are hardly the only organizational opportunities, however, for Wellesley women to learn social capitalism. There are twelve varsity sports, each of them offering both leadership challenges to captains and cocaptains and a powerful sense of belonging and participation to all team members.

Wellesley students also work together in campus governance. According to the college's Web site: "Students, through election to the College Community Senate and through voting representation on College Committees, share responsibility in the decision-making processes of the College. Students serve on committees of the Board of Trustees, on the Board of Admissions, and on important departmental committees. Students regulate their lives in the residence halls through House Council and manage student activity funds used to support more than 160 student organizations."[28]

With a student-faculty ratio of nine to one, it is not surprising that Wellesley also offers students mostly small classes (the average is eighteen to twenty-one students per class). In such classes, again, students have important opportunities to function as members of a group, working together, rather than just as a passive audience. In the right setting course work can be a way of developing skills for future social capitalists.

Obviously, this small college offers its students a dazzling array of opportunities to develop the habits and skills needed to build interpersonal networks, which, Robert Putnam believes, are eroding in contemporary America. Every way a Wellesley College woman turns, she has the opportunity to be a member and a leader of a club or society or organization. In this respect my visits to small colleges across the country have convinced me that Wellesley is a truly typical example. If, in our larger, suburbanized, TV-addicted society we are moving toward isolated individualism, as Putnam suggests, in small colleges we have a remarkable stronghold of collective activity.

Putnam also describes another type of social capital, one that builds bridges between groups, as opposed to strengthening the bonds within an individual social network. In chapter 6 I will discuss at some length the ways in which what have been called the "new liberal arts" flourish in small college settings. Briefly, it is my thesis that the more intense, focused, smaller college environment is one in which diversity can be made more ubiquitous; that if a small college is truly multicultural, that diversity is experienced more universally and more deeply than in a larger, more diffuse collegiate setting. At a small college that has achieved some sort of genuine plurality of population, where students from a range of cultures study, live, and recreate together, Putnam's bridging social capital is cultivated, nourished, even required.

At small colleges students learn to bowl together. In the context of Putnam's *Bowling Alone* small colleges not only offer communities in themselves but play a key role in what may be an increasingly needed process of educating students to live together in communities for the rest of their lives.

Interdisciplinarity and Community

Burton Clark's study of small colleges and the kind of communities they constitute led him to conclude that "[a condition to the creation of community] is smallness of size, which allows informal as well as formal links across the specializations and internal divisions inherent in formal organizations. An aggregate of strangers brought together to pursue a common purpose within a small organization is more likely to develop a community than is an aggregation set to multiple purposes in a large enterprise."[29]

Clark's focus on the informal and formal links among academic specializations makes a crucial point about community in small colleges. It is, after all, the community of *learning* which is central to colleges and universities.

Within the world of academic endeavors there are two very different sorts of intellectual communities, both essential to the creation and dissemination of knowledge. The first is a community of specialized scholarly colleagues; the second is a community across the disciplines of scholarship.

Large research universities offer the first sort of opportunity: a community built upon shared scholarly interests. The charming but antiquated image of the research scholar, in the humanities, social sciences, or natural sciences, sitting alone in her study or lab, perhaps surrounded by pipe smoke, thinking then writing deep, original thoughts is almost never accurate. Human knowledge is usually advanced by people working, formally or informally, in groups. Darwin's work on evolution was connected to the work of Baron Georges Cuvier, Chevalier de Lamarck, Patrick Matthew, and Alfred Russell Walker. Albert Einstein's discoveries were built on the science of James Clerk Maxwell, Michael Faraday, and Antoine-Laurent Lavoisier. The collective aspect of the advancement of human knowledge is, if anything, more pronounced today. It is enormously valuable for research scholars to be surrounded by others—faculty colleagues and graduate students particularly—who understand and can help advance their research. Contemporary electronic communications make it possible to build this sort of research community at a distance. But no real substitute has yet been found for wandering down the hall to a fellow astrophysicist's laboratory to test out an idea or grabbing a cup of coffee with another scholar in Jacobean drama to mull the origin of character in a play by Cyril Tourneur. This sort of proximate community of fellow scholars is one of the glorious riches of large universities, and it is one of the important preconditions for a fertile environment for new scholarship. Its absence is one of the liabilities of virtually all small colleges. Living and working in a community of fellow research specialists not only helps generate and support important research; it can also be a boost to good teaching: if one teaches in a department with four other astrophysicists, one is going to be strongly motivated to keep up-to-date about the most recent developments in the field.

So, the first sort of community of scholars is built on shared academic interests. The second is nearly opposite, built on a diversity of scholarly specialization, and it is the particular strength of smaller institutions.

A personal anecdote: I, like most small college teachers, had the experience of moving, precipitously, from one sort of scholarly community to the other when I went from my Ph.D. studies to my first regular teaching position. At Northwestern University, where I taught for a year after finishing my graduate work, I was one of four faculty members in British Renaissance drama, in an academic department of over one hundred tenure-track faculty and advanced graduate student teaching assistants.

When I moved from Northwestern to Cornell College in Mount Vernon, Iowa, I was the sole faculty member working in British literature before the eighteenth century in a five-person English (and American) Literature and Creative Writing Department! I had no colleagues in Renaissance drama; I was assumed to be competent to teach Chaucer, Spenser, Milton, and Donne as well as Shakespeare and Webster. If, at Northwestern University, I had written an article on John Webster, there were a handful of colleagues who could knowledgeably read it and make informed suggestions and comments; at Cornell I was the only person in the department who had ever read *The Devil's Law Case*. But I soon came to realize that I had not lost a scholarly community but traded kinds. If there were no Renaissance drama folks in my new building, there were other, different, but equally intellectually stimulating colleagues. There was a poet with whom I could discuss what it meant when Webster or Shakespeare went from prose to verse within the same scene. There were two political scientists with whom I could discuss Shakespeare's British political theories or Tourneur's wild image of Italian political intrigue. There was a sociologist with whom I could discuss issues of dysfunctional social and familial relationships. If I went to the only dining hall / café on campus for the weekly faculty lunch, which was attended by 90 percent of Cornell's teachers, my table would typically include biologists, painters, mathematicians, an historian (who was also the college chaplain), and someone from student affairs. We could talk about the latest all-college curricular proposal or the work of the campus long-range planning committee or a particular pedagogical challenge ("How do you get smart but shy students to say something in a class discussion?"). Sometimes we might chat about something like the relationship between nature and human nature, and I would mention *King Lear's* conjunction between a stormy climate and a turbulent mind, and the biologist would comment on the biological origins of altruistic behavior, the mathematician would remark on something he had heard in church the past Sunday, and the student affairs person would muse about student behavior in relation to alcohol use, which would remind me of *Othello* and Cassio's foolish drunkenness.

I belabor this story to make a key point. In a small academic setting faculty members miss the colleagueship of fellow specialists but have, instead, a constant intellectual cross-fertilization with other academics whose ideas are stimulating and exciting precisely because they are not those of fellow specialists. The interdisciplinary opportunities of small colleges are not restricted to traditional liberal arts institutions: a faculty member at the Minneapolis College of Art and Design (MCAD), for example, cited as his first reason for coming to MCAD, "I love the interdisciplinary approach to teaching, and felt that for my area . . . it would be a great fit."[30] Speaking of liberating teachers and teaching, Gamson comments on the "common desire to 'make connections' not normally made in college settings. Making connections among the disciplines was one [such linkage]."[31] Being a faculty member in a small department at a small college means being in constant contact with fellow scholars from across the academic spectrum. This may be in a formal context, such as serving together on the Curriculum or Educational Policy committees or, more pervasively, in casual settings: at breaks or meals, at social events, working out or on faculty sports teams, in line at the Registrar's Office, walking across campus, everywhere, all the time. There is an important kind of understanding which grows from learning, along with fellow scholars, more and more about one's particular academic specialty, be it astrophysics or Jacobean drama. There is another kind of understanding, no less important, which comes from being stimulated to see the connections—similarities and differences—between, say, physics and literature (e.g., the first tends to work best when it creates a language in which each symbolic utterance has one and only one referent; the latter works well when its utterances cultivate multiplicity and ambiguity). Small colleges, by virtue of their smallness, stimulate and even demand a constant and steady interdisciplinary conversation among scholars.

What is true for faculty members is, of course, equally true for students. There are advantages to the large university setting, where, for example, one might be one of twenty trumpet performance majors. But at a small college there are equally valuable opportunities for undergraduates who are constantly exposed to fellow students from across the institution. Again, in a variety of settings—classroom, extracurricular, social, residential, and accidental—small college students can't escape fellow students with academic (and other) interests very different from their own. Students at the College of New Rochelle, for example, cited both small class size and, more important, the small size of the college as a whole in affirming that every student on campus knew every other student, regardless of her major or extracurricular interests.[32] An English major and a physics major might be the sports columnists for the student newspaper. The hundred DJs at the Wellesley College student radio station are going to include women studying all across Wellesley's curriculum. On most largely residential campuses students are not segregated in housing by academic interests (although some schools do have "French houses" or "international affairs floors" and the like).

Simple physical proximity plays a role in this pervasive interdisciplinarity: an entire small college will be contained within a few square blocks. By contrast, on the Twin Cities campus of the University of Minnesota the performing arts are across the Mississippi River from the engineers, and the social work majors are in St. Paul, while the College of Liberal Arts is in Minneapolis. In such a dispersed academic setting students may have little opportunity for intellectual interaction with others who do not share their academic interests. But across town, at Macalester, the future social worker, engineer, and musician will all have classes within a few yards of one another.

Finally, of course, this sort of community of cross-disciplinary perspectives is not just faculty-to-faculty or student-to-student: it also enriches the relationships *between* students and their teachers. At a small college of, say, a thousand students and eighty faculty members, it is a certainty that students are going to come to know well teachers outside the subject areas of their majors. Small colleges, say Michael McPherson and Morton Shapiro, put "professors in contact with manageable numbers of students in a setting that is on a human scale."[33] Faculty members are going to be well acquainted with many students from outside their teaching special-izations. At several of the colleges I visited, I asked students if they thought they knew, at least by sight, *all* the faculty at their college. In sev-eral cases—Centenary, Warren Wilson, Minneapolis College of Art and Design, and Wellesley, among them—they were confident they did. At many small colleges entering students are assigned faculty advisors ran-domly, regardless of the students' professed potential interests and the faculty members' departments. Faculty advisors for clubs and organiza-tions (and at many small campuses, virtually every faculty member has at least one such connection) will work closely with students of the widest ac-ademic interests. Research has suggested the importance of such contacts. E. J. Pascarella found that "the evidence suggests that what transpires be-tween students and faculty outside of class may have a measurable, and possibly unique, positive impact on various facets of individual develop-ment during college."[34] Arthur Chickering and John McCormick, study-ing what factors influence change in college students, found that "student-faculty relationships reflected strong and consistent correlations with change. At colleges where contacts with faculty members outside of class occurred more frequently, Autonomy, Impulse Expression, and Complex-ity [positive outcomes] increased and Practical Outlook decreased."[35] And the first of the "Seven Principles for Good Practice in Undergraduate Edu-cation" promulgated by the Johnson Foundation, the American Associa-tion of Higher Education, and the Education Commission of the States is: "Good practice encourages student-faculty contact. Frequent student-faculty contact in and out of classes is the most important factor in student motivation and involvement."[36]

Institutions with a universal core course, or a core of courses (e.g., Colby-Sawyer and Centenary), will usually staff that core with faculty from across the disciplines, and commonly students will take sections regard-less of any particular academic special interest. Faculty and students will serve on committees, and at small colleges virtually all faculty will serve on such committees, with students, often from across the campus.

At small colleges students and faculty sacrifice some of the excitement and productivity of intellectual communities based on shared scholarly in-terests. They gain, in return, a different kind of community of enrichment through interdisciplinary diversity. As Eva Brann says, U.S. colleges "need smallness, so that people may run into each other often for spontaneous conversation."[37]

Community and Mentoring over Time

If small colleges encourage the building of intellectual communities across academic disciplines, they also enhance the opportunities to create communities that cross temporal limits. Small colleges stimulate a kind of delicate yet powerful learning relationship across time. In this respect they offer an interesting parallel to the highest reaches of graduate education at research universities.

One of the delights and strengths of American graduate education, in research universities, is the kind of long-term, protracted, mentor-apprentice relationship that grows between graduate students and their faculty, often for years. True, it is a rare Ph.D. candidate (and her family) who does not at some point complain that it is taking *too* long to finish her doctorate. But it is equally true that most graduate faculty value watching the scholarly and professional growth of their disciples over a substantial period, and most graduate students recognize the very positive effects of a long-term relationship with a senior scholar. Wellesley president Walsh observes that at research universities this kind of protracted learning relationship exists almost entirely at the graduate level; at small colleges it can be found extensively among undergraduate students and their professors.[38]

At a small college teachers and their students are going to interact over a substantial amount of time. "You see them," as a group of faculty at Southwestern University noted, "over and over again; you see them grow."[39] Obviously, in their major fields students are going to get to know a relatively small handful of faculty members very well. If one is a physics major in a school with a physics faculty of three—or even five or seven—and the major consists of some eight to twelve courses, as is common, it would not be unusual to take as many as four or even a half-dozen courses from the same instructor. Such a hypothetical physics student might well have taken the introductory physics course in the first year from the same professor who teaches the senior-level advanced seminar four years later. This pattern of working closely with one or a small number of professors in the major discipline is similar to what happens in graduate school. (As is the increasingly common practice of faculty/undergraduate coauthorship of scholarly publications, thanks to a heightened emphasis on "undergraduate research.") Quite likely, the small college closeness between student major and faculty mentor is sometimes duplicated at larger places. Even in a physics department of twenty-five, there is a chance that a student might take at least a couple of courses from a single favorite professor.

Such long-lived, learning mentorships outside one's major are rare beyond small colleges. But at smaller schools it is common for students to take multiple courses outside the student's major discipline from one instructor: our physics major might well take an English course in the sophomore year to meet a humanities distribution requirement and another from the same faculty member as a senior elective. In a typical small college with roughly a thousand students and seventy-five faculty members and a graduation requirement of thirty to forty courses, it is virtually inevitable that the undergraduate experience will involve returning to a handful of professors for multiple courses. At one institution I visited, I asked a random group of six students, in a wide variety of majors, how many of them had taken at least four classes from one professor. *All* of them had. At another I asked the same question to a group of five, and only a single sophomore had not (and she had already had three classes from one faculty member). Then I asked if there was a second teacher from whom they had taken at least three classes, and in both cases there was a unanimous positive response.[40]

There are two potential drawbacks to this pattern of students taking many courses from a relatively small group of faculty members at small colleges. First, the professors may be weak. Although students are unlikely to choose to take repeated courses from poor teachers, if a student finds herself majoring in a department of three mediocre teachers, there isn't much choice. Second, if a student takes a half-dozen courses from the same teacher, there is a certain loss of diversity of pedagogical perspective, which can be a liability. Most small colleges are aware of both dangers and work hard to minimize them. In the first case mechanisms such as faculty development programs, careful hiring and promotion processes that reward good teaching, and the like are focused on identifying and correcting individual and departmental pedagogical deficits. In the second, many small colleges limit the number of courses a student can take in any one department, even that of the major, and work self-consciously to guarantee that no department will be so small or so single-minded as to deny students variety of perspective. One small college has a regulation, for example, that it will not offer a major in any area that does not have at least a minimum of three faculty members. Both these possible liabilities are genuine; I believe that they are outweighed by the advantages of close, continued, learning relationships sustained throughout the undergraduate years.

As noted earlier, at small colleges faculty members typically have significant, and often multiple, duties outside the classroom and department. If our hypothetical physics major is a senator in the student government assembly on campus and the English professor happens to be the advisor for that group, they will interact in that setting as well. The pervasive involvement of small college faculty in student clubs and extracurricular organizations promotes continued contact over the undergraduate years. My visit to Morehouse College happened to coincide with the first day of classes for the second semester. A faculty member with whom I spoke just after the first meeting of one of his courses remarked that he knew every single student in that course—though none of them had ever taken a class from him before: he knew each of them from other contact.

Finally, perhaps most important and wholly impossible to measure, are those "spontaneous conversations" that Professor Brann described. Smallness guarantees a certain proximity, which invites a culture of continuing contact. Most small colleges will have a single place on campus for all students and faculty to go have a cup of coffee or a soft drink. At the café the physics major is going to bump into her freshman writing teacher, even if she never takes a second course from that teacher. They are going to cross paths walking across the campus quadrangle going to and from class. They are going to find themselves next to each other in the line for refreshments after the annual holiday concert or on adjoining Stairmasters at the campus fitness center or seated next to each other at a play or lecture.

The pattern is one in which each student will likely have a handful of faculty with whom she is in contact for most of her undergraduate career; each faculty member will have a similar cluster of students who are known for all or most of the baccalaureate years. This characteristic is both gratifying and edifying for a faculty member. It is rewarding to observe the callow freshman one taught in her first semester grow into a confident, successful graduate. Indeed, that is one of the keenest pleasures most small college faculty members find in their work and one reason why most small college graduations are celebratory for the faculty as much as for the graduates and their families. It is also important, as a teacher, to see what has become of those one teaches. At the graduate level faculty can watch their doctoral students follow in their footsteps. At the undergraduate level that is less likely, but the freshman writing instructor can notice whether or not that physics major who was in the freshman composition class is writing for the student newspaper and, if so, whether or not she is writing well. The biology teacher can observe whether or not the philosophy student who took Bio 101 to meet the lab science requirement can speak intelligently three years later in a debate on ecological issues. In short, at a small college faculty members get to see, on a close daily basis, the results of their teaching.

Continuing undergraduate contact between student and teacher is equally valuable for the students. When students take multiple courses from the same faculty member, they have a chance to observe how different patterns of analysis and teaching are appropriate to different subject matters: if one has the same teacher for freshman composition and for poetry writing, one learns from that "controlled" pedagogic situation something about the differences between these two approaches to manipulating words. Moreover, they have a chance to measure their own intellectual progress against the steady template of the same instructor. A student who takes a senior physics seminar from the same teacher who taught her introductory physics lab would know how far she has come because she is moving through a familiar landscape.

Some students I interviewed also noted that, after they had taken several classes from a single instructor, they could "stop worrying" about what that instructor was specifically "looking for" in papers and tests and start concentrating, instead, on just mastering the material.

The small college undergraduate has, in the cluster of familiar teachers, a group of potential mentors and advisors to whom she or he can turn for advice about graduate school or potential professions—or, commonly, nonacademic issues such as family issues or living arrangements. Obviously, too, for both students and teachers this sort of long-lived relationship is very helpful when it comes time to seek or to write letters of recommendation to employers or graduate schools. Such advising and counseling relationships are likely based on voluntary affiliations with a favorite teacher or faculty member whom the student has gotten to know as an advisor or coach. Because they know each other over time, small college faculty and undergraduates constitute a kind of developmental community, a teaching and learning relationship with depth and duration.

The Liabilities of Community at Small Colleges

The closeness and intensity of small college communities is not without a dark, or at least clouded, side. Living in small, tightly contained communities such as little towns and small colleges can be like living in a fishbowl. When small colleges are located in small towns, as they often are, the effect is magnified. Individuals at such institutions who are in a position of public interest—college presidents or chancellors, deans of students, major sports coaches, perhaps even the director of theater or the conductor of campus musical groups—are never out of the public eye. If the football team loses badly on Saturday, the coach will hear about it in church or at brunch on Sunday. There is a reasonably good chance that the faculty member who receives tenure, or who is denied, will hear congratulations, or commiserations, from the checkout person at the grocery store or the travel agent or the insurance office. The president of a small college in a small town will learn quickly that, even in the midst of the weekend or a vacation period, it is unwise to step outside the house unshaven or wearing a tie-dyed T-shirt if she doesn't seek a countercultural image in the community.

Even when the small college is in a large city, on the campus the same lack of privacy can be troublesome. At Wellesley College in Boston or Westmont in Santa Barbara it is not likely that the checkout person at the Stop-and-Shop or Safeway will know one has been granted or denied tenure, but it is a virtual certainty that everyone on campus—students, secretaries, colleagues from all across the disciplines, and administrators—will.

This situation can be particularly acute when individuals at small colleges might reasonably want some privacy. If such persons are charged, say, with sexual harassment or if they charge someone else with such an offense, it is likely that "everyone will know." Indeed, if a faculty member goes out on a date with another faculty member and it doesn't go well, and they don't go out again, this will not remain a secret. If two students get into a fight in a dormitory or in the lunch line, there is nowhere either of them can go to avoid the other thereafter on campus. When I was a beginning assistant professor, I was helpfully told by my department chair that our college had only recently become more tolerant about alcohol consumption but that most folks still made sure to disguise empty wine bottles in their trash cans. In this chapter I have characterized small colleges as communities because everything and everybody tends to be connected. Most of the time this is a blessing; occasionally, it is a curse.

A somewhat less obvious concern in small collegiate communities is institutional myopia. Individuals at small colleges can easily become insular, and institutions can do so as well. So, for example, when I visited Morehouse College in Atlanta, one faculty member (himself a Morehouse graduate) said that his biggest concern for the college was that its students could become provincial. By this he meant that such students could grow to believe that the way the college did anything and everything was not only the best of all possible ways; it was really the *only* way.[41] Consultants at small colleges or those representing accrediting agencies visiting small and isolated institutions (I have been in both situations) know that too often the answer to the question "Why do you do it in this way?" is "Because that's how we do it."

Sometimes such myopia can infect teaching performance. In small departments it is much easier than in large ones to ignore contemporary scholarly trends with which one disagrees or about which one has just not taken the trouble to become informed. In a three-person department that has not hired a new member in a decade or two, there might well be little pressure to adjust teaching to new scholarly, pedagogic, and academic movements. Deans of small colleges frequently speak of the difficulty of changing the culture of nonfunctional departments, in which a small number of professors can often effectively resist efforts to hire new women and men with different perspectives or pedagogical inclinations. In my site visits to institutions and in reading about them and other small colleges, I commonly encountered pockets of individuals who have become so fixated on the collective and individual idiosyncrasies at their own institutions that they are not open to considering the merits of other options. In some ways small colleges are *harder* places to change than larger places, for exactly these reasons. In this respect they work in self-defeating opposition to one of their most inviting assets, the ability to be more nimble and responsive than larger, more cumbersome organizations.

Small colleges can seem excessively self-contained to students, particularly those who avidly seek the resources of larger institutions. Especially in small town settings, but even in large cities, small colleges are not going to be able to provide a steady stream of major arts, culture, and intellectual events found on major campuses. Nor are they as likely to be able to provide the range of handy internships or service-learning opportunities so readily available at large universities, especially in cosmopolitan settings. Richard Ekman of the Council of Independent Colleges notes that a potential challenge to small institutions is this possible isolation as well as the heightened need to work especially hard to make the sorts of connections to the larger world which come much more naturally and easily in metropolitan settings and at major universities.[42]

As the intermezzo that follows this chapter demonstrates in a particular case, there are many fine students, faculty, and administrators who find small colleges constricting. Some splendid faculty members, as this narrative demonstrates, are simply unable to flourish at small colleges, especially in small towns. This is not, in any sense, some sort of personal or professional defect, any more than it is defective for others to find unattractive or unacceptable the lures of large research universities. The limitations of small communities are real, and they can be stultifying. Since this set of limitations follows inevitably from the virtues of small college communities, there really is no way to eliminate them. Some of the insularity and self-centeredness of small colleges can be mitigated and modified: for example, sabbaticals and other leaves that take individuals to other institutional settings often have a potent positive effect in reducing the sense that one's own college is the center of the collegiate universe. Travel to professional meetings for brief periods can have a similar beneficial consequence. Student attendance at conferences and events at different and distant campuses has the same effect. And some small colleges encourage students to spend a term as a visiting student at another institution (the National Student Exchange facilitates such temporary relocations). Campus visitors from other places, with other perspectives, can be eye-opening. Still, those who are acutely uncomfortable in the fishbowl of small, self-contained communities and those who are discomforted by an almost inevitably exaggerated sense of institutional importance probably will not be happy at a small college. Those who are less disturbed by these liabilities can enjoy the many benefits of the close-knit family of small college communities.

◆ ◆ ◆

William Perry defined nine stages through which students might progress in college in their journey toward mature consciousness. The last of Perry's learning stages is "commitment." At that stage one has moved from unthinking acceptance of authoritarian positions through rebellion and ambivalence to a deeper understanding of a place where one can stand and the reasons for finding and holding such a position. Perry concluded that, in order for college students to achieve this last and highest learning stage, "the most important support seemed to derive from a special realization of community. This was the realization that in the very risks, separateness and individuality of working out their Commitments, they were in the same boat not only with each other, but with their instructors as well."[43] Small colleges offer such a special realization of community. It is not without its dangers, but its potential rewards are rich and deep.

Oakley speaks of colleges as "small face to face residential communities which maximize the degree to which the extracurriculum reinforces the curriculum."[44] Having examined some of the specific meanings and characteristics of small colleges as face-to-face communities, we turn in the following chapters to this process of "reinforcement" in which the various elements of the small college experience mesh to produce an educational experience of "integrity."

Less than Positive

Because of the mixed nature of this narrative, I have disguised the names of the individuals and institutions described here.

Dr. Janie Olson-Schmid came to Upper Midwest College (UMC) as the third member of a three-person Department of Theatre. She had done her graduate work at the University of Montana, where her terminal degree had been in theater studies, with a dissertation on an important pioneer in reader's theater for women. Although her particular interest was in directing, especially in the area of musical theater, she understood that in a small department at a small college she would be expected to do a little of everything. It was less clear to her what that would mean in terms of the scheduling of her personal and professional life. She had been an undergraduate at a small liberal arts college in Nebraska and had previously held a one-year part-time appointment at a small college. In addition to directing a play each year, her teaching load included courses in acting, oral interpretation, costuming, TV acting and directing, and reader's theater. She also had five advisees and supervised the small costume shop run by the college's theater department.

Although her interests were overtly focused upon performance, Dr. Olson-Schmid had published two papers (one of which was a version of her doctoral work) and written two book reviews for regional journals. She had a substantial record of contributions as a panelist at both regional and national meetings, contributing, for example to a panel on "Developing Goals, Objectives, and Ideals for the Theatre Division Mission Statement" at the national convention of the Speech Communication Association.

Each year at UMC Janie directed a play. Generally, her choices had been relatively lightweight (e.g., *The Music Man* and *All in the Timing*), but she had also undertaken such weighty works as *Coriolanus* and *Tartuffe*. Within the limits of a small department at a small, liberal arts college, with few students seriously contemplating a profession in theater, her productions were quite well received by colleagues, students, and within the general college community. Her teaching also was well regarded. At the time of her third year review, for example, her colleagues wrote that students found her "approachable, inspiring, collaborative, and creative." She was described as a well-respected director and a skilled costumer. Her department chair praised her as an "excellent teacher." Each year the academic vice president awarded Dr. Olson-Schmid a merit pay increase, not at the very top of the scale but always well above average.

Janie Olson-Schmid liked her students and was initially energized by the range of her responsibilities. But after three years she began to tire under the constant demands to spend evenings directing plays and supervising the Costume Shop and days teaching, advising, and in department and committee meetings. She also came to feel that her scholarly productivity was drying up. She felt she just didn't have the time and energy to prepare papers for professional meetings or for publication in addition to all her campus commitments. Although she had made many good friendships within the faculty and still enjoyed her students, she began to consider relocating to a job in which she would be able to focus her considerable energies a bit more tightly and, perhaps, more productively.

Dr. Olson-Schmid's situation at UMC was additionally complicated by personal factors. She had been accompanied to the small, rural town in which the college was located by her husband, Joseph. Joe Olson had a degree in landscape design, a subject not taught at the college and for which there was virtually no market in or around the small farming community in which the couple found themselves. They decided to rent a farmhouse outside of town, and for a year or two Joe was content puttering around this property and picking up a few small gardening, landscaping, and redecorating jobs. His second passion was in the field of alternative medicine, and what he really wanted to do was teach yoga and therapeutic massage. He had offered these subjects through the local community education program, but, not surprisingly, the market for such enterprises in a small, rural agricultural town was also small. Increasingly, it became obvious that Dr. Olson-Schmid's husband would find nothing like full or appropriate employment in either landscape design or alternative medicine. Although their income from her full-time and his occasional jobs was adequate, it was well below what they had hoped they would be able to earn as a couple. Perhaps a more crucial factor, however, was the frustration Joe increasingly came to feel as a result of his inability to find a serious vocation in the UMC region.

After many long and serious conversations, Joe and Janie decided it made sense for her to seek another teaching position, at a larger university in a larger community. Given her energy and the successes she had achieved in four years at Upper Midwest, this quest was not a difficult one, and in January of her fifth year Janie was offered a position at a regional comprehensive university in a small city in the upper South. A visit to the prospective new employer convinced Joe that he would have many more opportunities to continue his own growth and work in yoga in this more cosmopolitan environment. With feelings of disappointment, mixed with anticipation and eagerness, Dr. Olson-Schmid notified her department chair that she would be leaving after the current academic year. She expressed her gratitude to the college's students, faculty, staff, and administration and said that the past five years had been "a time of great professional and personal growth." The college dean wrote her a sincere note, thanking her for "your real and important contributions to our campus and especially our students, during your time here. We were fortunate to have you with us." The UMC community was sad to see Janie depart, and she, and to a lesser extent her husband, also felt some sadness at leaving. But leave they did.

6 | The Integrated Campus

Integrity of life is fame's best friend
Which nobly, beyond death, shall crown the end.

JOHN WEBSTER, *The Duchess of Malfi*

Integrity

Imagine the following scenario, which, while probably a touch tidy, is not flamboyantly unrealistic in the context of a small college undergraduate experience:

> Jenny Spelvin is a theater major at a small liberal arts college who has a strong interest in dramatic literature. So, she was excited when she heard that two members of the faculty were going to do something different this fall semester. Professor Nancy Meyer, from the English Department, was going to include John Webster's Jacobean tragedy *The Duchess of Malfi* (c. 1614) in her course on non-Shakespearean British Renaissance Drama, and Professor Rich Olson, in the Theater Department, was going to direct the play during the same term. Naturally, Jenny registered for the course, and in the second week of school she tried out for the play and won the role of the Duchess.
>
> *The Duchess of Malfi* is a drama that focuses on an aristocratic and strong-willed woman who falls in love with the steward of her household, an honest and sweet man who is her social inferior. The Duchess's choice offends her brothers, who torment her horribly and destroy her and—later—her family and finally themselves.
>
> The role was a demanding one for Jenny, but she relished the challenges. She was particularly fascinated by the dramatic conflict between the restrictive, even oppressive social norms personified by the Duchess's demonic brothers and the solid, strong and unrelenting determination of the martyred Duchess. This was a theme very close to some of the issues Jenny had been discussing this term in the Women's Issues Discussion Group sponsored by the campus Women's Center (of which Professor Meyer is the advisor). There had been several discussions at the group about the ways in which it was necessary for women to chal-

lenge social conventions, even those that sometimes seemed extremely comfortable to most people.

Jenny had a personal interest in the conversation about women challenging social norms because she had settled into a not-very-satisfying relationship with Tom, a philosophy major a year ahead of her class and a fellow resident of her coeducational residence hall. Although Tom was no tyrant, he had rather conventional ideas about male-female relations. Jenny was fond of Tom but was increasingly persuaded that their relationship needed to be redefined in a manner that was more respectful of her—her ideas, her needs, her intellect, and her interests.

This is not a very subtle tale, but it makes a point. In this yarn a mythical but not unbelievable college student is having a remarkably integrated, connected experience. Her curricular work includes studying the Webster play in the classroom. Being in the same play, on stage, is an exciting cocurricular opportunity. Participation in a Women's Center discussion group that is focusing on a set of issues raised both in the course work and the theatrical performance adds an extracurricular dimension. (I am defining *cocurricular* as activities outside the classroom which have a direct connection to credit-bearing course work—e.g., being in a play while studying dramatic literature—and *extracurricular* as activities that enhance the students' educational experience but are not directly related to the curriculum.) And, finally, relating classroom, stage, and discussion group to private living arrangements brings in what might be awkwardly called the noncurricular, or residential, realm.

Each of these tiers of Jenny's undergraduate experience is reinforcing and illuminating the others. She has the opportunity to live out in her personal life the lessons she is learning in her course work; she has the equally important opportunity to bring into the classroom and stage and discussion venues the world of her daily living experiences. We do not often enough appreciate what a rare, even artificial condition this is. Most of us, most of the time, do not have this sort of opportunity to create or live the kind of well-rounded life which small colleges—especially residential small colleges—permit, encourage, and even require. In the intermezzo that follows this chapter, a seasoned "student affairs" administrator reflects on the ways in which his work in residential life and co- and extracurricular programs has been inextricably knit to the curricular life of the public liberal arts college where he spent his career.

Francis Oakley, former president at Williams College, captures this opportunity for a connected collegiate life with persuasive eloquence: "Education is not a process that can wholly be confined to classroom, laboratory, studio or library, but one to which the diverse experience and richly variegated moments of life in a residential community must all combine to make their particular contribution. Extracurriculum as well as curriculum; play as well as work; fellowship as well as solitude; the foreign as well as the familiar; discomfort as well as ease; protest as well as celebration; prescription as well as choice; failure as well as success."[1]

In this respect the small college experience can be, for the undergraduate, like a work of art. It puts a "frame" around life and, in effect, forces it into a comprehensible, rational framework. Works of art have an internal coherence and unity too often lacking or blurred in "real" life. Everything in them should have an understandable relationship with everything else: those white squares of floor tile in Vermeer's *The Love Letter* match the color of the leering maid's headdress and the shape of the letter; the relationship of Polonius and Laertes is a mirror of Hamlet's confused father-son situation.

Jenny's experience, to circle back to *The Duchess of Malfi*, is one of integrity. *Integrity, integration,* and *integer* all have the same etymological root, the Latin word for "whole." Jenny's undergraduate experience is an integrated whole. She has the chance to be "integrated" and therefore to have "integrity." Jerry Gaff (vice president of the American Association of Colleges and Universities) has remarked that one of the defining features of small colleges is that it is possible at such places to think in terms of the coherence of the curriculum as a whole as well as the coherence of the entire collegiate program. And that, he notes in turn, makes it possible for small colleges to develop distinctive, "signature" offerings.[2]

An integrated collegiate experience is not guaranteed to every undergraduate at a small residential college all of the time. Many a biology major has studied the delicate interdependence of the systems of the human body in the afternoon and then behaved in a fashion that seems to ignore all that has been learned about these systems at the neighborhood bar that night. But the biology student did have the opportunity to put together lecture, lab, and libation. That "putting together," doing the intellectual, emotional, and spiritual work of integration, is the challenge we make, year after year, class after class, student after student. In the words of Zelda Gamson, speaking of a small college (Saint Joseph's in Indiana), "along with a recognition of intellectual integration, perhaps even preceding it, is a sense of personal integration."[3] She observes that "one of the problems with current undergraduate curricula is the failure to pay adequate attention to the connections among the subjects taught. This is a serious failure; for a long time, the essence of a liberal education has been seen to be the development of an integrative habit of mind."[4]

Similarly, the Carnegie Foundation's study of the college curriculum across American higher education in the late 1970s noted the importance of paying attention to connections between curricular subjects and the overall weakness within our postsecondary system in making, overtly, such links.[5]

Putting things together is the work of liberal learning.[6] One is reminded of the musical *Hair,* the popular Broadway emblem of my generation, which included a song that asked, "How can people be so heartless, how can people be so cruel, especially people who care about evil and social injustice?" Such people lack integrity: what they think and the way they live their lives are not unified. In *Scholarship Reconsidered: Priorities of the Professoriate,* Ernest Boyer suggests that, particularly at smaller liberal arts colleges, faculty "scholarship" can focus on integration, putting things together. He notes that at major research institutions the discovery of new knowledge is perhaps the major form of faculty scholarship or research. But there is an equally important task involved in thoughtful and creative reflection upon the relationships between disciplines and discoveries.[7]

It has become clear in countless studies that smaller learning communities are a particularly rich soil in which thoughtful integration can develop.[8] Places where the functions of daily living (eating, sleeping, brushing our teeth, and doing the laundry) are inextricably linked to the functions of collegiate learning (going to class and participating in co- and extracurricular activities) nourish the kind of dialog among life's activities which builds integration, integrity, and wholeness. As one of the faculty members with whom I spoke at Centenary College put it, the entire collegiate experience is "all blended together."[9] Surely that sense of the sanctity of a small community that did its work and its living together has long been revered in our culture; for example, it undergirds the Benedictine monastic ideal.

President Dale Knoble of Denison University has said to entering students at that college: "You have plenty of time to live as well as learn at Denison. And my premise is that they shouldn't be too separate. If you really do learn, if you are really engaged by what you explore with this faculty, it should show up in your living—not just later, but now . . . In fact, you will see living together on this campus and in this community as an exceptional opportunity to live what you learn, to keep your actions in line with your thoughts and your words."[10] Richard Hersh, similarly, notes that small residential colleges undo the dichotomy between the classroom and the rest of student life, which, he believes, is when the best education happens.[11]

The notion of the connection between integrity and learning is at the core of Parker Palmer's popular book *The Courage to Teach*, a book mostly about college teaching, less about the lives of college students. Palmer's central thesis is "we teach who we are . . . As I teach I project the condition of my soul onto my students." He contends that educational reform must begin with integrity, at the moment when "people come to a juncture where they must choose between allowing selfhood to die or claiming the identity and integrity from which good living, as well as good teaching, comes." He suggests we must have the courage to make "the decision to live an undivided life" in order to re-form ourselves as teachers.[12] Small colleges make the offer to those who dwell within them to live an undivided life.

For many students a large, urban, commuter university is a wonderful and stimulating introduction to the complexities and richness of modern life and living. But for others—or some of the same, at a different moment in their lives—the small self-contained community of a residential college is a particularly productive laboratory in which we learn to make the connections that give our lives integrity. A student leader at Warren Wilson College, reflecting on that institution's mission triad of classroom academics, campus work, and community service, commented that the college "forces you to learn amazing things!"[13]

Integration and Opportunity

All colleges and universities offer their students opportunities to participate in a wide range of collegiate activities. Small college students (and faculty and staff) have a remarkable chance not only to participate in many and diverse endeavors but also to connect them. And, as institutional size decreases, the chances for individual participation in multiple and meaningful collegiate activities actually increase. As Virginia Smith and Alison Bernstein point out:

There can be only one student body president whether the institution enrolls forty thousand or two thousand students. And yet the quality of the experience, the contribution to the development of a sense of personal responsibility, and the opportunities for working with others may be as useful and valid in the smaller institution as in the larger one. Opportunities to work on student newspapers and curriculum committees and to participate in performing groups, sports and budget review committees do not increase with the number of students. In an institution with two thousand students, the chances that the students will have some possibility of taking leadership positions might reasonably be set at 1:20. At the college with forty thousand students, the ratio explodes to about 1:400.[14]

One excellent and typical illustration of this aspect of small college life is intercollegiate athletics. As noted earlier, most smaller institutions are members of National Collegiate Athletic Association (NCAA) Division III, although there are plenty of exceptions. Generally, Division II institutions are larger than Division III ones, and Division I are larger than Division II (table 6.1).

The smallest institutions (Division III) offer a *larger* number of intercollegiate sports than do Division I or II. They have more student athletes than the Division II institutions and only 72 fewer varsity athletes on average than Division I universities, with 7,100 fewer students overall.

Viewed from a slightly different perspective, this means that, among the 1,036 colleges and universities that were members of the NCAA in

Table 6.1 Characteristics of Division I, II, and III Institutions

Division	Average Enrollment	Average No. of Athletes	No. of Sports	Average Percentage of Student Participants
I	9,224	398	14	4.3
II	3,275	320 (with football) 170 (without football)	12.5	5.3
III	2,088	326	15.6	15.7

Source: NCAA Membership Report, 2001.

2001–2, 15.7 percent of students at Division III schools were varsity athletes, 9.7 percent at Division II institutions with football and 5.3 percent at those without, and 4.3 percent of the students at the Division I level had the opportunity to play intercollegiate sports at the varsity level. At the upper end of the size continuum these figures become more dramatic. Even at the largest universities there are no more than about 700 varsity athletes, sometimes in student bodies of 35,000 to 45,000. A basketball squad at the University of Michigan is not going to be larger than at Albion; the women's volleyball team at Berkeley will probably not outnumber that at Mills. At the very large institutions—say, the Big 10—less than 2 percent of the students have the opportunity to participate.

Many Division III schools have a "no-cut" policy, which permits any student willing to try out for a sport, and stick with its workouts, to be on the squad. Such a policy, coupled with the "nonprofessional" level of competition, means that at most small colleges virtually any student who wants to be a varsity athlete can be.

What is true of intercollegiate varsity athletics is equally valid in many other endeavors. For example, in a cocurricular arts participation field such as music, proportional opportunities will be much richer, and the requisite level of specialized talent relatively low, at small colleges. Most smaller residential colleges have an orchestra, band, and chorus. Some will have additional ensembles: pep band, jazz band, and gospel choir. At small colleges with a particularly strong musical tradition—for example, St. Olaf or Oberlin—a very high proportion of the entire student body is involved in some sort of musical performance group (and, of course, they will be much more selective at the highest level). But even in a more modest setting, with, say, a modestly sized orchestra, band, and chorus, a significant proportion of the student community has a chance to participate in musical performances, whether or not they are majors in music.

At a university with a strong conservatory program in music or theater—for example, Northwestern University—a student majoring in electrical engineering or philosophy is not likely to be a member of the concert band. Nor is she likely to try out for, and win, a lead in a major University Theater production. But at small colleges physics majors are concertmasters, philosophers are quarterbacks, and sometimes quarterbacks are concertmasters. At Centenary College, for example, the student recruitment view book boasts: "You do not have to be a music major to sing in the choir or a theatre major to act in a production. You do not have to be a communication major to work at the campus radio station or write for the student newspaper."[15] A wide range of other participation opportunities are similarly open to nonspecialist students at most small colleges.

Obviously, there is a significant downside to the distinctly amateur status of small college athletics, performing arts, journalism, and other activities. No connoisseur of music is likely to confuse the Northwestern University Concert Band with that of Northwestern College in Minneapolis; no dedicated sports fan will mistake the Duke University basketball team for that of Warren Wilson College. Indeed, the comparison is invalid: a music program like Northwestern University's or a basketball program like Duke's or a school of journalism like the University of Missouri's is designed to train reporters, musicians, and athletes in specialized professional skills. At Northwestern College and Warren Wilson music and sports and the student newspaper are seen as opportunities for undergraduates to enrich and expand their experiences through participation in endeavors in which, in many cases, they either have no career aspirations or are overtly "giving things a try." (Sometimes, of course, small college athletes or artists do find professional success: Spike Lee and Samuel Jackson are both graduates of Morehouse College who went on to find success in film; Guilford College's Tony Womack has had a solid major league career in professional baseball.)

Finally, small colleges are proud of the range of student activities and clubs catering to special interests and hobbies they offer. In this respect, more than in areas such as the arts and athletics, they resemble larger institutions. Morehouse College, for example, notes that its students can join any of over 40 extracurricular organizations with an emphasis on leadership development.[16] Wellesley offers "more than 160" student organizations, including the Snowboard Club, the Women for Caribbean Development, the Investment Society, and a jazz and blues choral group.[17] At Warren Wilson cycling and whitewater paddling are varsity sports, and students can participate in organized kickboxing, African dance and drumming, yoga, and contra dancing.[18]

Small college faculties and staff members share in the range of opportunities available to their student colleagues. At many small institutions, for example, members of the campus community are encouraged to participate in campus musical groups (Cornell College in Iowa, e.g., has a campus community chorus). And many of those organizations and clubs have faculty and staff advisors and/or participants. At Guilford College the most popular show on the student radio station is hosted by a professor of psychology. At my own institution, the University of Minnesota, Morris, the vice chancellor for financial affairs is the advisor for the equestrian club.

As institutions of integrity, small colleges invite their students, faculties, and staffs to connect what they do in the classroom with the rest of their lives. And they offer rich opportunities for participation in a variety of amateur and special interest activities.

The New Liberal Arts

Campus integrity, the connectedness of learning and life, has significant and sometimes unexpected consequences in the curriculum, in the positions colleges take on political issues, and in matters of individual and collective ethics.

Martha Nussbaum's award-winning book *Cultivating Humanity: A Classical Defense of Reform in Liberal Education* summarizes and crystallizes, from a philosophically nuanced perspective, a prominent theme in contemporary discussions of liberal learning.[19] She offers a balanced and thoughtful defense of curricular reform and the inclusion of areas such as African American studies, women's studies, the study of non-Western cultures, and human sexuality within a Senecan definition of *liberal education* as the learning that can create free citizens, "citizens who are free not because of wealth or birth, but because they can call their minds their own" (293). Nussbaum offers three characteristics of such a liberating higher education experience: Socratic self-examination; the cultivation of citizens of the world; and the creation of "narrative imagination," defined as the ability to envision oneself as another.

Obviously, there are partisans of positions both to the intellectual left and right of Nussbaum. She is, for example, scornful of some of the more extravagant claims of extreme Afrocentrists (e.g., that Shakespeare was a black man) and equally intolerant of some of the more radical trends of literary criticism, which she understands as calling into question the very possibility of "learning," or the existence of any objective thing to learn other than a kind of maze of evolving cultural constructions. And, of course, on the other side there are equally vigorous advocates of a definition of liberal learning which excludes the sorts of new curricula Nussbaum defends. These proponents of a more conservative vision of liberal learning (e.g., Harold Bloom and the National Association of Scholars) cling to a more traditional curricular vision that focuses centrally on the mainstream Western European cultural inheritance.

Nussbaum's thoughtful moderate liberalism is generally carrying the day in most American liberal arts colleges. Courses in non-Western cultures, indeed various versions of graduation requirements in "multiculturalism," have proliferated, and women's studies and African American studies have generally won the battle to be taken seriously.

What is the special role of the small college in this large discussion? It is a curious one, in some ways strikingly counterintuitive. I argue that in some ways a small, relatively isolated college offers students a better chance at an education in which diversity—in both the curriculum and in living arrangements—plays a significant role than does a large, urban university. This paradoxical point can be illustrated by a comparison of two sister institutions that I know well professionally, the University of Minnesota, Twin Cities, and the University of Minnesota, Morris. The latter is a small, public liberal arts college, the former a huge public research/land grant university. Both campuses have a minority population of roughly 15 percent. On the Twin Cities campus, with its 40,000 students, this equates to about 6,000 students of color; on the Morris campus, which has about 2,000 students, it amounts to about 300. On the bigger campus the largest single minority group is African American students, but it would probably be difficult to find *any* ethnic, cultural, racial, or religious minority that is wholly unrepresented. On the smaller campus about 125 students are American Indians, 110 are African Americans, and there are a smaller number of Hispanic and Asian students.

At Morris about a third of the faculty are not white Americans, and they represent a surprising range of backgrounds: the 120-member faculty includes Christians, Jews, Buddhists, Muslims, and teachers from other religious traditions as well as professors from both Western and Eastern Europe, Asia, Latin America, and Africa. Less surprisingly, the Twin Cities campus has a spectacularly diverse and cosmopolitan faculty and professional staff. The Twin Cities metro region itself is an increasingly multicultural community, with, for example, a very large recent in-migration of both Somali and Hmong populations; the town of Morris, by contrast, is culturally homogeneous. Outside the college population there are fewer than a half-dozen residents of color. The nearest synagogue is a three-hour drive, and, even including Jewish faculty and staff, there are not a half-dozen Jews (me among them) in Morris or its county and even fewer Muslims or Buddhists.

Clearly, the Twin Cities university is demographically more diverse than the Morris campus, if not proportionally then in raw numbers. And there has been a substantial, and significantly effective, effort to promote multicultural concerns, both in the curriculum and in the noncurricular daily life of UM-TC students. Thus, from one perspective one could legitimately argue that a student who actively seeks diversity in and beyond the classroom would be well served by attending the larger campus.

Yet a strong case can be made that the smaller college community, in the smaller town, actually is every bit as likely to generate the sort of substantive multicultural contacts that would satisfy Nussbaum's desired "citizen of the world" and "narrative imagination" educational experiences. Geoffrey Canada, who was a minority student at Bowdoin College, observes that "different groups coming into intimate and sustained contact with one another, can be well served by the small liberal arts college."[20] The key here is the sort of enforced proximity generated in a very small community and the corresponding opportunities for de facto segregation in a very large one. Virtually all of the students at the Morris campus live either on campus or within a tiny few-block radius. Twin Cities students are spread across a large metropolitan community, which includes neighborhoods that are wholly integrated but many more that are monocultural. In a single-college, all-undergraduate, wholly liberal arts curriculum, in which 15 percent of the undergraduates are students of color, it is a certainty that all students, whether they are majoring in philosophy or physics or psychology, are going to find themselves constantly in small class settings with students from different backgrounds. At a major research university that sort of guaranteed classroom diversity is far less certain. The student of electrical engineering may well count on an entirely different classroom demographic than the student of veterinary medicine (in fact, the first will be in classes dominated by males, the second will have many more female student peers). The National Survey of Student Engagement asked students if they had had serious conversations with students of a different race or ethnicity or with students with very different religious or political backgrounds. Students at baccalaureate / liberal arts category colleges answered "often or very often" significantly *more often* than students at doctoral or master's institutions.[21] Students in Minneapolis and St. Paul may eat in residence hall dining facilities, or they may opt for downtown soul food restaurants or Scandinavian bakeries, or they may cook for themselves with supplies from a Somali grocery around the corner or the supermarket of an affluent, homogeneous, white, upper-middle-class suburb. In short, the diversity experience at a large multifaceted campus of a major research university in a large city may well be either a hit-or-miss venture or a matter of choice: one can opt in, or one can opt out; the choice is up to the students. It seems logical that in too many cases the students who would benefit most from the development of narrative imagination, who come to college farthest from being citizens of the world, would unfortunately tend to opt out.

By contrast, in the intense, hothouse atmosphere of a small college, particularly the small college that is geographically isolated, with virtually no extra-campus options, students are going to have to learn to live with one another, in and out of class, or not be able to live at all. White students in Morris are going to do their laundry with students of color because there is only one public Laundromat in the community and four or five sets of coin-operated washing machines in thoroughly integrated campus residence halls. There is one dining hall on campus and one McDonalds, one Pizza Hut and one Subway in town. The town has one movie theater, the campus one café. If anyone in Morris wants to go to a recreational gym, the one at the college, with one locker room for all men and another for all women, one competition swimming pool, and one cardiovascular exercise room is the only choice. One way to put this case graphically might be to say that in a well-integrated small isolated college, the "narrative" of understanding the lives of individuals from different backgrounds requires much less "imagination." A student at such a college will learn something of how different people live because they are all living on top of one another and could not avoid one another if they tried. Richard Ekman, president of the Council of Independent Colleges, points out that in a small college setting it is impossible for students to gravitate only toward others in their interest or racial group, as they can and do at large institutions.[22]

Certainly, the act of living in an integrated dorm is not the same as imagining life in Somalia, Amazonia, urban Japan, rural China, or post-Communist Russia. But what can be guaranteed in Morris, and not in the Twin Cities, is that students will be constantly interacting, in meaningful social and intellectual ways, with students from dramatically different backgrounds by virtue of the very smallness of the college.

Interesting quantitative data supports these conclusions. At both Minnesota campuses students were asked upon entering college if they had socialized with someone of another race in the previous year. At Morris a much smaller proportion (46 percent) said yes than in the Twin Cities (57 percent). But at the conclusion of their undergraduate careers, when asked if they had had a close friend on campus with a different racial background from their own, 66 percent of the Morris students responded affirmatively, compared to 56 percent on the more metropolitan Twin Cities campus.[23] This is a very significant turnaround.

In this sense, then, racial, cultural, and ethnic integration can be understood to be a function of the overall coherence and connectivity of the institution. When students' curricular, cocurricular, and extracurricular experiences—their classes, pastimes, and living arrangements—are woven together, their education is designed to foster the kinds of self-examination, world citizenship, and multicultural imagination Martha Nussbaum describes as essential for contemporary educated women and men.

Of course, it goes without saying that the sort of fishbowl experience of multiculturalism I have been describing depends entirely on a collegiate population at that small and isolated campus which has some genuine diversity. By contrast, one might examine a third campus of the University of Minnesota in Crookston. There, despite good faith efforts on the part of the administration, faculty, and staff, the student body is largely drawn from the monocultural local community. At that campus students live as closely with one another as in Morris, but generally they live close to other white, rural, Christian, English-speaking young people. Their enforced community is, in effect, the single-culture community that some students in the Twin Cities are able to choose. And, when Crookston students were asked the same question about close friends with a racial background different from their own, only 31 percent—less than half the proportion in Morris—said yes.

Furthermore, even in the smallest and most diverse community, patterns of habitual or self-imposed segregation can develop. A small college can make students eat in the same dining room, but few, in the twenty-first century, tell them where to sit. There might be only a single gym, but one group may choose to swim, while another plays a pickup basketball game and a third lifts weights. Small colleges have a built-in opportunity to help students become citizens of a larger world, but they cannot afford to be complacent in believing that this opportunity is actually being delivered to all students most of the time. Wellesley president Diana Chapman Walsh remarks that one of the challenges of small colleges seeking to cultivate a diverse student body and a global outlook is that of simultaneously "holding some center, keeping an open, free exchange of ideas."[24] Thoughtful, effective programs need to be developed and implemented to make sure that these opportunities are being productively exploited. Jim Hunt, provost and dean of the faculty at Southwestern University, comments that "to be a small college and to be diverse is hard, but it is best."[25] What he means is that it can be hard to achieve diversity in a small college, especially a geographically isolated one, but, when that effort is successful, the smallness of the institution multiplies the effects of cultural pluralism on students.

In terms of curriculum there is again a certain inherent opportunity at small institutions. At many small colleges all first-year students take a "common course," a universal freshman seminar. The larger the institution, the less likely that there can be that sort of universally shared common curricular experience. Even if the topic of such a common course is not remotely connected to the "new liberal arts" curriculum (although frequently it is), it nonetheless provides at least one universally shared curricular experience.

If programs in women's studies, African American studies, non-Western studies, and studies of sex and gender are to be found in small colleges, there is an excellent chance they are closer to the central curricular core of the institution than might be the case within a large university context. Small colleges do not, as a rule, have institutes, centers, or freestanding programs. If there are faculty and courses and majors, there is probably a department. And students majoring in such a department are far more likely to be subject to all-college distribution and graduation requirements than might be the case within a self-contained, more specialized university center. One way of saying this is that at a small college it is very hard to "marginalize" anything because the periphery isn't very far from the center, and there isn't much room for a very distant margin.

While there is certainly no guarantee that a small college will have a more diverse faculty than a large university, it does seem likely that, given equivalent levels of faculty diversity, a large proportion of students at a small college are likely to benefit from that variety and range of professorial exposure. Thus, if the average student on the Morris campus in Minnesota graduates with between thirty and forty courses in the baccalaureate years, she will have taken these courses from a pool of about 120 full-time faculty members (and no part-time instructors or graduate assistants). If the same student attended the Twin Cities campus, she would have taken the same number of courses and drawn from a pool of over 1,500 full-time faculty and a plethora of part-timers and teaching assistants. This suggests that, if a small campus can build a diverse faculty, it has a much higher level of assurance that a significant number of undergraduates will actually benefit from that diversity. This is, of course, no certainty, but one suspects that a student at a huge major university could arrange her curriculum so as to take all—or at least most—classes from faculty members of color or virtually none. The option of such discrimination does not exist in a smaller pedagogical universe.

The "new liberal arts," like the old, must always be understood as an opportunity, not a guarantee. If the function of liberal learning is intellectual liberation, we must always remember that being free is an active task, not a passive gift. At the most conscientious and diverse college or university students can only be invited to broaden and open their minds: they cannot be forced to. I contend, however, that in many ways this invitation, like many others, is most beguiling and most likely to succeed when it issues from a small college.

Integrity and Engagement

Seen through one lens, the characteristic of institutional integration is deeply connected to the concept of student "engagement." As institutional integration refers to the thoughtful relatedness of multiple aspects of collegiate life, student engagement is a concept that invites us to consider the degree, depth, and multiplicity of activities in which students are truly involved in college. The first suggests the importance of connections between curricular, residential, cocurricular, and extracurricular elements; the second speaks of the pervasiveness of students' connections to the campus and through the campus to the world beyond.

Student engagement has been the subject of intense scrutiny and interest in recent years. Hersh, for example, makes the overt equation that smallness equals involvement equals educational success.[26]

A number of key issues for most campuses have emerged. Do most students live on campus, or in close proximity, or do most live with their families or have families and residences of their own? Students who do not live on or close to campus, as noted earlier, find it more burdensome to attend cultural and social events at the college. Do students work off campus? There are many colleges today where over half of the students have off-campus jobs (e.g., the University of North Carolina–Asheville). In many cases these jobs are consequential—full-time or twenty to thirty hours per week. On-campus work, whether funded by the institution, state, or federal resources, tends to be somewhat less disruptive than a "regular" job, both formally (e.g., fewer hours) and informally (e.g., most students who work in an academic office or for a professor will have little trouble seeking extra time away from work to prepare for finals). Students at smaller colleges are more likely to work on campus, and less likely to work off campus, than those at larger institutions.

The annual National Survey of Student Engagement provides comparative information about the connectedness of students, their expectations of college as first-year students compared to their judgments as college seniors, and their motivation for and perceptions of college education. Table 6.2 presents the responses of first-year students (FY) and seniors (SR) in two categories: all NSEE-responding schools (366 institutions and 206,000 students) and schools in the Carnegie baccalaureate–liberal arts (BA-LA) category (about 20 percent of the total). Note that not all small colleges are in the BA-LA category, and not all schools in that category are small colleges, but the overlap is significant, and this category is the closest by far to the group of schools discussed in *Old Main*.

Also related to residence and work are age and full-time/part-time status. Although it is certainly not a hard and fast rule, often the students who are living at home and working off campus will be older than the traditional eighteen- to twenty-one-year-old contingent of college attendees. The older college student—typically called "nontraditional" a decade ago—remains an increasingly important and growing segment of the college student population, in small colleges as well as large. Some smaller schools now see a quarter or a third of their students in this category. This is particularly evident in institutions that devote a large portion of their curriculum to vocationally oriented studies and, hence, are attractive to adults who may wish to upgrade their career options or shift jobs. It is my opinion that many small colleges do not do as well by such students as they do with their traditional eighteen- to twenty-one-year-olds.

Not surprisingly, a thirty-five-year-old who lives off campus and has a job is more likely to be doing college work on a part-time basis than a nineteen-year-old living in a residence hall without the demands of external employment. Table 6.3 shows a number of these factors in relation to part-time/full-time status.

Table 6.2 National Survey of Student Engagement, 2002: Selected Summary Results

Student Engagement	Class	NSSE 2002 Mean	Baccalaureate / Liberal Arts Mean	Effect Size
Academic and Intellectual Experiences (1 = never; 4 = very often)				
Worked on a paper or project that required	FY	3.04	3.17	.15
integrating ideas or information from	SR	3.33	3.47	.19
various sources				
Put together ideas or concepts from different	FY	2.47	2.58	.13
courses when completing assignments or	SR	2.82	2.89	.08
during class discussions				
Discussed grades or assignments with an	FY	2.60	2.75	.17
instructor	SR	2.81	2.93	.13
Talked about career plans with a faculty	FY	2.15	2.23	.08
member or advisor	SR	2.45	2.74	.30**
Discussed ideas from your reading or classes	FY	1.80	2.01	.26*
with faculty members outside of class	SR	2.08	2.34	.29*
Worked with faculty members on activities	FY	1.53	1.71	.22**
other than course work (committees, orienta-	SR	1.81	2.12	.33**
tion, student life activities, etc.)				
Discussed ideas from your readings or classes	FY	2.74	2.92	.20*
with others outside of class (students, faculty	SR	2.86	3.02	.19
members, coworkers, etc.)				
Quality of Advising (1 = poor; 4 = excellent)				
Overall, how would you evaluate the quality of	FY	2.91	3.06	.16
academic advising you have received at your	SR	2.86	3.15	.31**
institution?				
Enriching Educational Experiences (0 = no; 1 = yes)				
Work on a research project with a faculty	FY	0.51	0.66	.30**
member outside of course or program	SR	0.28	0.36	.18
requirements				

Table 6.2 (*continued*)

Student Engagement	Class	NSSE 2002 Mean	Baccalaureate / Liberal Arts Mean	Effect Size
Time Usage (hours of work: 1 = 0 hr; **4 = 11–15 hr; 8 = more than 30 hr)**				
Working for pay on campus	FY	1.62	1.80	.14
	SR	1.88	2.20	.20*
Working for pay off campus	FY	2.33	1.59	−.34**
	SR	3.65	2.46	−.43***
Participating in cocurricular activities	FY	2.10	2.49	.28*
(organizations, campus publications, student government, etc.)	SR	2.04	2.58	.38**
Institutional Environment **(1 = very little; 4 = very much)**				
Providing the support you need to help you	FY	3.01	3.20	.22*
succeed academically	SR	2.86	3.10	.21*
Attending campus events and activities	FY	2.76	3.02	.26*
(special speakers, cultural performances, athletic events, etc.)	SR	2.51	2.83	.33**
Quality of Relationship **(1 = unfriendly; 7 = friendly, supportive)**				
Relationships with other students	FY	5.66	5.76	.07
	SR	5.70	5.77	.06
Relationships with faculty members	FY	5.39	5.71	.26*
	SR	5.55	5.91	.28*
Relationships with administrative personnel	FY	4.88	5.08	.13
and offices	SR	4.57	4.69	.07
Satisfaction **(1 = poor; 4 = excellent)**				
How would you evaluate your entire educa-	FY	3.19	3.33	.19
tional experience at this institution?	SR	3.24	3.42	.26*

Note: These results from the NSSE are all "statistically significant," in part because of the very large sample size. The column labeled "effect size" is a measure of the significance of the difference. Items in which the effect size is particularly noteworthy are indicated by one or more asterisks. Aid in preparing and interpreting these statistics was generously provided by Jon Anderson of the University of Minnesota, Morris.

All these factors, in their multiple interactions, have a potent effect on how students experience college. For some students college *is* their job—indeed, their life: the primary occupation of their days and nights. One group of such students interviewed for this project won my affection by telling me that they spent hours sitting around the residence hall lounge and student café arguing about poststructuralism or the lasting geopolitical effects of Bismarck. And there are other students for whom college and academic work is but one responsibility of many and sometimes not the most important. It is difficult to convince the mother of a sick child that writing an English paper comparing and contrasting narrative and lyric poetry is more important than caring for her child—perhaps because it isn't.

Thus, the older, part-time, nonresidential working student is usually far less deeply linked to the college. Such a student is less likely to be engaged in extracurricular activities such as musical groups or special interest

Table 6.3 Characteristics of Part-time and Full-time Undergraduates at Four-Year Institutions

Characteristic	Student Percentage	
	Part-time	Full-time
Age: 25 years old or older	67	13
Dropped out for some period since entering college	58	16
Married, divorced, separated, or widowed	53	10
Currently employed full-time	59	4
College grade-point average of B or higher	61	55
"Very important" goals		
Career success	57	63
Financial success	40	43
Intellectual development	70	69

Source: Carnegie Foundation for the Advancement of Teaching, National Survey of Undergraduates, 1984.

clubs. These students may well not see the college as their primary source of socializing and friendship, and sometimes they will simply not have the time to stop by a professor's office during office hours to chat about an issue left unresolved in class or a paper due next week. Many studies have demonstrated conclusively that students strongly linked to the institution outside the classroom are more likely to succeed in college and persist to graduation than are less fully engaged peers.[27] Of course, part-time, older, working, and, hence, less engaged students are far more likely to be encountered in nonresidential community colleges or on the campuses of major metropolitan universities than at smaller institutions, but they certainly are a fact of collegiate life virtually everywhere in contemporary American higher education. Given that I myself married after two years of undergraduate college and thereafter lived and worked off campus, I am not prepared to affirm that such students are a liability as much as a growing and important challenge for small colleges.

In summary, compared to college students generally, those at smaller colleges were more likely to have reported engagement, in that they

—worked on a project that integrated ideas;

—put together ideas from different courses;

—discussed work with an instructor;

—discussed ideas outside of class;

—worked with faculty members on activities other than course work;

—gave high marks to the advising they received;

—worked on a research project with a faculty member;

—either have studied or want to study abroad;

—have done independent study;

—worked for pay on campus (and they are less likely to have worked off campus);

—participated in extracurricular activities (were less likely to have commuted to class or to have provided care for dependents);

—felt their colleges provided good academic support;

—attended campus events; and

—had good relationships with other students, faculty members, and administrative personnel.[28]

A finding in Alexander Astin's data supports the claim that students are more satisfied with the faculty and the educational program at small liberal arts colleges, "attributable to the . . . college's small size."[29] A similar set of findings about the range of activities and their connections is reported by Winter, McClelland, and Stewart in their study of one liberal arts institution ("Ivy College") in comparison to a state teachers' college and a community college.[30] These researchers were seeking to ascertain what effects liberal learning produced in students and then to refine what particular causes produced these effects at Ivy College. In very abbreviated form their findings were that two characteristics of Ivy College were critically important. The first characteristic was "diversity of choices, opportunities, and other students," which produced participation in organized activities with other students. The second characteristic was "demand to integrate broad and diverse experiences, [which] increased critical thinking and confident leadership," two of the most important liberal arts competences. Their conclusion, then, is that integrating experiences and a high level of participation produce significant gains in leadership abilities, critical thinking, and personal maturity.

Student engagement is enhanced by the wide range of opportunities for participation at small colleges and is an important predictor of student success and persistence. In turn, the depth and diversity of involvement in a range of in-class and out-of-class campus activities increases the likelihood that a student will have a cohesive collegiate career. Such an integrated college experience calls students—and faculty and staff—to Nussbaum's "new" learning, characterized by self-examination, global awareness, and the narrative imagination to envision oneself as another.

Integrity of Life

The first definition of *integrity* in the *Oxford English Dictionary* is the sense in which I have been using the word here—a condition of wholeness and completeness; integration. But, of course, in contemporary usage the word also has an ethical denotation, what the *OED* calls "soundness of moral principle."[31] I believe there are at least two ways in which the wholeness of the experience potentially afforded by small colleges can cultivate moral soundness.

First, by striving to build a collegiate experience in which curricular, extracurricular, cocurricular, and residential experiences are mutually reinforcing and seamlessly consonant, colleges can achieve a kind of institutional moral integrity. When, for example, a professor at Warren Wilson College leads a discussion in an ethics course about the value of hard, honest work and the importance of an ethos of service to one's fellow humans, the college provides an integrated triadic program that overtly links that class to work and to service. The college is practicing what it preaches. Every time a member of the Southwestern University community enters the McCombs Campus Center, she will read in very large letters on the building's wall that one of the core values of the college is promoting a passion for intellectual growth, another is respecting the worth and dignity of others, and yet another is the pursuit of justice and the common good.

Second, of course, institutions that model the integration of life's learning, activities, and relationships can teach students who want to learn this lesson how to go about it. Colleges of integrity can produce as graduates men and women of integrity. I agree with Cardinal Newman that no college or university can make a person *want* to be virtuous: "Quarry the granite rock with razors, or moor the vessel with a thread of silk; then may you hope with such keen and delicate instruments as human knowledge and human reason to contend against those giants, the passion and the pride of man."[32] But a small college of integrity can help teach individuals who want to be good how to do it.

Yav

Dr. Eric Iovaccini is universally known to colleagues and friends as "Yav." At the end of the 2002–3 academic year he stepped down from the position of vice chancellor for student affairs at the University of North Carolina (UNC)– Asheville, a position he held for a quarter-century.

Dr. Iovaccini grew up in southern New Jersey, where he attended Vineland High School, immortalized in the film *Eddie and the Cruisers*. Vineland had some two thousand students in the three class years (sophomore through senior) it offered when Yav was a student. In high school he was a student leader: a varsity athlete, class president, and member of the Honor Society.

Yav picked Gettysburg College as his undergraduate college. There, too, he was active in student life. He played baseball, served in student government, was a leader in his fraternity, and eventually took a leadership role in Gettysburg's student-directed honor system. His involvement in campus student leadership and governance was one reason Yav decided to go to law school. He received his law degree from the University of Nebraska and practiced with a small firm in Lincoln for two years. One of his major assignments was doing the legal work for Union College there, and he developed an interest in higher education law, in particular serving as a legal advocate for students. He was subsequently offered a job at the University of Wyoming in the office of student affairs, largely dealing with student legal issues such as the Buckley Amendment and Title IX. At Wyoming he was advised that a continued career in higher education would get a boost from a doctorate, so he pursued and earned a Ph.D. degree in higher education from Wyoming while on the staff. In 1978 Yav came to Asheville as the chief student affairs officer.

Yav points out that there are really two important and distinct administrative leadership positions in student affairs. The "dean of students" is someone who knows students individually and serves as their advocate and caregiver. The "vice president for student affairs," on the other hand, is an institutional policy maker, dealing with budgets, legal issues, and similar overarching managerial issues. At a small institution, he notes, usually the same person does both jobs, even though at times there can be some contradictory responsibilities.

It is Yav's sense that during his twenty-five years at UNC-Asheville he has become less the dean and more the vice president. Partly, of course, that is a function of age and experience: in his mid-fifties, he is no longer a contemporary of the students with whom he works, and with his quarter-century experience he is a wise old hand at the university. But he also believes that external factors, which are pervasive in American higher education, have moved him in this direction as well. Increased federal and state regulations, increasingly complicated personnel practices, and demands of "accountability" are partly responsible. Also, he believes, the sorts of issues with which student affairs offices currently deal most commonly are increasingly sociopolitical matters—drugs, alcohol, mainstreaming students with high psychological medication needs, issues involving gay students, racial diversity—more than personal matters. From his perspective in student affairs Dr. Iovaccini has concluded that often parents (and students) pick small institutions believing that they will take better care of students, particularly students who need such care. And at a small university he actually sees the students (and their parents) when such problems occur: "When the crisis happens, people like me have to *be* there, not just talk to the press."

Still, Yav feels that today he spends more time with faculty colleagues than with students—serving on committees and task forces, consulting with them individually. At small institutions, he points out, there is more respect for student affairs professionals, since both the faculty and student affairs staff see the students outside the classroom. Still, he feels, faculty today are less inclined to get involved in the extracurricular lives of their students than in earlier periods in American higher education—typically, they live farther from campus and have more scholarly and personal interests and obligations, for example. And fewer and fewer of them come from a small liberal arts college background themselves.

Like faculty, students today are tied less closely to the campus than in the past. Many have demanding jobs and/or family responsibilities. Virtually all have cars, cable TV, a more suburban lifestyle. The growth of public sector collegiate institutions, the near-universality of higher learning, and the "buyer's market" in college admissions all have contributed to the less-engaged student. Today's students, Iovaccini believes, are less committed, on average, to the total collegiate experience than earlier generations. Full-time students who start college immediately after high school and proceed straight through their undergraduate careers are still common in private liberal arts colleges but increasingly rare in the public sector.

Another development Yav sees is the increasing assertiveness of parents in issues involving the students. He receives a growing number of phone calls and visits from parents playing an active role in managing their progeny's college careers. And their expectations for those careers have grown as well: parents believe it is the college's responsibility to see to it, for example, that students go to class and remain safe. And they are quick to call, even threaten legal action, if those expectations are thwarted.

Yav notes that his closest relationship within the university has tended to be with his academic counterpart, the chief academic officer at UNC-Asheville. He has team-taught with academic deans and occupied an office adjacent to that of the vice chancellor for academic affairs, with whom he interacts on a daily basis. He considers the vice chancellors for academic affairs and student affairs important allies and notes that at most large universities these two officers are usually not even in the same building.

Dr. Iovaccini has stayed at UNC-Asheville both for personal and professional reasons. In particular, he has enjoyed watching the institution change and grow and playing an important part in that evolution. He has enjoyed relationships with academic colleagues and has been stimulated by some of his other responsibilities as well. For example, he has been instrumental in helping to envision and design new residence halls, a fitness center, and a student commons, all opportunities he believes he would not have had at a large university. As he steps down from the chief student affairs position, Yav plans to pick up a leadership role in the college's growing international programs, with a particular interest in programs in Italy, a country in which, along with the United States, he holds dual citizenship.

7 | Blurring the Boundaries

America does remarkably well in producing a wide assortment
of educational experiences. Colleges come in many sizes.

DEREK BOK, *Higher Learning*

During the course of my visits to schools for this book, I developed a sharpened perception of interesting and worthwhile efforts to blur the borders between large universities and small colleges at the beginning of the twenty-first century. (May I suggest that a sharpened perception of a blur is an uncomfortable sensation?)

A number of small colleges seek to create the diversity of programs and the broad range of academic and extracurricular programs of larger institutions; some big universities are looking for ways to offer students the advantages of human scale and academic community found in small colleges. Certainly, neither sort of institution is trying to become the other, nor is it repudiating the essential values and missions of its type. Nor would any rational observer of higher education assert that one sort of institution is inherently better or more effective for all students than another sort. Small, quick, lithe athletes might try to gain muscle mass; big, strong ones may work on their speed and coordination. But football players are not seeking to become gymnasts, and marathon runners don't wish to be weightlifters. For many students the wealth of resources at a large research university is the perfect stimulus for undergraduate learning; for others the focus and integration of a small college is just right.

Nor, of course, can a large university become a small college by building an honors program, any more than a small teaching college can become a major research university by giving more attention to faculty scholarship. A student cannot acquire a research university baccalaureate experience at a small college any more than a small college can realistically offer to duplicate the breadth of a large university. Sometimes admissions offices or officers at both sorts of schools become overzealous and claim the best of both worlds for prospective students. Sometimes car dealers suggest that their product combines the fuel economy of a Civic, the speed of a Porsche, and the brute force of a Hummer. Wise consumers of colleges and cars are skeptical of such claims.

It is both interesting and instructive to take a closer look at the ways in which colleges and universities, large and small, have supplemented their core missions with values traditionally associated with other kinds of post-secondary institutions.

Small Colleges with University Qualities

For a variety of reasons many small institutions have developed programs that emulate some of the characteristics of large universities. Of course, many formerly small colleges have simply evolved into large and complex institutions. As noted in chapter 2, for example, it is common for former small teachers' colleges to develop into large, graduate degree–granting regional comprehensive universities; Northern Illinois State Teachers College, for instance, has grown into Northern Illinois University, with nearly twenty-five thousand students.

Others, however, have clung tenaciously to a small college core while adding supportive programs clustered around it. One good example is the College of New Rochelle (CNR) in suburban New Rochelle, New York. Founded as the first Roman Catholic college for women in the state of New York in 1904, the college was for sixty-five years a small, traditional, undergraduate Catholic women's school. Over the past half-century its size has varied from four hundred to one thousand students. The traditional liberal arts core college, today known as the School of Arts and Sciences, currently enrolls about 475 students, still exclusively women.[1]

In the late 1960s and 1970s CNR moved assertively into several new areas of operation. First, it created a graduate school in 1969. In 1972 the college launched the School of New Resources, an undergraduate program for adult learners. It is now the largest of CNR's schools, with forty-seven hundred students. Finally, the School of Nursing was established in 1976 and today offers baccalaureate, master's, and certificate programs. All the schools except the original School of Arts and Sciences are coeducational.

The campus facilities in New Rochelle, occupied by the college since 1904, are today home to the School of Arts and Sciences and some of the students from the other four programs. But most of these non–Arts and Sciences students are located on six other campus centers throughout the

Greater New York area. There are today nearly seven thousand students enrolled in various College of New Rochelle endeavors, but, as noted earlier, only about 475 of them are housed in the traditional, undergraduate, core unit.

This entrepreneurial expansion has been successful for the college in at least three ways, according to those I interviewed in New Rochelle. The new schools have brought resources to the college which have enabled it to remain financially sound (the consensus is that the graduate, nursing, and New Resources schools help to support the traditional liberal arts school); the expanded programs provide faculty and other sorts of human and curricular resources that exceed what might be reasonably expected of a college of 475; the programs provide important community services to a wide range of constituents.

Because the bulk of CNR's newer programs take place off the traditional campus in New Rochelle, the relationship between these endeavors and the School of Arts and Sciences seems a delicate one. The campus itself has very much the appearance and culture of a small, private college. If one asks faculty and staff, as I did in several instances, "How large is this college?" the answer will typically be, "The School of Arts and Sciences is around 475, and the college as a whole is around 7,000."

A different response emerged when I met with two groups of Arts and Sciences students at CNR, one a first-year honors section of a required introductory course, the other a group of upper-division women. When these students were asked about the size of their institution, about half of them answered *only* in terms of the School of Arts and Sciences; the other half responded along the lines that "there are about 475 in our college and maybe a couple of thousand in nursing and the other programs." My conclusion was that the College of New Rochelle has kept its historic liberal arts core program well insulated from the other programs, which have developed more recently. To the students and faculty in the School of Arts and Sciences, the identity of the College of New Rochelle was still primarily that of a small, Catholic women's liberal arts college. Except at the upper echelons of the administration, those connected with the traditional baccalaureate liberal arts program understood themselves to be a unit apart and, in a sense, to constitute the "real" College of New Rochelle.

College publications emphasize both the intimacy of the college and its expansion. Thus, the institutional fact sheet discussing the founding of the college concludes, "Today, the College of New Rochelle has grown to four schools . . . with seven campuses and a student enrollment of approximately 7,000."[2]

A somewhat similar arrangement exists at George Fox University in Newberg, Oregon. The university is home to about fourteen hundred traditional baccalaureate undergraduates. In addition, George Fox has created a Department of Professional Studies, which offers four majors to adult learners, takes into account credit for life learning experiences, and has classes that meet one night per week. The department offers courses not at the central Newberg campus but in Portland, Eugene, Salem, and Clackamas in Oregon as well as Boise, Idaho. George Fox also offers twelve graduate programs at the master's and doctoral levels, both in Newberg and on its Portland branch campus. And the institution has acquired a theological seminary, now called the "George Fox Evangelical Seminary," also housed at the Portland site. This cluster of programs enrolls roughly the same number of students as the traditional Newberg undergraduate enterprise.[3]

As at the College of New Rochelle, George Fox University sees these newer expansions of its traditional undergraduate mission as serving significant community needs for adult learners and for those seeking careers in the evangelical pastoral field. It also sees such programs as an economic engine that can help propel the institution as a whole and preserve the fiscal viability of the older undergraduate college in Newberg.

George Fox's expansion is different from that at the College of New Rochelle in two important ways. First, the size relationship between the older baccalaureate enterprise and the newer ventures is close to fifty-fifty, compared to CNR's one-to-fourteen ratio. Second, because almost all the non-baccalaureate programs at George Fox are "off site," their emotional and intellectual impact on the Newberg students and faculty seems slight. When asked about institutional size, teachers and students alike responded in terms of the undergraduate offerings. Without overt prompting, few mentioned the degree completion, graduate, or seminary options. Students with whom I spoke seemed to have no idea about the size, scope, or location of these programs, and faculty, by and large, were vague as well. During my visit to campus only senior administrators tended to see the university as a whole, and even they tended to see the Newberg campus as one thing and everything else as something else.

Again, as at the College of New Rochelle, I sensed little competition or hostility between the traditional undergraduate programs and the entrepreneurial ventures, which have grown up more recently around that core. As at CNR, the new programs seem to have succeeded both in meeting important educational needs of the region and in providing a more secure economic base for the institution as a whole.

A third variation of this pattern was developed at Saint Leo University in Florida.[4] Originally chartered as a college in 1890, Saint Leo began with a program of liberal arts and commercial course work which resulted in a "Master of Accounts" degree. In 1920 the college converted to a prep school, but in 1959 it began awarding college degrees again, now the associate's credential. In 1967 it granted its first bachelor's degrees. Only six years later, in 1973, Saint Leo began offering college courses to military personnel, located on regional military bases. Today it is the sixth largest provider of college work to the U.S. military. With programs offered on bases throughout the Southeast and at Florida community colleges, Saint Leo enrolls 6,000 students in these programs and 1,700 in traditional undergraduate programs at its "home" campus. Its "Center for Online Learning" enrolls another 2,860 students. In 1994 Saint Leo began offering an MBA program as well.

As at the College of New Rochelle, Saint Leo is dominated, in terms of sheer student numbers, by individuals, mostly military personnel, who are not within its traditional baccalaureate, campus-based programs. But, more like George Fox, these programs are physically and geographically so distinct from the undergraduate college that their visibility is minimal on campus to students and faculty engaged in the traditional core.

The evolution of these three colleges into more complex, and larger, institutions is far from unique. Similar examples are common: Whittier College in Whittier, California, has a School of Law in Costa Mesa; Antioch College has grown into a university today, with five campuses in four states and a well-known rocky record of occasionally overambitious expansion. The more common history is that of a small college growing into a larger university in such a way as to cause the initial institutional core to disappear into the new, larger entity. The College of Charleston, for example, was for the first two hundred years of its existence a small, local, private institution. But in 1970 it became part of the public system of higher learning in South Carolina and has since grown to over ten thousand students. Today, in its public utterances and in its internal image among students, faculty, and administrative staff, the college is a fairly seamless institution with a five-figure student headcount. Except in dimming historical consciousness and in a lovely low-country campus core physical plant, there is really no enduring "small college" remaining at the College of Charleston comparable to the School of Arts and Sciences at New Rochelle, the undergraduate Newberg program at George Fox, or the resident baccalaureate college at Saint Leo University.

Consortia are another way in which smaller institutions seek to secure some of the virtues of larger universities.[5] By banding together, a cluster of small colleges can offer some of the programs and services otherwise only available at major university centers; they can "offer students more options without significantly changing their size, structure or basic purposes."[6]

So, for example, one of the oldest and most successful of the consortia, the Five Colleges (Mount Holyoke, Amherst, Hampshire, Smith, and the University of Massachusetts–Amherst), provides continuous bus service connecting the thirty thousand students at the five campuses and offers majors not available at the individual institutions through the consortium (including astronomy and dance).

Another major consortium, the Great Lakes College Association (GLCA), which consists of twelve colleges in Indiana, Michigan, and Ohio, offers an impressive variety of programs, including a major conference in black studies every year.

The Associated Colleges of the South (ACS) includes sixteen institutions, including three of the school sites I visited for this book, Morehouse, Southwestern University, and Centenary College of Louisiana. The ACS offers programs in cost containment, diversity, environmental programs, educational technology, global and international initiatives, library cooperation, a summer faculty development initiative, women's studies, and a tuition exchange program among members.

Similarly, the Associated Colleges of the Midwest (ACM) makes available to its fourteen member colleges off-campus programs, faculty development, information exchange, and even some programs in external relations. Whereas a single college, no matter how devoted and wealthy, might offer, for example, a handful of institutionally sponsored international programs each year, a collective of a dozen or more small schools, such as the ACS, GLCA, or ACM, can multiply these offerings dramatically through the mechanism of each institution sponsoring a few programs and making them available to students throughout the consortium.

The Conference of Public Liberal Arts Colleges (COPLAC) annually offers a faculty development seminar at one of its member institution campuses, focusing on a different discipline or area each year.

In some cases very diverse sets of institutions can band together to
make available to their students a range of choices and educational experiences. For example, the Greater Greensboro Consortium, which provides
cross-registration, includes Bennett College (an historically black women's
college), Elon University, Greensboro College, Guilford College, High
Point University (all traditional church-related liberal arts colleges), Guilford Technical Community College (a public two-year institution), the
University of North Carolina–Greensboro (at one time called Women's
College of the University of North Carolina but now a strong regional public university), and North Carolina A&T State University (a public, historically black university, with special strengths in engineering).

Another mechanism by which smaller institutions seek to provide
some of the benefits of large schools is through cooperative programs with
universities. In a typical arrangement Centenary College offers a dual-
degree program in engineering with Case Western Reserve University, Columbia University, Texas A&M University, and Washington University in
St. Louis. After three years of liberal studies at Centenary, students pursue
professional engineering courses at one of the cooperating universities,
and at the end of five years they are eligible to receive a bachelor of arts degree from Centenary in physics or mathematics and a bachelor of science
degree in engineering from the university.[7]

Public small colleges often have similar arrangements with the larger
public universities or systems within their states: thus, the University of
Wisconsin (UW)–Superior offers to its students opportunities to travel
abroad through the University of Wisconsin system's programs. The "Wisconsin in Scotland" program, for example, enables UW-S students to join
with those from other campuses of the university to study British history
and other subjects near Edinburgh at Dalkeith House. Like Centenary,
Superior also offers a dual degree in engineering, in this case with the
University of Wisconsin–Madison as well as Michigan Technological University.[8]

Every small college I visited in the course of writing this book is a member of some sort of collective or consortium, and many are members of
several, ranging from very loose groups of similarly religiously affiliated or
geographically close institutions to important and substantive cooperative

arrangements. A typical example is Westmont College, which is a member of the Association of Independent California Colleges and Universities, the Council of Christian Colleges and Universities, the Christian College Consortium, the Independent Colleges of Southern California, and the Annapolis Group (a national group of small liberal arts colleges) and has a dual-degree engineering program with four universities.[9]

It is my impression that, following an initial gush of unrealistically enthusiastic aspirations for small college consortia in the 1960s and 1970s, expectations for these groups have become more modest in recent years. The consortia have obviously filled important and continuing needs. But, at the same time, the challenges of such cooperative endeavors as student/faculty exchange, course sharing, and joint purchasing have proven more tenacious than earlier optimism may have suggested. Today small colleges almost universally find consortium arrangements a helpful benefit and a useful way to expand the opportunities they can offer their students and faculty, but few see them as central to their basic characters. In my interviews across the country those with whom I spoke mentioned consortial arrangements at some point—for example, in discussing library technology and interlibrary loan or off-campus programs—but not once were such confederations cited in the context of the core mission of colleges.

The explosion in educational technology is perhaps the most ambiguous of the mechanisms that might bring to small colleges the benefits of larger universities. In some ways digital information processing offers enormous opportunities, especially to small institutions. In other ways it poses daunting challenges.

According to the National Survey of Student Engagement's 2002 report, students at baccalaureate–liberal arts colleges tend to use the Internet to discuss or complete academic assignments at about the same rate as students at doctoral and master's institutions: 53 percent of seniors responded that this was often or very often the case at the baccalaureate liberal arts colleges; 57 percent at doctoral/research universities; 54 percent at master's institutions.[10] At the same time, as we saw in chapter 4, faculty at smaller institutions do less non-face-to-face teaching than their colleagues elsewhere in American higher education.[11]

Diana Balestri, in an insightful essay on information technology at small colleges, notes that "no one living or working for a small liberal arts college is untouched by the presence of digital technologies."[12] But she also notes that it has been very hard to assess the benefits of that technology. She asks if information technology can aid the liberal arts transformative learning experience and notes that at smaller institutions teaching and learning are enhanced by residentiality, chance encounters between teachers and learners, and the like. It has been argued by thoughtful observers of American higher education that the small, Socratic undergraduate seminar is the quintessence of the small college learning experience. Eva Brann's descriptions of the St. John's model, for example, make such a case compellingly.[13] But that is a model that, by its very nature, derives its educational effectiveness by a kind of pseudo-inefficiency: discussion moves into dead ends, lurches forward by fits and starts, and digresses unpredictably, and such discussions are exactly when some of the richest learning happens. Most technologically sophisticated instructional aids do not accommodate well to such a pedagogy.

Information technology brings to the small college research opportunities formerly only to be found at large universities: among other things, most small college students now have electronic access to the libraries of large universities. And, of course, anyone with an Internet-linked computer has access, whether in Berkeley or in Deep Springs, California, to the huge (and raw) mountain of data available therein. Indeed, electronic technology enables students and faculty at Deep Springs to communicate instantly with their colleagues in Berkeley. In this regard academic computing helps to level the scholarly playing field between small and large institutions.

On the inevitable other hand, however, there are ways in which smaller institutions have suffered in comparison to larger ones as a consequence of information technology. Computing is expensive. Hardware is costly, software is too, and the personnel costs associated with academic computing are staggering. And this is an area in which "economies of scale" really do seem to be in play. A college of five hundred students is going to need a director of academic computing, just as a university of fifty thousand does. And that director at the small college is certainly not going to be paid 1 percent of her counterpart at a big school. Small schools are going to need licenses for software such as SPSS or Lexus/Nexus, and, while they will cost less, the expenses are not proportional. It will not cost as much to wire the five hundred–student campus for fiber optic Internet access as the much larger campus, but, again, it will certainly cost more than 1 percent of the larger institution's expenditure. Moreover, major research universities have learned to cover significant parts of their computer costs through external grants and soft funding. It is a rare research grant that does not include a hefty sum for computing costs. Most smaller colleges do not see external research funding at a level corresponding to their larger sibling institutions and therefore have to bear more of the costs of academic computing internally. Some institutions have moved to funding instructional technology through a student fee. A hundred-dollar tech fee at a major research university is going to buy more computing, proportionally, than the same fee at a small college.

An appropriate cautionary note on electronic teaching is raised by Paul Neely, who observes, "If such teaching is to displace the traditional forums, . . . it is likely to follow a clear order: first, professional and vocational courses that are required as part of employment, thus addressing the many motivational problems of distance teaching; second, the colleges and universities where teaching modes most closely resemble television watching, namely, large lectures before passive students; and third, and only then, the colleges where the educational process and campus life are heavily based on the personal interaction of students and faculty."[14]

Like Balestri, I find it very difficult to assess the overall costs and benefits of instructional technology in the small college sector. On the one hand, computers open to teachers and learners at small colleges some academic options and opportunities that were not available in the past. But, on the other hand, that technology disproportionately touches the often precarious budgets of small colleges, so that often they struggle to afford the benefits of this new set of learning tools.

Large Universities with College Qualities

Just as many small colleges have sought to maintain their traditional characters while simultaneously adding some of the advantages of larger size, big universities have frequently attempted to create programs that bring within their folds some of the values of smaller institutions. Commentator Paul Neely phrases it rather strongly: "Special honors colleges within the university, set up as if to say a student can be part of a school like Swarthmore but stay in Fayetteville, pretend to offer the best of both worlds."[15] I would be considerably less skeptical and say that one can bring some of the advantages of Swarthmore to the University of Arkansas, and vice versa, without deception or pretense and to the benefit of each school.

A personal illustration: in the mid-1970s I left my position as an associate professor of English and chair of the Honors Committee at a small Iowa college to assume my first administrative post, as director of the honors program at the University of Maine. Soon after I arrived in Orono, the president of the university met with me and offered as my "charge" his vision of what a good honors program could do for the institution. What President Howard Neville said was, "I would like for the honors program to be like a good small college in the midst of the university." I soon discovered that President Neville's view of honors programs was far from idiosyncratic.

During my years working in collegiate honors programs, including a term as president of the National Collegiate Honors Council, I discovered that the word *honors* can cover a very wide range of collegiate offerings. At one extreme students can receive graduation "honors" simply for achieving a high grade point average or perhaps for doing a senior independent project in the major. At the other pole are full-blown "honors colleges," which can come close to achieving virtually independent status within a university.

Joan Digby's *Peterson's Guide to Honors Programs* offers an excellent descriptive snapshot of the range of honors programs at some 350 colleges and universities across the country.[16] The handbook *Beginning in Honors* of the National Collegiate Honors Council offers a more theoretical taxonomy.[17] Of particular relevance to this discussion are the self-contained honors colleges, which often move close to recreating the conditions of small independent institutions housed within far larger university settings. (Conversely, some honors programs at smaller colleges offer students a heightened emphasis on research and scholarship, emulating the core values of large universities.)[18]

The Honors College of the University of Houston was founded in 1993, evolving out of an honors program that began in the late 1950s. It describes itself thus: "For the 300 students who join each fall, the Honors College offers all the advantages of a small college without sacrificing the wealth of resources and rich diversity of a large university . . . The Honors College offers a full array of services including scholarships, tuition waivers, residence halls, and internships."[19] Administratively, the University of Houston's Honors College is considered one of fourteen colleges within the institution. It has its own dean. Significantly, it hires its own faculty (students take courses both within the Honors College and across the university). The Honors College awards the baccalaureate degree and has its own set of graduation requirements, orientation programs, extracurricular events, advising mechanisms, and special programs. The college has a "population" of about nine hundred undergraduates.

Houston's Honors College is one of the most fully developed in the nation, but it is by no means unique. Students enrolled in Clemson University's Calhoun College take at least one course every semester within the program, often an interdisciplinary seminar. Many of them reside together in honors residential space; the program offers a wide range of educational and recreational co- and extracurricular activities.[20]

Similarly, the South Carolina Honors College of the University of South Carolina is "an Honors College offering a peerless academic experience unifying the benefits of a small liberal arts college with the opportunities of a comprehensive university."[21] Offering its 850 students some one hundred courses a year, the college has its own dedicated classrooms, student lounges, and housing for some four hundred students. In class size, student characteristics, faculty qualifications, curricular expectations, and student/faculty interactions, it overtly compares itself to "a fine liberal arts college." The Robert D. Clark Honors College of the University of Oregon serves about five hundred students and "offers the advantages of a small, liberal arts college as well as the University's rich resources and curriculum. The Clark Honors College brings together excellent students and selected faculty members in a program that is both challenging and supportive."[22]

It is important to note that, in each of these cases, there is no effort to suggest that the university honors college is not, in fact, embedded within a university setting. None of these units claim that their students will have a small college experience at Oregon or Clemson or Houston. Nor do they repudiate the fact that honors students at those universities will have countless opportunities to harvest the rich offerings of large universities.

Honors colleges in many large university settings seek to offer some of the important communal cultural and educational values of small colleges to students of outstanding promise and/or motivation. They promote their small classes, interactive learning pedagogies, interdisciplinary curricula, opportunities to reside in close proximity to students who share the same classes, and close and repeated contact with a relatively small group of faculty members who are, presumably, devoted to undergraduate teaching and learning. Other universities have tried to create many of these conditions without specifying a clientele of "honors" students.

Perhaps the most famous and influential, although also one of the most short-lived, of these efforts was Alexander Meiklejohn's Experimental College, which existed from 1927 to 1932 at the University of Wisconsin. Meiklejohn's book *The Experimental College* details both the pedagogical idealism that animated this project and the academic political pettiness that stunted then killed it.[23]

Meiklejohn came to the University of Wisconsin at the invitation of a new president, Glenn Frank, with the explicit expectation that he would create a program with the potential to reform undergraduate learning at the university. What Meiklejohn and his collaborators developed was an integrated program for the first two years of baccalaureate education. It was a program that was dramatically experimental, both in curriculum and in pedagogy. A group of students (all male, because it was hoped they would all reside in a common dormitory) would work through a common set of readings and assignments together through the "lower college" (first and second) years. The curriculum that evolved focused the first year on the study of Athenian Greece in the era of Pericles. The second year focused on the United States, with *The Education of Henry Adams* as a central text. Between the two years students were to investigate and write a descriptive report on a contemporary American community of their choice —commonly, their own home community. Faculty members, called "advisors," did not lecture, and there were no examinations. Instead, students wrote extensively and met in very small sections with advisors for weekly conferences. Meiklejohn's focus was on independent thinking, which led the college to develop a program that placed significant responsibility on individual learners for their own education—and lifted the traditional collegiate regulations, such as required class attendance, from their shoulders.

In his book Meiklejohn describes at length a group of students in the Experimental College, ranging from highly motivated scholars to flighty young men, all with a strong interest in "college life" as well as academics. The aim was to create a program that worked for a variety of students, some of whom were not particularly well prepared or academically serious.

The question of institutional size was a central one in the vision of the Experimental College: "We have said that for educational purposes it is desirable that student groups be small. It seems even more important for the same purposes that the teaching groups, the faculties, be small" (250). The entering classes tended to be one hundred or fewer; only about thirty faculty members participated during the five-year life span of the college. Altogether, fewer than four hundred students completed the two-year Experimental College curriculum.

To the extent it was possible to make it so, Meiklejohn's Experimental College was a remarkably self-contained unit. Students did not need to take classes outside the college, and it was presumed that, after finishing their freshman and sophomore years there, they could proceed with no impediment to complete their baccalaureate degrees elsewhere within the University of Wisconsin.

Reading Meiklejohn's description of his experiment some three-quarters of a century afterward, it seems evident that the college was a demanding experience for both students and advisors. Equally evident is the increasingly rough sailing the college experienced within the faculty of the University of Wisconsin during its brief life. It is clear that the majority of Meiklejohn's colleagues considered his "experiment" a threat and an affront, and it suffered the political fate of an experiment that failed. On the other hand, the Experimental College was a resounding success in two important aspects. First, it seems clear that many of the students who participated found the experience a richly rewarding educational venture. Second, the Experimental College was a visible and much-noted effort, which spawned countless offspring in the years that followed. Thus, another small college within a large university which grew out of the Meiklejohn experiment, the Western College program at Miami University of Ohio, established in 1974, seeks to provide about 250 students "the individualized education of a small liberal arts program" with an interdisciplinary curriculum.[24]

Even today, a quick scan through the Internet seeking various sorts of university innovations in curriculum and in teaching turns up multiple references to Meiklejohn and to the Experimental College. For example, an ERIC Digest article on Learning Communities written by Karen Kellogg states: "The origin of learning communities dates back to 1927 when Alexander Meiklejohn formed the two-year Experimental College at the University of Wisconsin . . . Although this first attempt at a learning community was short-lived—only six years—it provided the foundation for the learning communities we know today."[25] As suggested by this article, one cluster of efforts to recreate aspects of the small college environment within larger institutions which have been increasingly important in the past decade are "learning communities." While a variety of endeavors are described under this heading, they have several characteristics in common:

—a group of students who take multiple courses together—sometimes as few as two courses, sometimes an entire semester's course of study

—courses that are team-taught and team-designed

—students and faculty together linking these curricular efforts under interdisciplinary themes

Learning communities have proven a powerful curricular innovation at institutions ranging from community colleges to major research universities: as one example, a dozen community colleges in central California have banded together into a "Regional Learning Communities Consortium"; likewise, the Federated Learning Community at SUNY–Stony Brook focuses on psychology, medicine, myth, philosophy, and biology through the exploration of social and ethical issues in the life sciences.[26]

Yet another example of a learning community effort is the Freshman Interest Group (FIG) program at the University of Oregon (UO). The program is described at the university's Web site as

a group of twenty-five first-year students who take two or three thematically linked courses together in the Fall term. These classes meet General Education requirements and comprise between 7 and 12 credits of the student's fall schedule. FIG classes are linked together through College Connections, a 1-credit course taught by one of the faculty who teaches an academic course in the FIG. The College Connections course meets once a week and is designed to help students make a smooth transition from high school to college. This course also provides greater mentoring and support from experienced UO students.

An overlapping but somewhat different development is the "living/learning center," which adds a shared residential experience to the learning community. The Ralph L. Collins Living/Learning Center at Indiana University is described on the school's College of Arts and Sciences Web site as "a residential unit of the College of Arts and Sciences [which] supplements a student's regular University programming with its own accredited courses, arts programming, social service activities, and academic support and enrichment programs. The residents of Collins work to create a community in which academic excellence, creative work, and a commitment to community service are given full support." Overtly citing the small college comparison, the university asserts that Collins "provides an alternative living environment for motivated undergraduates. It combines the advantages of a small college community with the rich resources of a large university. It emphasizes a close, fruitful relationship between formal academic learning and the day-to-day residential experience."

The University of Missouri combines the learning community FIG with the residential option, in more than eighty Freshman Interest Groups in which "groups of 15–20 freshmen are assigned to the same residence hall community. They enroll together in three core courses and one class that focuses on essential skills for college success and the particular FIG theme."[27]

The university has also created twenty-seven "sponsored learning communities" ranging from "Women in Engineering" to "Agriculture" in which students reside together, on the basis of particular intellectual or educational interests, and are encouraged to co-enroll with their residence hall fellows in shared course work. It also offers three residential colleges in Fine Arts, Leadership, and Natural Science and Mathematics.

In what is not an unfamiliar figure of speech by this point, at the University of Michigan, living/learning communities are said to

—facilitate personal relationships among students and faculty;

—believe that increased learning and student retention is accomplished by building a nurturing, welcoming atmosphere;

—encourage student participation in a variety of activities that foster a learning environment; and

—provide a small college setting with large university resources.[28]

In this brief description of honors colleges, experimental colleges-within-universities, learning communities, and living/learning centers, a unifying theme is the effort of large collegiate institutions to bring into their midst smaller units that mirror some of the character and culture of small colleges. The obvious proliferation of these endeavors indicates that they have been widely perceived as successful—both as student recruitment incentives and as instructional experiments. My personal experience has been primarily within the honors community, but I have spent time over the past two decades on several campuses that offer the other programs as well (e.g., Oregon, Miami of Ohio, and Indiana University). My subjective sense is that the majority of these programs are at least partially successful. Frequently, for example, honors programs can document higher retention rates than the universities within which they are housed, sometimes approaching those of small colleges. At the same time, some limitations are obvious. Registration at the University of Michigan is going to be a different process than at Albion College; attending a basketball game at Indiana University is not likely to be confused with the same activity at Wabash College; the physical environment at the University of Oregon is unmistakably not that of George Fox University.

Seeking the perspective of a leader of a large university on these issues, I spoke with Mark Yudof, chancellor of the University of Texas and former president of the University of Minnesota. Yudof agrees that there has been an effort to "blur the borders." He notes that, while at the University of Minnesota, he often said he was trying to capture for that huge land grant campus "a bit of Carleton." And he believes these efforts, of both the large universities and small colleges, have had notable successes. But he also concludes that there are, finally, limiting factors for both sides of the equation which suggest it is possible to go only so far: Swarthmore is never going to have the range of engineering programs of Berkeley or Wisconsin or Arkansas; the University of Minnesota will never be able to afford the level of personal attention to every student possible at Carleton.[29]

Institutions large and small can try, and partially succeed, in importing some of the more attractive characteristics of differently sized schools. The virtues of smallness (and largeness) are apparent throughout U.S. higher education, but these benefits can be difficult to achieve when institutions strive for qualities that do not flow easily from their overall size and mission. Universities may, with cleverness and hard work, create learning communities: small colleges often simply are such communities.[30]

A Conversation

This dialog between a small college president, Anne Ponder, and a professor of philosophy, Dr. Amy Knisley, both of Colby-Sawyer College, seems to me to reveal a good deal about the perspectives of both participants toward their quite different roles in the small college setting. It also says much about their relationship of mutual respect and trust. Certainly, the intensity with which the college CEO knows the teachers and the deep personal involvement in their recruitment and cultivation are characteristic of smaller, focused academic communities.

President Ponder: Halfway into the initial interview with this prospective faculty member, and I knew that she belonged here. I knew that, if she came to this small college, she would be a central figure in making this college better. I found a way during the search process to tell her that she belonged here.

During her seven years here—not quite two student generations—she has already demonstrated what I knew instinctively when I met her. What a splendid teacher and colleague. She has been recognized already as the winner of the college's distinguished teaching award. She has served as the faculty representative to the board and as faculty athletic representative. She has earned her first sabbatical. I tell her now that I hire faculty to be colleagues for her. The daughter of a professor of history who later became dean at a small college in the mountains of another beautiful state, Professor Knisley can articulate wonderfully her reasons for being here.

Professor Knisley: My dad likes to tell this story: "Your mother and I didn't want to be authoritarian with you kids. 'Ask and explain' was our policy—*ask* you to do things instead of ordering you and *explain* why it needed to be done. But sometimes, like when we were trying to get you, your brothers, and your stuff all into the car for a twelve-hour drive to the beach, 'ask and explain' just didn't do the trick. That's when I'd become daddy dictator. 'Just do it—*now*—because I said so!' So one time, when you were about six, you'd just asked me 'why' you had to do something, and I said, 'because I said so!'—you looked up at me with your hands on your hips and said, 'But Dad, what if you're *wrong*?'

So when you told us you were going to major in philosophy in college, I wasn't a bit surprised."

This is not my memory, it is my father's, but after several hearings I feel as if I remember it, and the image has entered into my self-concept: Amy the child philosopher. It helps me understand a line *I* tell about my "choice" of major in college: "I didn't choose philosophy; *it chose me.*" I'd worked since I was fourteen, so I didn't approach college as a way into a career—I would always work at something and didn't need to go to school for that! My *mind* drove me to college, my restless mind. After college it drove me on to a Ph.D. program in philosophy, where I stumbled into what has become my career for now: teaching philosophy at a small college.

This career was unintended but hardly inexplicable. I attended a small residential college myself and grew up a faculty brat, roaming the campus of a small college founded in the nineteenth century. Now I traverse a campus of similar size and antiquity in hilly New Hampshire—as the faculty member, not the child. *Then,* I felt I had license to the campus that the students would never have—I almost pitied them. They wouldn't be around long enough to find the secret back stairwell in the student center or the long fissure at the bottom of the pool's deep end or the tiny grove of hemlocks on the north side of boys' hill. Now, however, I know that students at small residential colleges transmit an intimate delight in their campus spaces, from generation to generation, accessible to no one else. *They live there.* They make the place and feel made by it— held, nurtured, cultivated. Their collective experience of the campus imbues it with tone and character that remain constant, even as its central population is constantly changing.

So, although I don't know why philosophy chose me (and at such a tender age!), I do understand why I have chosen a small college as my place of work. Its scale, its pathways and daily rhythms, its private spaces, conspire to create a community. I know and am known by many. Then, as now, I inhabit a community of life and work in which our knowledge of each other supports the college's broader business: knowledge of everything else.

President Ponder: Philosophy found her, and then this small college found her. Her life is centered here, especially in the months when the college is in session. Her achievements here are ours—her work here, her rightful inheritance.

8 | Small College Futures

> Quality rather than quantity is the great need
> of American education today.
> FRANK AYDELOTTE

Surveying all of God's creation, the Augustan poet Alexander Pope found "a mighty maze, but not without a plan." Somewhat less ambitiously, I find that same mix of complexity and coherence when I think about the future of small colleges.

In this chapter I will first consider the concerns and the dreams of small college people—students, faculty, staff, trustees—as they look ahead into the twenty-first century. Then I will suggest some strategies that those who study contemporary small colleges hope will strengthen our colleges in the coming years, an aspiration I share. Finally, I will mull how the future of small colleges is linked to other, overarching social concerns many observers have about the scale of American life in the new millennium. In this discussion, as throughout, I focus on the fact that what all small colleges share is, first, their smallness, but that at the same time there is enormous variety in the focus, nature, history, people, and resources among schools of similar sizes.

At each of the colleges I visited, I asked students, faculty, staff, and trustees two related questions. First, I asked what concerns they had for their college, and places like it, for the coming decade. Then I asked the happier question: what opportunities did they see for their institution and for other small colleges in the next ten or twelve years—what were their dreams and hopes? I invited students to imagine returning to campus for their tenth reunion, what they feared they might find, and what their most optimistic projections were for that reunion.

Fears

What are people at small colleges worried about? Not at all surprisingly, money. Fiscal concerns certainly dominated the challenges cited by all constituents. As Association of American Colleges and Universities vice president Jerry Gaff has observed, small colleges across the country are struggling with funding, especially those not in the top tier of prestige and endowment (although I would be hard-pressed to affirm I heard any less worry about money from colleges that are rich than from those that are comparatively impoverished).[1] Those concerns are expressed in several ways.

First, in several cases concerns about financial aid were central. One group of students at Morehouse, for example, cited the need for increased funding for student scholarships. These concerns were echoed by trustees at Centenary College, who are acutely aware of the financial pressures of tuition discounting.[2] At Minneapolis College of Art and Design faculty members expressed worry about the cost of their college and the average thirty thousand dollar debt with which young artists were graduating.[3]

Other fiscal worries abound. On virtually all campuses mention was made of at least a few facilities in need of renovation (an administration building at Southwestern University, e.g., and a student center at Centenary College). At institutions ranging from the richest to the poorest, concerns about the size of the endowment were voiced. It seems that no one, from faculty members at Warren Wilson College to administrators at Grinnell—with an endowment about forty times that of Warren Wilson's —believes that their institution's endowment is large enough to provide financial security. Faculty members at George Fox University worry that too many institutional decisions are made on the basis of financial impact. Although faculty salaries improved in relation to those of the other professions during the second half of the twentieth century, there is widespread consensus—especially among faculty members themselves—that there remains significant room for improvement. There is a fear in both the private and public sectors that, as state funding grows ever tighter and as the stock market shows no inclination to repeat the surges of the 1990s, salaries will not continue to improve. Many students are concerned that class sizes may grow as faculty positions are threatened.

Public institutions note declining legislative appropriations and fret; private colleges are equally concerned about declining endowment values. Both see increased tuition as inevitable but unattractive, and both sectors view increasing rates of tuition discounting (the proportion of tuition income needed to fund financial aid) with alarm.

In many cases worries about the challenges of finances blend with concerns about student enrollment. At Morehouse College, for example, trustees wonder if there will continue to be a sufficient applicant pool of bright, highly motivated African American males. Colby-Sawyer president Anne Ponder believes that the issue is one of communicating the balance between costs and values: making the case that the expense of attending a small institution is justified by the kind and quality of the education found there. Several senior administrators at Wellesley College expressed similar concern about the college's ability to articulate persuasively to prospective students and their families that the quality of a Wellesley education justifies the high tuition rates there.

Enrollment issues, in turn, combine with concerns about finding a "niche." Small college presidents and many of their constituents are worried that their institutions, and those like them, have not been as effective as they could be in communicating the virtues of the smaller college sector. President Russell K. Osgood at Grinnell observes that small liberal arts colleges are competing for a shrinking pool of students and facing increasing competition from public institutions, which almost always seem to place a high value on growth and large size. Many of the individuals I interviewed at private small colleges expressed similar concerns about competition from public colleges and universities and their difficulty communicating the distinctive values of the private higher education sector. Lee Cuba, the dean of the college at Wellesley, believes that Honors Colleges at large universities are successfully persuading students that they offer small college virtues at public university prices. At Minneapolis College of Art and Design a faculty member noted the challenge of "communicating the worth of what we do" to students and to the culture at large.[4] As President Walter E. Massey at Morehouse observed, small liberal arts colleges have a kind of "fragility" in today's collegiate market.

This cluster of fiscal concerns—costs, scholarships, facilities, salaries, enrollment, niche, competition—ran through conversations about worries at small colleges, but it was not the only thread in that discussion. Two other areas, the first concerning faculty and the second students, were also recurrent themes.

At several, but not all, of the colleges I visited, faculty recruiting was mentioned as a serious problem. In particular there is a perceived challenge to recruit new teachers who sincerely want to work in smaller institutions, with their emphasis on teaching in relation to research, closeness to students, professional interdisciplinarity, and similar vocational predilections. Do new young scholars from the nation's graduate schools want such a faculty life, and do they have any realistic understanding about what such a life's rewards and challenges will be? President Jake Schrum at Southwestern finds faculty recruitment a significant challenge, as does President Ken Schwab at Centenary College. Faculty members at Warren Wilson College also raised this issue.

The last quarter of the twentieth century was a time of dramatic over-supply of potential faculty in relation to workplace demand. Occasionally, a field such as computer science, reading education, or management/marketing would experience a surge of positions and a dearth of appli-cants. But for much of this period college teaching positions were so hard to find, even for highly qualified applicants, that institutions worried little about filling them with capable professors. In the early years of the twenty-first century the job market remains very tight in many areas, especially within the humanities. The most recent data gathered by the Modern Lan-guage Association shows, for example, that the number of Ph.D. recipi-ents continues to exceed the number of positions available in English and the modern languages.[5] But in many disciplines and subdisciplines, as well as in some areas of the country perceived as less desirable, the chal-lenges of recruiting top-quality teachers are clearly growing. Thus, faculty and administrators at Centenary College worry that potential professors might not want to relocate to Shreveport, and those at the University of Wisconsin–Superior share a similar concern about recruiting faculty to the Duluth-Superior region.[6]

It is going to be important to small colleges to monitor and reverse this trend: such institutions depend deeply on their ability to offer top-quality teaching and easy, productive interactions between professors and stu-dents. For small colleges to have trouble finding good teachers is like air-lines having difficulty securing pilots.

One encouraging initiative that seeks to address this challenge is the Preparing Future Faculty (PFF) program. This endeavor has been admin-istered by the Council of Graduate Schools and the Association of Ameri-can Colleges and Universities, with support from the Pew Charitable Trusts, the National Science Foundation, and private gifts.[7] The PPF pro-gram has evolved over the past decade into a national initiative in which forty-three doctoral institutions are paired with close to three hundred "partner" institutions, most of them considerably smaller (e.g., in 2001 Duke University was paired with Durham Technical Community College,

Elon University, Guilford College, Meredith College, and North Carolina Central University). Graduate students working toward their doctorates who aspire to a career in college teaching are given opportunities to study and, more important, to observe on site the lives of college teachers in a variety of institutions. PFF participants have a chance to experience the challenges and rewards of faculty life in a diverse range of campus settings, almost always including one or more small colleges. To date, over four thousand doctoral students have participated in this program.[8] This represents a substantial group of graduate students who might well not have had prior experience in smaller institutions and who enter the professorial job market with a greater and more realistic understanding of faculty life in small colleges because of their experiences in PFF.

An unexpected concern that emerged often in my campus visits had to do with the character of students and student culture in the current sociopolitical and economic climate. Invariably, faculty, students, and staff spoke glowingly about the students at their institutions. But two worrisome concerns about student culture issues darkened that rosy picture.

First is the general notion of student (and family) consumerism about college choice and college life. As President Douglas Orr at Warren Wilson notes, students have come to expect what he calls "a twenty-four-hour Student Center lifestyle" (i.e., something always going on, all day, everyday) which is a challenge for small institutions to maintain. So, although both Centenary College and Southwestern University have recently built splendid campus fitness centers, for example, both their presidents worry that they felt they *had* to because students and their parents looked for such facilities, and, in a highly competitive student recruitment marketplace, woe to the college without them. Given the greater ability of large institutions to achieve economies of scale for buildings, facilities, and programs of this sort, it's increasingly difficult for smaller institutions to compete with them.[9]

I also encountered a widespread, but hesitant, concern about the level of personal emotional or psychological problems, or "baggage," which undergraduates were bringing to small colleges. At several institutions, and in particular among administrators in student affairs, there was a sense that small colleges see a rapidly increasing enrollment of students with such difficulties. The consensus is that a relatively small number of students is involved but that even a small number of students with serious personal problems can be highly disruptive, especially in small communities, and equally highly demanding of already heavily taxed staff time and attention.

Explanations of this phenomenon are various. One student affairs professional noted that young people with serious psychological problems are much more likely, at present, to be placed on medications and then "mainstreamed." It is certainly also the case that in some situations the Americans with Disabilities Act has been understood to restrict the ability of colleges to deny admission to students with histories of severe emotional problems, even if they want to.

Moreover, small colleges have advertised themselves extensively as places where young people will not get lost, where they will get individualized attention, and where there is a close and constant personalized level of interaction between the institution and the individual student. They may boast about careful and personalized advising programs. Many of the religiously affiliated institutions present a pastoral face to the public. This image of a caring community has invited parents and students to see small colleges as especially appropriate institutions for troubled young men and women who might be unable to flourish or even survive at larger, more impersonal universities. More than one individual with whom I spoke had perceived a surge in parental involvement in the academic and social relationship between students and the college.

Coupled with this concern is the conviction I encountered (although rarely among teachers or students) that faculty members are less willing to engage themselves in the lives of such students than in the past. Some attribute this to an increased focus on personal, scholarly development among young professors. Others attribute it to a sensible fear of legal or institutional liability should "amateur" counseling go awry.

These issues of student culture do not seem to me to be epidemic. They emerge more as concerned reflections of people at caring small colleges. Certainly, it is the case that the very size of small colleges enables them to be more individually attentive, and this is, in fact, one of their true and great virtues. But my campus visits have suggested to me that such attentiveness needs to be framed in a manner that encourages students' independence and growth and discourages their dependence. Perhaps the administrative staff at Southwestern University has hit upon a wise strategy in its decision to stop using the word *nurturing* in describing their college and to speak, instead, of "empowering."

Hopes

Aspirations are the flip side of worries—for those linked to small colleges the hope that in the future the challenges that face their institutions will be met. Like other people, many small college students, faculty, and staff hope that the stock market will recover, that state legislatures will become more generous, that scholarship aid will increase, buildings and infrastructure be improved and well maintained, salaries raised, class sizes shrunk, applicant pools deepened, faculty recruiting and retention made even more successful, and student life improved. An interesting set of additional aspirations also emerged from my discussions, especially in the areas of community relations and service, visibility/communication, and college programmatic integration.

As I noted in chapter 3, some small colleges are located in major urban areas, while others are found in tiny towns, and many are somewhere in between. Regardless of their geographical position, most American colleges and universities have always been conscious of their relationships with—and responsibilities to—the communities within which they find themselves. Although occasionally institutions have found themselves at odds with their cities and towns, generally they retain a strong sense of service to the community and region. But my visits to small colleges suggested to me a distinctly heightened aspiration on the part of most college constituents to strengthen and deepen the bonds of service which traditionally have linked town and gown. Twenty-first-century colleges seem to have a strong desire to do more with and for their neighbors. This aspiration takes many forms.

A number of colleges have renewed their efforts to encourage volunteerism, especially—but not exclusively—by students. In addition to the customary venues of student volunteerism, many small colleges now include a mandatory community service project as part of new student orientation—probably not a very realistic program at institutions with first-year classes of over a thousand students. Others (such as Warren Wilson College) have incorporated such work as part of overseas and off-campus endeavors. Since the 1980s, spring and fall break service ventures have flourished at many kinds of institutions, and this trend appears to be spreading at the small colleges. Thus, for example, students at the University of North Carolina–Asheville have used their spring vacation to build a Habitat for Humanity house; students and faculty from Guilford College likewise have traveled to impoverished coastal islands in Georgia and South Carolina for a similar venture.

Another manifestation of the aspiration to build stronger links between campus and community is the explosive growth of service learning: incorporating community service projects into the academic work of the classroom. My favorite service learning project was the class in applied mathematics at my (far northern) campus which solved a classical spatial relations problem by devising the most efficient route for municipal snowplows to follow after a storm. The students learned the math; the town's road maintenance crews followed the new, more efficient routes.

Some smaller institutions are imitating larger ones by creating business incubators, hosting regional economic development conferences, and offering enhanced continuing education opportunities, among other things.

Part of the motivation for this renewed interest in linkages to their publics is undoubtedly self-serving as well as community serving. Strong campus-public relations help public institutions win political favor and help all colleges, public and private, with donor and alumni relations. It is good for student recruiting for a college to be seen in a positive light in its region. But I also detect a surge of genuine altruism in colleges' hopes to build stronger ties off campus. Many small colleges, especially in smaller towns and in less developed areas of the country, seem to have shifted from a kind of embarrassment about their locations (e.g., Superior, Wisconsin; Grinnell, Iowa; Newberg, Oregon) to a healthier and more mature pride of place. And, as some of the last remaining nineteenth-century small college moral paternalism is evaporating, schools are looking anew at the issue of ethical and character development, not in loco parentis but within the contexts of developmental psychology and holistic learning. Westmont College, for example, according to both former president Dave Winter and current president Stan Gaede, believes that it is in an advantageous position because contemporary American society is seeking places of learning which overtly try to help build character in students.

A second, and related, hope I often heard from those at small colleges—students and faculty as well as administrators—had to do with visibility. When I asked a group of professors at Warren Wilson College about their dream for the future, one responded (to laughing assent from his colleagues), "To be better known than Berea!" At Centenary trustees were eager to expand the circle of people who are familiar with the college. They want their visibility to be high in Atlanta, New Orleans, and the Dallas /

Fort Worth metro area. Colby-Sawyer College trustees similarly were clear that the college needs wider recognition across the entire New England region. Other small colleges—for example Southwestern University—are eager to be seen as "national" institutions. On campus after campus I heard wistful variations on the theme "if only people really *knew* about us." But, as large schools become ever larger, they tend to consume a growing share of public and media consciousness. Most everyone in Ohio knows the score of the last Ohio-Michigan football game; how many follow Antioch's progress in volleyball? And, of course, nobody except the participants is likely to know the outcome of the Minneapolis College of Art and Design's intramural softball games. When Duke or Vanderbilt hires a new president, it is at least back-page national news; not so for George Fox or Colby-Sawyer. It is not very likely that a national media or political celebrity often will be lured to be the graduation speaker at the University of Wisconsin–Superior.

A number of the concerns expressed in small colleges today are linked to visibility issues. These certainly include financial resources, student recruitment, and articulating and holding a niche. But the very smallness of small colleges renders them increasingly inconspicuous, especially in an era of few localized media outlets and faster and broader national and global communications. How can a small college in the Swannanoa Valley of North Carolina or a 450-student College of Arts and Sciences at New Rochelle or an innovative program to integrate classroom, cross-cultural, and service opportunities in Georgetown, Texas, hope to make the evening news or *USA Today?* Grinnell president Russell Osgood makes the case that it is essential today for the presidents of the strongest and *most* visible colleges to seek a larger audience aggressively. They must, he argues, use the relative prominence they enjoy to make the case for all their collegiate peers. To a remarkable degree small colleges want, as much as anything else, to be noticed.

Another dream often cited by those I interviewed was that of greater integration—what I have called in chapter 6 "integrity." At Colby-Sawyer College one theme of a recent campus-wide master planning initiative was stronger linking of career preparation and liberal learning. Westmont College works to bridge a deep Christian faith and a spirit of open academic inquiry. President Stan Gaede remarks that Westmont seeks to communicate the same message in the classroom, required thrice-weekly chapel, extracurricular clubs, residence halls, and on the athletics playing fields. Faculty, students, staff, and President Doug Orr at Warren Wilson expressed a very strong desire to bring together more closely the college's historic triadic mission of scholarship, service, and work. And at Southwestern University an initiative similar to Warren Wilson's called the "Paideia program" aspires to help every student link classroom, cross-cultural contacts, and character building into a unified collegiate experience. As I suggested in chapter 5, the opportunity to build such a unified, linked, integrated learning environment is a distinctive characteristic of small colleges. College presidents, faculties, students, staffs, and trustees express powerful yearnings to achieve such coherence throughout all their activities.

Finally, and perhaps most tellingly, I found that at small colleges all around the country there is a deepening concern, even a fear, that some pressure—fiscal, political, or cultural—could force institutions to change, not evolutionarily but essentially. And, correspondingly, there is a dream on small campuses that at their core these colleges can stay the same. It is not that small colleges are reactionary, although they perpetually react to the changing world of knowledge around them. It is not that they are conservative: most, after all, affirm that they are devoted to an educational experience that is liberating. But they are, if not conservative, *conservationist*. These colleges are devoted to the preservation of the core values of their missions, and they see these values as being linked to questions of size and scale. What most small colleges want—and I suggest later in this chapter that this is an uncharacteristic American desire—is to stay small. A trustee at Centenary College put it this way: "My dream for the future is that we'll still be Centenary College." A faculty member at Southwestern University expressed a similar hope when he said, "My dream for ten years from now is that we'll still have the same kind of dreams."

Strategies

It would be useful at this point to detail a set of strategies by which small colleges could surmount their challenges and achieve their aspirations. Alas, it would also be fraudulent. A recurring motif in my examination of these institutions has been the ways in which they differ from one another as well as the values and attributes they share. The unique character of small schools mandates unique pathways to achieve their individual goals.

So, for example, both George Fox University and Westmont College are small West Coast evangelical Christian liberal arts colleges. Both see increasing fiscal strength and security as a key objective in achieving their vision of faith-based liberal learning. But, whereas George Fox has moved aggressively into enterprises such as continuing education in the Portland metro area, programs for adult learners, and a school of theology, Westmont has scrupulously avoided moving beyond its historical student constituency, its traditional liberal arts curriculum, and its small single campus in Santa Barbara. George Fox sees its diversification as a sound financial strategy; Westmont sees its sharp focus on residential undergraduate liberal education as an equally effective fiduciary tactic. The success both institutions are having in endowment expansion and student recruitment suggests that both are right—for themselves.

Thus, perhaps, the first and maybe most important strategic lesson to be learned from this study is that each small college must invent or discover its own pathway to survival and success. Each must do the work of perpetual self-definition and the strategic thinking that follows from clarifying its mission. What is just right for one might be catastrophic for another. In spite of the booming market for consultants, it is impossible to import institutional plans (and legitimate consultants do not attempt to do so). Nevertheless, there are some principles and tactics that would be helpful, even wise, for small colleges to consider as they move into the future.

Developing and strengthening appropriate networks of connections is surely one such action. As the framers of American federalism realized, there is strength in confederation. Many small colleges have derived significant benefits from building consortial relationships, such as the Associated Colleges of the Midwest, the Great Lakes College Association, and the Associated Colleges of the South (see chap. 7). Another set of productive relationships has been established between small colleges and large universities in programs such as Preparing Future Faculty and the 3-2 Engineering options discussed in chapter 7. The Council of Public Liberal Arts Colleges (COPLAC) is proving a useful support network for its member colleges around the country, as are the state and national associations of independent colleges, such as the Council of Independent Colleges (CIC). Some private, historically church-related colleges, after decades of distancing themselves from their sectarian roots, are moving to reinvigorate them in new and timely modes (Southwestern University under the leadership of President Jake Schrum offers an example of such reinvigoration). And, as noted earlier in this chapter, stronger connections between college and community or region are a persistent aspiration of small college presidents and others. Other promising possibilities include exchanges of students and teachers, joint purchasing accords, exploitation of instructional technology links, shared special facilities (e.g., astronomical observatories or wilderness field stations), and shared management data. Such links can only root small colleges more securely in their environments. And these alliances can boost lobbying efforts and enhance institutional visibility through the sharing of costs, joint publications, and the like. In networks that provide support and strengthening contacts, small colleges have a powerful mechanism for surviving and improving.

A second strategy, which is nearly universally useful, has to do with mission and focus. It has been demonstrated (e.g., by the regional accreditation process) that having a clear, defined raison d'être is very important to all colleges and universities but particularly the smaller ones. The University of Texas can be many things to many people—a football power to some, an economic development engine to others, a research and new technology producer to one cluster of constituents, an undergraduate teaching school to another. No small college can long sustain diffusion of its core mission.

Strong colleges not only must have a mission; they need to stick to it persistently. While frozen inflexibility is no virtue, vacillation about the core purpose of a college is hardly better. The history of colleges that have radically redefined their missions repeatedly—for example, Parsons College and Mount Senario College—is not a happy one. On the other hand, Wellesley has since its origins defined itself as being at the intersection of academic rigor in the liberal arts and helping women find the skills and knowledge to make a difference in the world. Three-quarters of a century after Jesse Macy helped create the discipline of political science at Grinnell, the phrase *social gospel* still resonates there. Westmont does not budge from a commitment to liberal learning within a Christian faith-based community. Warren Wilson affirms its historic belief in the triad of scholarship, service, and work, decade after decade. Morehouse College espouses a vision of liberal learning for men who will lead the African American community. Minneapolis College of Art and Design sticks to preparing students for professional practice in art.

Institutions that know what they are also know how to make their case with prospective students and parents; with donors, legislators, and neighbors; with evaluators; with the public; and, especially, with themselves. President Stan Gaede at Westmont observes that small colleges with a clear mission and an identifiable niche will thrive in the coming years, but those without such a calling will be in jeopardy. Who will pay high tuition for shapeless mediocrity, he asks?

Small colleges do not have to appeal to everyone: they don't need tens of thousands of applications annually or billion-dollar capital campaigns. They don't need to try to answer the needs of every potential supporter. But they do need a compelling case to appeal powerfully to enough students to fill the freshman class and to sufficient donors to fill the coffers. They have to be able to show why a student should pick X college from the universe of potential schools or why a philanthropist should make the same choice. And the successful colleges do this by being distinctive. They say, "If you are seeking *this* quality, we are your choice; if you are seeking *that* one, look elsewhere." A strong, clear, focused sense of identity and purpose is a small college's greatest treasure.

Small colleges also need to affirm their collective case. Each institution would do well to define and explain itself, but each also must help others argue the rationale for the entire class. There are voices in the higher education community who argue that the American public sees "smallness" as a vice, not a virtue.[10] I do not think this is entirely true; it seems a remarkably un-nuanced assertion. But even if it is only true in part, only small colleges themselves can modify this opinion. It is part of the job of people at small colleges to be persuasive publicly about the contributions their small institutions make to the rich texture of American higher education. Small colleges are accustomed to seeing one another as the "competition" for students, attention, funding, and the like. This is partly true and probably to some extent inescapable. But we need to work harder to see one another as part of the same team, with many of the same goals, needs, and values. As public television advertisements legitimately proclaim, "If we don't do it, who will?"

Small colleges have in the past been, and need to continue to be, sources of important innovation for American higher education. No college or university is easy to change, but small ones have less inertia and are, in the rather ponderous world of postsecondary institutions, the "light cavalry." A modest experiment (e.g., Carleton's academic calendar or Grinnell's first-year seminars or Southwestern's Paideia program) can have widespread visibility across an entire campus and much farther afield.

Small colleges need to listen more alertly and carefully to students when it comes to issues of size. On all the campuses I visited, I talked with students (usually student leaders), and they were never without an opinion on matters of institutional size. Invariably, that opinion was both a strong and a conservative one: their college should stay its current size or revert to the size it recently had been. This is not a surprising finding. Students pick small colleges because of their size, not in spite of it. They want to be at a college of the size they selected. Interestingly, this is as true of the 2,700 undergraduates at the University of Wisconsin–Superior as of the 450 College of Arts and Sciences students at the College of New Rochelle, the 750 students at Warren Wilson College or Colby-Sawyer College (where one student asserted, "If the college had been 1,000 students, I wouldn't have come"). Too often strategic plans and decisions about college size are made outside the orbit of student consideration—probably a shortsighted and unwise institutional process.

The Not So Big College

I have discussed small colleges in the contexts of other small colleges, of larger universities, and of American higher education as a whole. But higher education itself is but a part of the fabric of contemporary society, interwoven in complex and intricate ways with all of our culture. Where do small colleges fit into the ethos of our nation in the new millennium?

One very strong motif in American culture, now and in the past, is a belief that growth—almost any growth—is good and that bigger is better. We pay admiring attention to the highest skyscrapers, the fastest airplanes, the widest expressways, the states that are the biggest cheese producers or have the highest populations or the lowest point on the continent. We tend not to visit the second-highest waterfall or geyser or mountain. The basketball team that takes second place in the annual NCAA Division I tournament is a disappointment, as is the runner-up in the Olympic figure skating competition. We want to "super-size" our fast-food meals. Perhaps because we inhabit a continent that only a few centuries ago seemed endless and (to Western European eyes) mostly empty, it seems somehow un-American not to want to grow.

This faith in expansion and bigness pervades higher education. Two-year colleges often want to become four-year institutions, even when they are thriving at the associate degree level. Four-year colleges grow to universities. Institutions that give master's degrees aspire to grant the doctorate. Annually, some colleges brag that they have admitted their largest first-year class in history. A president of the University of North Carolina system remarked that, if that state's public liberal arts college (the University of North Carolina–Asheville) was doing a good job by providing a top-quality liberal education to twenty-five hundred students, it would be four times better if they could enroll ten thousand.[11] To many it is an act of faith that colleges (like corporations) either grow larger or die.

But, obviously, many of the institutions studied here embrace a different set of values. A senior administrator at Westmont College, for example, says bluntly, "We would rather be better than bigger." As I noted earlier, virtually all the students with whom I met wanted their college to stay the same size or even to revert to a smaller population. Faculty members affirm that a small enrollment is important to them for restricting class size, permitting close advisement, and providing opportunities for optimal relations with their students. Many perceptive observers of the higher education scene (including Boyer, Astin, Breneman, and Clark) have found positive values correlated with smallness.

This belief that, when it comes to higher education, bigger is not always better and that growth is not always good may run against a strong current of our culture, but it is not a unique philosophy. There is another set of contemporary values within which faith in the importance of small colleges can be firmly embedded. From as far back, perhaps, as the Jeffersonian pastoral ideal, there is a streak of the American ethos which affirms the virtue of the small, human scale of life. Millions of Americans dutifully tune in every week to listen to Garrison Keillor's satiric but very fond stories of small-town life in Lake Wobegon, on the edge of the prairie. Bill Bryson's similarly satirical, similarly fond, best-selling book *The Lost Continent* (1989) is subtitled "Travels in Small-Town America."[12] Chicagoans and New Yorkers subject themselves daily to grim commutes in order to live in picturesque little suburban communities such as Englewood Cliffs or Glencoe. The entrepreneur who leaves the huge corporation and finds true happiness in some garage shop handicraft business is an admired and mythic figure.

What follows are illustrations from four startlingly different areas of our lives—sociology, agriculture, economics, and architecture. These perspectives echo what we have heard from those at small colleges about their institutions, their fears and dreams.

Small Town in Mass Society (1958) by Arthur Vidich and Joseph Bensman is a classic sociological text of the mid-twentieth century.[13] Studying a real community, disguised under the pseudonym "Springdale," the work examines the relationship between a small, rural community and modern mass industrial society. Vidich and Bensman found that residents of Springdale believed that urban Americans were "caught up in the inexorable web of impersonality and loneliness" and contrasted urban values with their own: "honesty, fair play, trustworthiness, goodneighborliness, helpfulness, sobriety and clean living" (30). In the small town the sense of community was powerful. Echoing a phrase I heard again and again at small colleges, they said, "Everybody knows everybody." They felt that "being in the community gives one a distinct feeling of living in a protected and better place" (31–32).

The authors felt that the self-image of residents of Springdale actually conditioned their way of life. Because they *believed* that residents of small towns were friendly and helpful, they *acted* friendly and helpful and thus validated their beliefs. Are the impressions that small colleges seek to disseminate about themselves—in their admissions material, for example— likewise self-fulfilling? Because small colleges say they foster more intimate student-teacher relations, do students and teachers seek to live up to such overt expectations?

Like many of the small colleges examined in this book, small towns nestled within mass society publicly espouse a position advocating social equality. Also like small colleges, Vidich and Bensman found small towns have a refined "etiquette of gossip" and, indeed, gossip was a significant and constant activity—the less happy side of the affirmation that "everybody knows everybody" (41–42).

In a finding that would sound remarkably familiar to those affiliated with small colleges, especially administrators, the authors found that small communities are increasingly controlled by forces outside themselves (e.g., state and federal authorities). Thus, the ability to influence the direction of local affairs tended to depend upon the effectiveness of access to external sources of power and finances.

Vidich and Bensman conclude *Small Town in Mass Society* by noting that the proportional role of smaller communities in midcentury America had shrunk considerably and continued to decrease. But they also noted that, especially to their residents, such small communities preserved a unique reservoir of values and relationships that remained precious within the large, impersonal world of urban mass culture.

Fifteen years after the publication of *Small Town in Mass Society*, economist E. F. Schumacher made an even stronger case against what he called

"giganticism" in the influential and popular book *Small Is Beautiful*
(1973).[14] Theodore Roszak, in the book's introduction, notes that Schumacher insists "that the *scale* of organization must be treated as an independent problem," a main theme of my study of small colleges. Like
Schumacher, and like Vidich and Bensman, he associates bigness with
impersonality, insensitivity, and a lust for abstract, concentrated power.
Small, Roszak contends, is "free, efficient, creative, enjoyable" (4–9).

Schumacher's discussion is rooted in the economics of environmentalism. He makes the case for "small-scale technology, relatively non-violent
technology . . . technology with a human face" (21). Like Roszak in his introductory comments, Schumacher is not afraid to suggest a philosophical
undergirding to his defense of smallness: "There is wisdom in smallness
if only on account of the smallness and patchiness of human knowledge,
which relies on experiment far more than on understanding" (36). Smallness, Schumacher contends, breeds environmental and social responsibility; largeness encourages irresponsibility and disrespect: "men organized
in small units will take better care of *their* bit of land or other natural resources than anonymous companies or megalomaniac governments" (35).

Several of Schumacher's points about small environmental economics
parallel our observations about small colleges. Thus, he notes that "as
soon as great size has been created there is often a strenuous attempt to
gain smallness within bigness" (64), precisely the phenomenon I discussed in chapter 7, wherein large universities seek to rekindle the values
of small colleges within their expansive borders. Similarly, Schumacher
echoes the theme of small college opportunities for an integrated collegiate experience, arguing that small size recognizes and takes advantage
of the truth that "all subjects, no matter how specialized, are connected
with a centre; they are like rays emitted from a sun" (94).

Sounding very much like a small college view book touting community,
Schumacher contends that "most of the sociologists and psychologists in-
sistently warn us of its [vastness's] inherent dangers—dangers to the integrity of the individual when he feels nothing more than a cog in a vast
machine and when the human relationships of his daily working life become increasingly dehumanized." He argues that "the only really effective
community is from man to man, face to face," and that "nobody really
likes large scale organization: nobody likes to take orders from a superior
who takes orders from a superior who takes orders" (242).

Schumacher's thesis—"Man is small and, therefore, small is beautiful.

To go for gigantism is to go for self-destruction"—became both an inspiration and a rallying cry for environmentalists and for others who sought alternatives to corporate and governmental growth (159). Even today, it continues to hearten advocates of small colleges.

A similarly outspoken and charismatic figure arguing eloquently for smallness of scale is the agriculturalist, ecologist, and philosopher Wendell Berry. Berry is perhaps at his most compelling in *The Unsettling of America: Culture and Agriculture* (1977).[15] Berry's book is a vigorous defense of that "class of independent small farmers who fought the war of independence" which has "been exploited by, and recruited into, the industrial society until by now it is almost extinct" (5). Berry argues against U.S. agricultural policy that sees food production as a "constantly expanding market" or, worse, a potential weapon. Against agribusiness he sets the ideal of the small farm and farmer: "The old idea is still full of promise. It is potent with healing and with health. It has the power to turn each person away from the big-time promising and planning of the government" (14). Berry equates large-scale farming with increasing specialization that, he argues, is destructive of community, and, conversely, he sees human-sized communities as being linked to a sense of the connectedness of life: "The community disintegrates because it loses the necessary understandings, forms, and enactments of the relations among materials and processes, principles and actions, ideals and realities, past and present, present and future, men and women, body and spirit, city and country, civilization and wilderness, growth and decay, life and death—just as the individual character loses the sense of a responsible involvement in these relations" (21).

Like those who seek to defend small colleges, Berry responds to the argument that agribusiness offers economies of size, which he believes results in a dangerous concentration of production and power in the hands of a relatively few specialists: "In Washington, the word on farming was 'Get big or get out'—a policy which . . . has taken an enormous toll." And, he argues, such growth is insidious: "bigness is totalitarian . . . the aim of bigness implies not one aim that is not socially and culturally destructive" (41). Like those who have questioned the value of seeking economies of scale of mega-universities, Berry asks those who advocate large-scale agribusiness farming, "Where are the people?" (73). Like Schumacher, he argues from a philosophical/theological position that giganticism is inhuman: "That humans are small within the Creation is an ancient perception, represented often enough in art that it must be supposed to have an elemental importance" (97–98). He is prepared to link the particular focus of his attention—agricultural policy—to much larger issues: "body, soul (or mind or spirit), community, and the world" (110). Berry's overarching thesis is that large-scale agriculture is senseless and destructive and that small farms and small farming nurtures the ecosystem and the spirits of the people who practice it.

Finally, architect Sarah Susanka argues that smallness can be a virtue even in the daily physical surroundings within which we live. Her 1998 book *The Not So Big House* was a surprising bestseller.[16] In a work that is as visually attractive as it is intellectually stimulating, she argues for craft and quality in domestic construction and against home design that gives first priority to monumentalism and square footage. "A house that favors quality of design over quantity of space satisfies people with big dreams and not so big budgets far more than a house with those characteristics in reverse" (4–5). She contends that, where smallness can feed the spirit, largeness for its own sake is enervating: "So many houses, so big, with so little soul . . . are bigger houses really better? Are the dreams that build them bigger, or is it simply that there seems to be no alternative?" (7). Susanka makes a compelling case that what counts in domestic design is not sheer space but the quality of what space there is: "What defines the character of a house are the details" (12). She recognizes the difficulty of discussing smallness as a positive attribute, noting that the language in which one can delineate quality is far more hazy than the language of quantity, but insists that small, well-designed, well-built houses fit human needs far better than the cold, impersonal "starter palaces" that fill new suburban developments.

Like the other advocates of smallness, Susanka links her area of specific interest, residential architecture, to larger social contexts. She believes that the sort of home she seeks to design, "the not so big house, . . . offers a way to bring the soul back into our homes, our communities, and our society's fabric" (193). It is noteworthy how often these authors link smallness with soulfulness.

Susanka believes that residential structures need to link mission with scale. She looks first at what a home is designed to do, for whom, then asks how large it should be. The answer, of course, for both homes and for colleges is "exactly big enough to do what it seeks to do in the very best possible way."

Old Main

At the dawn of the twenty-first century Americans are ambivalent about matters of size, in colleges and in much else. As our cities and our malls grow and grow, we seem to yearn more and more deeply for the general store on a mythic Main Street in some elm-shaded small town where there is no rush and there are no strangers. We move to Minneapolis or San Diego and shop at Wal-Mart or Home Depot yet suspect that things would be somehow better back in Mount Vernon at the local small-town hardware shop.

Such ambivalence is no sin and seems deeply rooted in the human character. Both largeness and smallness have their virtues and their liabilities, and our lives are richer for embracing them both. As we have seen in the preceding pages, this is especially true in the world of American higher education. Large universities offer a range of learning and a depth of expertise that can be endlessly stimulating. Small colleges embody the values of human-scaled communities and the possibilities of an undergraduate education of integrity. In them we teach, learn, and work with people we know and care about deeply. And the learning that goes on at such places can at its best permeate all areas of collegiate life: the classroom, the performance hall, the athletic field, the dormitory, the laboratories, the office, and the bench under one of the elm trees, out on the grassy quadrangle, in front of Old Main Hall.

Olya

Here is what it is all about: what happens to a good student at a good small college. This current college student has obviously developed powerful connections to her small college, its people, and its programs. In doing so, she has developed an impressive sense of her own character and her place in the world as well as a realistic and idealistic plan for the next phase of her life after college. She is intense, passionate, self-aware, dedicated. I believe that, if small colleges can continue to graduate young people of this caliber, our futures are strong and secure.

I interviewed several dozen students during my site visits. Olga Milenkaya (Olya), a student leader at Warren Wilson College (WWC), was particularly engaging but not atypical. I asked her an additional series of questions for this "Intermezzo."

---

1. *Tell me a bit about your background. I know you emigrated as a child. How old were you? From where? Where in the United States did your family move?*

I was born in 1982 near Novosibirsk, Russia. I left Russia with my older sister and parents in 1989. I was seven. My mother is also from Siberia, but her parents are Ukrainian. My father is from Minsk, Belarus, and is ethnically Jewish. We lost our Russian citizenship and most of everything we owned upon leaving. We went through Austria and stayed in Italy, waiting for a U.S. visa. We were accepted as refugees and flew to San Francisco via New York City. We spoke no English. We settled in Mountain View and later moved down the road to Palo Alto. My sister and I started school right away. My parents are computer programmers.

2. *Where did you go to high school? public or private? large or small? Was it a positive experience? What did you like, and dislike, there?*

I went to Los Altos High School. It is public, in the neighboring suburb of Los Altos. The school has about fourteen hundred students. And, so, I would say that I had a positive experience in high school. That is not to say, however, that it was great or that I would ever do it again! Los Altos and Los Altos Hills are two very wealthy cities. The neighboring suburb of Mountain View, however, is less affluent. Image, wealth, power, all play a role in the hierarchy of high school students. Los Altos High School is a microcosm of the greater Silicon Valley. Most students are also fairly conservative politically and socially. In the beginning of high school I was shy and kept to myself. By the end I had established an ethic and opinion on the world. I had found my voice and used it. I was the outspoken leftist activist, and I enjoyed it. By my senior year I was president of the Environmental Club, and I worked at a local environmental nonprofit organization, organizing high school activists. Support for my activism came from a couple other dedicated students but mostly from the faculty. Los Altos High School is lucky to have some great teachers. I am still in touch with a couple, and that is a testament to how wonderful they really are. Many of the teachers have been there for a long time. There is low turnover, and that really helps the students. I can easily say that there were at least eight *great* teachers that I had in high school. They were not only good at teaching and, actually, sometimes weren't, but they were great people. One of the best characteristics that a teacher can have is a sincere passion and love for the students. Teachers, especially in high school, are more like role models and supporters than they are disseminators of information. Also, I despise the focus on standardized testing. My high school is big into competitive testing: SATs, AP tests, and state and national tests. I hate being taught by the test.

I got good grades. I played sports (track, cross-country). I took all the AP classes. I was happy to leave and move on to a real education.

3. *Why did you pick Warren Wilson College?*

I picked WWC because all other colleges were too normal. They did not have an environmental studies program that I wanted. They did not offer me a holistic education. WWC jumped out at me through its initial recruitment letter. It was on tree-free paper and printed with soy-based ink! The *Triad* [academics, work, service]! In brief: small, private liberal arts college in a rural setting, in the mountains, on the other side of the country, work, service, academics, *the best* environmental studies department, intimate and close-knit community, a place that walks its talk, egalitarian, unique, a place with a mission, farm, forests, history, culture. I wanted an alternative education but was not ready to let go of majors or grades or classes. I was still holding onto some notion of "academic rigor." The work program excited me but wasn't vital. (It has become a lot more to me now!) Originally, I just thought it sounded neat and was a way to establish a sense of community and togetherness and to minimize our participation in the exploitative global economy. I came here because I did not want to debate whether or not we had an environmental crisis. I wanted to debate how to fix it. I did not want to talk about Democrats or Republicans; I wanted to talk about bioregionalism, deep ecology, and other radical perspectives. I wanted a place rooted in its natural and cultural history, a place with character as opposed to the urban sprawl and social decay of Silicon Valley. I wanted something new and challenging. I wanted everything that was in the WWC promotional brochures. I applied for an early decision, submitting my application on November 5, 1999. Two weeks later I was in!

4. *What is your major? What activities have you been involved in? What work assignments have you had? Have you enjoyed your work? With what service projects have you been involved?*

Academics: Environmental studies. There are six concentrations to pick from (analysis, policy, education, sustainable forestry, sustainable agriculture, conservation biology) and an option to design your own. I designed my own concentration.

Work: I did janitorial work my first year. I worked on the farm my second year (general crew first semester, pig crew second semester). I am now splitting my work hours between two crews for my third year. I work in the College Archives and as the student trustee. Each year one person is elected by the student body to hold this position. The student sits on the board of trustees and has a vote like all other board members do. As I mentioned earlier, the work program has become very important to me. I learned countless things about myself and the world through the work program. If I had to pick the most valuable component of WWC, it would definitely be the work program. I have enjoyed it immensely! In some ways I regret not being on one crew for three or four years. People really become experts in those fields when they do that. I, however, ended up with different crews every year. I managed to somehow find the most diverse type of work. It is this broad spectrum of work that cannot be underestimated. From cleaning to good old-fashioned manual labor to politics to office work. I've loved all of it.

Service: As with most students here, service is the weak leg, the last priority. Interestingly enough, however, most of us did tons of service before coming here. I did countless hours in high school but somehow lost track of it all when I came here. Partly, I am just too busy. It is too easy to overcommit oneself and not leave room for service. Also, it is just easy to get really caught up in what is going on here. I have done several small service projects: I tutored women hoping to get their GED at a nearby prison, did river cleanups, did habitat restoration at a preserve, etc. I am going on a service trip over spring break. A group of about fifteen students, led by the landscaping crew boss, are going to the John C. Campbell Folk School to do their landscaping and camp out for the week. I'm really looking forward to that.

5. *What have you found most fulfilling and enjoyable about your college experience, especially in the context of Warren Wilson's small size? Any disappointments or frustrations?*

I don't know what to say. I love this place so much. And I am so bitter about it too. For a long time I thought that I was feeling contradictory emotions about this place. What I have realized, however, is that one must be critical of the thing one loves most. That is honesty. And I must be true to this place if I really care for it.

I am frustrated that the school is getting bigger and that I wasn't here when there were five hundred students, that I wasn't here to protest the growth to eight hundred. The school is getting more normal, more institutional, and less communal. I am frustrated that there are people here who are unhappy; they are mostly racial and social/political minorities. I am mad that I still don't know everyone's name here. I am scared that the work program will be boiled to nothingness. I fear that one day we will no longer have a farm. I am frustrated at the seemingly endless construction on campus, as a result of the growth of the college. I am disappointed with this place for losing sight of its original mission: to give an education to poor Appalachian guys. This place was once for the hardworking dedicated person. Now tuition, room, and board is twenty thousand dollars. I can't believe we, *a farm school,* have [a multinational corporation] as our food provider. Class sizes are growing. The Triad should be more integrated. The staff should not be treated worse than the faculty. Student Caucus and Staff Forum should be able to decide on policy, rather than make recommendations. And the list goes on.

The great thing about this place is that it's not a huge cookie-cutter university. The potential here is amazing! This place has a purpose and character. But, compared to what it could be, we are falling short.

I do love, however, that I do know Doug [Orr, the president] and Larry Modlin (the vice president of business). I love it that they play the guitar, that Larry makes stained glass in his free time, that I can call Louise (our dean of students) around midnight and be invited into her home for a chat. I love working, studying, doing service, and living with my community members. I love the passion that is here. The dedication, the *oomph!!!* The students are talented and inspiring. The faculty, staff, and administrators are sincere. The mountains are beautiful. I love the fact that I had never been on a mountain bike before I joined the team, and then, *wham,* two months later, I'm at Nationals, biking twenty miles in the snow, and I came in fourth! I love long quiet walks in the woods.

I've served on the following: EcoDorm Committee, Business Affairs Committee, Strategic Long-Range Planning Committee, and the task force for the rebuilding of our burned dorm. I am the liaison between Student Caucus and the business office. I learned to mountain bike here. Last fall we came in third for Division II schools [of the Southeastern Conference of the National Collegiate Cycling Association]. I was a resident assistant (RA). I go contra dancing every Thursday night on campus (I had never heard of contra dancing before I came here). A couple weeks ago I learned how to milk a cow. I am a vegetarian right now and have been for eight years but have decided to eat meat again. For my first time back to meat I have committed myself to eat WWC beef. This summer I am doing an eleven-week internship through WWC's Environmental Leadership Center. I will be working for the Audubon Society, doing puffin research off the coast of Maine. I also love to paint (oils), draw, and go backpacking.

I have enjoyed the people, the place, the work, the study, the challenge, the opportunities. I have made this my home.

6. *Can you tell me a bit about your professors?*

First, I must make it clear that my professors are both faculty and staff. They are not just the individuals in the classrooms but also my supervisors at work. And in many ways they are also the administrators, alumni, and trustees with whom I've interacted and therefore learned from. That is the beauty of Warren Wilson. Education is extended beyond the conventional classroom setting and into one's everyday life. I learn at work. I learn by doing service. I learn by my community involvement right here on campus. The entire WWC experience is a learning one. Professors are therefore, in the broad sense of the word, everyone I've encountered here. The people I have met here are amazing. These are individuals who have been mentors to me, whether they know it or not. These are individuals for whom I have a huge amount of respect. And these are individuals who've helped me figure myself out and the world.

7. *When do you expect to graduate? What do you plan to do after graduation? What would be your longer-range goals in your life and career? How do you think your small college experience will fit into those plans?*

I expect to graduate in 2003, with a B.A. degree in Environmental Studies. After that my plan is to move back to Russia. I want to stay with my grandmother. She lives in a small village in Siberia. I plan to stay for at least one year, maybe a year and a half. In essence I want to live off the land and try to become rooted, to understand the ecology, culture, and the interrelationship between the two. I want to learn about my family history and traditions. I want to improve my Russian. What does it mean to be Russian? What is rural culture like in a village that small? What's the ecology like? What is the relationship between villagers and their surroundings? I want to grow food, can it for the winter, hunt, and fish. A lot of this longing to return to Russia is an attempt to come to grips with me having left. Instead of being both Russian and American, I feel like neither. I want to rediscover my roots so, if I choose to leave, it will be my own decision.

One of the most valuable things that I got out of my WWC experience is the development of my ethic. This ethic resonates in everything I do and is very clear in the work I plan for myself in the future.

My long-term goals, as of now, are to go into ecological fieldwork and/or nonprofit management. Right now I see myself doing both on and off. I hope that this summer's experience doing fieldwork with puffins will help me decide if that's what I really want to do. Honestly, I don't know what I will do after Russia. I foresee it as being a life-changing experience, and I can't predict what that will do to me. Perhaps I will be starving for academic study and might go into grad school. I might not want to leave Russia. I might do a million things. We shall see.

| Small Is Different | A Guide for the Perplexed

Ernest Boyer's book *College: The Undergraduate Experience in America* concludes with an epilogue entitled "A Guide to a Good College." Intended as an aid to parents and college-bound students, this section represents a bit of a narrative swerve from the scholarly and abstract discussion and recommendations of the previous 286 pages but a valuable and interesting pragmatic distillation of much of the earlier material. The section of this book which follows seeks the same sort of effect, principally for new faculty at small colleges.[1]

Many of those for whom this postscript will prove useful will find themselves, by accident or by design, working in a smaller college or university. For some this will represent a return to a familiar ambience; for others it will be an entirely new institutional context. For most it will be a startling shift from a research university. One effective approach to such a new setting is that of the field-based anthropologist: think of the small college as a self-contained culture, explicable primarily through its own rules. The wise fieldworker tries to restrain or suppress the customs and patterns of her own cultural context and seeks the underlying mechanisms of the society under investigation unhampered by prejudgments.

What follows, then, is less a "taxonomy" than a guide for newcomers to small colleges. While lacking the specificity of a Peterson's bird guide ("look, over there, it's a southern, coed, Quaker-affiliated, moderately selective private liberal arts college!"), it may at least help the neophyte investigator distinguish fin from feather, or, to beat the anthropological metaphor into the dust, matriarchal agricultural society from patrilineal industrialism.

◆ ◆ ◆

Small colleges and universities are "different." They are different, as a class, from large universities, and they are different from one another. Much of this chapter will focus on the first of these sets of differences, trying to make useful generalizations but keeping in mind that small institutions may well resemble one another no more than they resemble their larger kin.

This idiosyncrasy is, in fact, one of the chief characteristics of smaller colleges. There is a sense in which the very "comprehensiveness" of larger institutions guarantees their uniformity: one such school is likely to "comprehend" pretty much the same as another. While there are certainly important (and endearing) individual traits that distinguish even our mega-universities, small colleges tend to be far more unique, even quirky. Because they are *not* even remotely comprehensive, their strengths and weaknesses—indeed, their inclusions and exclusions—are definitive and essential. Which languages are taught? Which sciences? How are humanities departments organized?

To take a concrete example, even in faculties of roughly the same size, departmental proportions and instructional personnel may vary dramatically. The specific arrangement can be crucial to an incoming faculty member. Thus, a new anthropologist at one small university may be joining a five-person Anthropology Department; at another she may find herself the sole practitioner of her discipline in a three-person Sociology/ Anthropology Department; at a few institutions such an anthropologist might be the only person in anthropology *and* sociology in a six-person Department of Social Science. My point is not that one of these arrangements is superior to the other but the stark importance of ascertaining *which* of them one is joining before, rather than after, the fact.

Small institutions are more idiosyncratic, too, because they are usually farther from the academic mainstream than major universities. Isolated societies tend to develop and evolve in highly individualized directions. Many faculty members at small colleges enjoy being somewhat removed from the intellectual fads (or, depending upon one's perspective, the latest developments) which tend to sweep through the disciplines, and they delight equally in what often appears to be a refreshing absence of careerism. Others, however, chafe at the sometimes undeniable parochialism and worry about losing touch with mainstream academe. Happily, a good number strike a reasonable and productive middle course: staying in touch with scholarly trends but not feeling compelled to be constantly au courant.

One key way in which liberal arts colleges differ from one another has to do with the extent to which they actually practice the "liberal arts," at least in the old-fashioned, curricular sense. Small colleges and universities, private and public, have been subject to severe strains during the past two decades, and they have often changed in response. Some would say that missions have "evolved"; other, more cynical voices proclaim defection. The former president of a fine private liberal arts college, David W. Breneman of Kalamazoo College, finds that the number of institutions truly belonging in this category has shrunk dramatically in recent years. He disqualifies institutions in which the majority of undergraduate degrees are awarded in "vocational" areas. This is a standard that some (including me) may criticize, but the point remains that at many liberal arts colleges the traditional subject matter disciplines have been overwhelmed or at least seriously challenged by career-oriented fields such as management, accounting, computer science, environmental studies, sports medicine, atmospheric science, administration of justice, and music recording technology. (All of these are areas in which it would be possible for students to major at institutions where I have worked, which were, in my opinion, genuine liberal arts colleges.) In practical terms young faculty members must be prepared to put aside "purist" definitions of liberal education or confine their job search to a small proportion of smaller institutions.

An important lesson is never to assume one small college is like another. It can be dangerously misleading to presume that an idyllic memory of undergraduate days on a small campus is a reliable template for the entire spectrum of institutions of, say, five hundred to three thousand students.

◆ ◆ ◆

Small colleges tend to have small departments, and this is a fact of constant consequence. A professor in, say, a History Department of four or an Economics faculty of three or, for that matter, a Music or Classics program with a staff of one (I worked at a good liberal arts college that did, in fact, have single-person "departments," complete with full-fledged departmental majors, in these two areas) will face a different kind of teaching load than does the member of a department of twenty-five, fifty, or a hundred. Most teachers at small colleges teach "out of their field," if by *field* we mean the subject specialty in which doctoral research was done. An English professor with a dissertation on non-Shakespearean Renaissance drama will probably teach Chaucer, Freshman Composition, Humanities I, and British Literature Survey; an ichthyologist will face classes in Introductory Biology; an Islamicist might teach courses with titles such as "Religion in America," "The Old Testament," and "Varieties of World Religions." Those of us who love small colleges delight in this demand for generalists. It keeps us alert and learning. But it also tends to mean that we find it easy to drift away from staying current in non-Shakespearean Renaissance English drama, ichthyology, and Islam.

It is also the case that, in many smaller institutions, faculty members will teach so far "out of the field" that they are, in fact, out of the entire ballpark. If the institution has a large core or interdisciplinary program, our hypothetical Ph.D. in Jacobean tragicomedy will find himself instructing a course in "Interdisciplinary Studies 101" or "Christianity and Culture" or "Humanities I: Classical Antiquity." Many thrive on such opportunities to integrate and "stretch"; many others find the experience disorienting, at least at first.

Another obvious implication of small departments at small colleges is the dearth of colleagues in a faculty member's specialty area. The ichthyologist or Islamicist will perhaps find herself the *only* scholar with such an interest on campus. So, for example, it is usually impossible to find a colleague on a small college campus who can give a careful and professional reading to a draft of an article or paper. It is easy to solicit the response of interested amateurs or a critique of the style, but the subject matter will usually be foreign to departmental peers. Graduate students are often habituated to deep and intense discussion of the latest research or theoretical development within their subdisciplines. On the small college campus the absence of such interactions may be lamented.

At most small colleges the normal teaching load is six to eight classes per year, three or four per semester. Usually, these loads are *not* reduced for unusual research assignments or other burdens, although course relief may be possible. In a given semester two or three of the courses taught will have different preparations—for the neophyte faculty member, this may mean three or so new preparations a term for a while. A bizarre but instructive anecdote: at one point early in my teaching career a sudden illness of one departmental colleague and a failure in the hiring process designed to add another to the college roster resulted in my teaching six different courses, each with a separate preparation, in the same semester. I survived; I still wonder if my students learned much that term.

Concatenating the size and the shape of a typical faculty load at a small college, we have a pattern that might manifest itself thus. A member of the Biology Department, with a Ph.D. degree in freshwater ichthyology, might teach a year-long introductory course ("Biology 101"), with lab, surveying both botany and zoology. First semester that instructor would perhaps also have a mid-level course such as "Principles of Animal Biology" and an advanced section in, say, "Animal Physiology." Second term would see the second semester ("Biology 102") of the introductory course, another more advanced offering, say, "Aquatic Ecosystems," and potentially an interdisciplinary contribution such as "The Sea in Science and Art." This hypothetical situation is by no means extreme. Add to such a schedule the potential for a dozen major and/or first-year advisees, service on a college-wide committee or two, work on a departmental curriculum review, weekly department meetings, monthly faculty meetings, and nomination to an ad hoc committee preparing for regional reaccreditation. This is a workload designed to combat boredom; it is not one likely to facilitate finishing that first scholarly book, research project, or article derived from a dissertation.

Most small college teachers are in their campus offices most of the day throughout the work week. Many do not even have a functional office elsewhere. Evenings and weekends on campus are not uncommon (attending the political science awards dinner, e.g., or a reception for parents on the Saturday afternoon of Family Weekend). The research university model of a division of time between campus office, classroom, private study, and research library or site tends to break down at the smaller institution, with the first two activities becoming dominant, even all-consuming.

• • •

Small academic departments also shape the social and general intellectual lives of academics in small colleges. The young academic in a research department of seventy-five, with its own building, parking lot, coffee and mail dispensaries, and the like, will find herself fraternizing mostly with departmental colleagues. In some situations only the occasional university committee assignment, an accident of residential neighborhood proximity, or a shared school or child care provider for kids will bring together institutional faculty from different departments or divisions. It may well be possible, at Ohio State University or the University of Minnesota, for a French teacher to spend an entire career without ever interacting with professors of geology or economics. This is far less likely, indeed, often downright impossible, at a small college. Most institutions with fewer than one hundred faculty members, for example, have democratic as opposed to republican faculty governance procedures: the monthly or weekly "faculty

meeting" is a meeting of the entire college faculty. Four or five departments, sometimes with no apparent organizing rhyme or reason, will be
housed in the same building; a central campus coffee shop will serve as
meeting place for the entire community. At one institution where I
worked, one building housed the Art Department and the campus art
gallery, the Leadership Programs office, the Management and Accounting
Department, an outreach program for senior citizens, a small conference
center, and the University Development office. At many small schools faculty members forge their deepest friendships—and sometimes their most
interesting and gratifying intellectual relationships as well—across departmental or divisional barriers. Indeed, those "barriers" are usually perme-
able membranes.

By way of a contrasting illustration, at the Twin Cities campus of the
University of Minnesota faculty and students of engineering are across the
Mississippi River, in Minneapolis, from the School of Law, and those in
social work and veterinary science are a pleasant bus ride away, in St. Paul.

Often the sorts of interdisciplinary or core programs cited earlier will
greatly facilitate such diverse patterns of personal and professional association. Many such courses are deliberately staffed and planned by faculty
members drawn from the widest possible departmental constituencies,
and at some institutions virtually the entire faculty is, over time, drawn
into these curricular ventures.

A good tip-off regarding this dimension of institutional culture for the
prospective faculty member is to heed carefully the staffing of the search
process. If interviewing for a position in political science involves extended
discussion with chemists, economists, theater historians, and professors of
sports medicine, it is a pretty good sign that the potential employing institution values and expects frequent and deep extradepartmental contacts.

◆ ◆ ◆

It is always important for new employees, within and beyond academe, to
ascertain with accuracy the standards and procedures by which they will
be evaluated. These standards and procedures will vary among small colleges, and there will probably be pronounced generic differences between
small and large institutions. Almost all higher education enterprises affirm that excellence of classroom teaching is an important criterion for
reappointment, promotion, and tenure. Some actually mean it. There are
still many small colleges in the United States today in which, practically,
pedagogical quality is the sole basis for major career decisions. In the ma-

jority of small institutions it is the most important factor or at least a very important factor. This means that classroom teaching should and may be evaluated with thoroughness and rigor: student course evaluations will be heeded; classroom visitations by deans or chairpersons will be regular and more than perfunctory. Note whether actual teaching, to actual students, is an important element of the hiring process: if it is, chances are it will also be a significant element in the review process as well.

This does not, of course, mean that research, publication, community service, and other factors will be excluded from evaluative decisions. It is therefore very important for a faculty member at an early point on the career path to come to a clear understanding regarding the relative weight of these criteria in the decision-making process and the means by which effectiveness—as a teacher, scholar, and community citizen—will be assessed. This understanding may not be easily reached. In many institutions official pronouncements in this area may not always conform to practice. At small, informal, nonunion campuses, the regulatory/descriptive "faculty handbook" is notoriously uneven; some are accurate, others flamboyantly unreliable. The wise newcomer will seek to discuss the evaluation and review process with a few trusted colleagues who have themselves relatively recently been through it as well as with those who will administer it. Find out what seems to have made a genuine difference, for good or ill, and be prepared to find that, more often than not, teaching makes the biggest difference of all.

Tangentially related to evaluation are salary and compensation issues. Expect the salary scale at most smaller institutions to be demonstrably lower than at larger and/or public institutions of roughly comparable status. While many small colleges and universities have generous benefits packages that supplement base salary, they are sometimes not as comprehensive as state-mandated programs in the public sector. Expect, too, that (in the private sector at least) salaries will be formally private but, in fact, virtually public knowledge and the subject of much semi-informed discussion within the campus community. It is rare for a private institution to publish faculty salaries, but it is even rarer for it to be difficult to get a pretty good idea of individual compensation levels. In sum you probably won't be paid much, your benefits status will probably be decent but not spectacular, and most everyone with whom you come in contact will know it.

It is also usually less expensive to live in a small college town than a major university center, and the events—athletic, cultural, intellectual—of the institution are often free or inexpensive to faculty members, a not in-significant benefit, especially in smaller, somewhat culturally or recre-ationally impoverished communities.

• • •

There is a pronounced difference in the kinds of relationships that develop between teachers and undergraduate students at large and small institu-tions. At the larger schools a faculty member may develop a close, mentor-ing relationship with a handful of strong undergraduate departmental majors. Usually, however, the closer relationships will be with graduate students. In a small college it is not uncommon for a teacher to teach the same students in courses throughout their undergraduate careers, from first semester to graduation. These students will not necessarily be majors in the teacher's particular field: it may be, for example, that an accounting major will take two or three theater courses and act in a handful of plays, under the tutelage of one drama professor. Many relationships, with stu-dents of varied scholarly bents, will develop at the small college. And often faculty members are deeply involved in student organizations and co-curricular activities. One of the joys of teaching at such schools is the fre-quent, recurring opportunity to watch undergraduates grow in intellectual and emotional depth during a period of four years. There is a kind of ma-ternalism about this relationship which some find cloying, but most see as deeply satisfying.

Some of its consequences can be amusing, some touching, and some downright irritating. There are institutions, for example, where it is con-sidered acceptable behavior for students to call professors at any hour of the night and day to discuss out-of-class personal problems, where the pastoral model of the student-teacher relationship is still held by a major-ity of the faculty, students, and staff. It is also the case that at many institu-tions the progress and foibles of shared students is a prime topic for fac-ulty conversation. For good or ill, the passage of higher education privacy legislation has seemed to have little effect upon professorial conversations about students at small colleges around the backyard barbecue grill.

• • •

Faculty at large institutions and at small ones have always played an im-portant role in the governance of institutions of higher education. At small institutions this role is likely to differ sharply from that at larger ones. A majority of the major institutional governance tasks remain the same, re-gardless of the size of the school: all colleges and universities need a curriculum committee of some sort, a personnel review process, a faculty athletic committee, a library committee, an admissions committee, an academic standards committee, or similar groups. At small colleges roughly the same number of tasks is therefore distributed among a much smaller pool of workers. While the volume of work is perhaps proportional to the size of the college, the breadth remains more or less constant. The faculty member at a small college may thus find herself serving on committees, study groups, task forces, fact-finding bodies, search committees, and similar institutional extra-classroom organizations in bewildering (and sometimes intimidating) number and range. In one sense this sort of "community service" often gives to the faculty of small colleges a demonstrable role in directing the destiny of the institution, which can be gratifying and educational. (At times it can be frustrating, to faculty and administrators, that being part of a small college also means that everyone should have a voice on every aspect of the college.) And such assignments, often contributing little directly to either teaching or scholarship, can be distracting. Every small college vows periodically to revamp its committee structure so as to eliminate this problem. The record of permanent solutions is remarkably slim.

◆ ◆ ◆

Many of the founding fathers (and they *were* virtually all "fathers") of small colleges sought locations for their institutions which safely removed impressionable young students from the temptations of city life. (Anecdotal evidence suggests those enterprising young people found plenty of quite satisfactory temptations in rural venues.) The consequences of this questionable choice may face the new faculty member at such schools.

First, at some smaller, more isolated colleges it may be necessary—and it is occasionally still required—that faculty live in the small town that houses their institution. The informality and potential closeness of such arrangements is inviting, especially for young families. It is not, however, without compensatory difficulties. If the college has "anti-nepotism" policies, it can be exceptionally difficult for a spouse to find satisfying employment. Also, these communities are often somewhat homogeneous, especially compared to major cities and large university towns. They do not tend to be culturally stimulating. If a steady diet of major dramatic and symphonic performances and first-class art exhibits is a necessity, life in Mt. Vernon, Iowa, or Gambier, Ohio, or Collegeville, Minnesota, may seem inadequate. Often the cultural opportunities of a small college community are those provided by the college itself, plus perhaps a single movie theater. Be prepared, too, for over-the-fence discussions of house painting and plumbing projects, kids' swim teams, and the scandal at the local church more often than analyses of the ballet performance last evening. The prevailing cultural and political climate in such towns, at least outside the immediate college community (and sometimes within it) is likely to be more conservative than in major university cities.

It is worth remembering that a *good* small college library may have 300,000 volumes. If that college is located many miles from the nearest city and/or university, access to significant library resources (or super-computer terminals or specialized laboratory facilities) can be exceedingly difficult. Careful planning may be necessary just to accommodate an occasional commute. Many librarians at smaller institutions are exceptionally helpful with programs such as Interlibrary Loan, but the graduate student who is accustomed to popping into a library of 3.5 million volumes to check an obscure citation will be easily frustrated in Deep Springs, California; New London, New Hampshire; or St. Leo, Florida. Of course, the increasing utility of electronic resources such as the Internet can do much to moderate this bibliographic dearth.

While the cultural connotations of working at a small school in relative geographical isolation are fairly obvious, the implications for personal social life are less clear. At some such schools a young, single instructor or one with an unconventional lifestyle may be uncomfortable. A faculty of, say, ninety members may have three or five members under the age of thirty and another half-dozen or so between thirty and thirty-five. There may not be many other individuals in this age group in town. A very young faculty member may feel more social affinity with mature undergraduates than with the majority of middle-aged colleagues. But often there will be strict codes or conventions governing social relations between students and teachers which discourage or forbid contacts more intimate than an informal afternoon softball game.

Some careful observers have also noted an interesting but sometimes disconcerting phenomenon regarding small college community mores: the pairing of political liberalism and social conservatism. There are those of us still around (albeit, tottering) who can recall settings in which it was acceptable to proclaim oneself a socialist or an anarchist (at least in theory) but still necessary to hide wine bottles in layers of newsprint buried in the weekly garbage set out for collection.

At many more urban schools, and for many individuals, these constraints are inconsequential, but for a few they are real and occasionally devastating. Well-rounded lives extend beyond the classroom and faculty office. Prospective faculty members are wise to ascertain if the extramural conditions of potential employers are a reasonable match with their personal needs.

· · ·

Sometimes those entering the professorate will ask if it is wise to accept a position at a liberal arts college or a small university "on the way to" a more desired job at a research institution. This is a difficult query to handle. On the one hand, any academic employment is probably preferable to none at all, at least over an extended period of time; a five-year employment hiatus in a resume will probably be a red flag in any hiring process. Then, too, many young academics come to a smaller institution intending to move on but find themselves captivated by the attractions and challenges of their "entry level" post and stay on indefinitely.

Others, however, for whom a small institution is a clear "second choice" tend to become unhappy in their work and consequently do not do very well. Certainly, being denied reappointment and/or tenure will not improve the likelihood of career advancement elsewhere.

Of course, there are many instances of a young professor coming to a small institution for a few years, building a good reputation as a teacher and scholar, and then moving on to a larger, more research-oriented school. There is much variability in the perceived quality of liberal arts colleges and in the open-mindedness of search committees. Certainly, it will be easier in most cases to secure employment at the University of Michigan coming from a job at University of California–Berkeley than from, say, Saint Mary's College of California. On the other hand, a candidate employed at Kalamazoo College may have an advantage based on regional familiarity. The more well known the institution, the more likely are favorable reactions from the search committee: a few years at Carleton, Oberlin, or Grinnell are unlikely to hurt a candidate at the state universities of Minnesota, Ohio, or Iowa.

Naturally, it will be important for those seeking to follow this route to make a substantial effort to maintain personal contacts with the "larger world" of professional scholarship and to keep publishing. Staying in touch with the dissertation advisor is a good idea; attending, even at personal expense if necessary, major professional meetings is certainly helpful, especially as a program participant.

A word of caution: while a lack of candor should never be encouraged, it is important to be very "diplomatic" about career plans that call for moving to a research setting. Surprisingly often, beginning college teachers assume that everyone in a liberal arts college faculty wants to be at a major university and are either working diligently to make such a transition or have become resigned to second-rate status.[2] Partially, no doubt, as a defense mechanism but mostly for more genuine reasons, the majority of us who work in smaller institutions do so not because we have to but because we choose to. Offhand comments about "moving up" will not be well received.

In sum, it is not unrealistic to envision one's early career years in a small college setting as a preface to appointment at a research university. It is important for those seeking such a path to build a scholarly resume that will be impressive to recruiters in coming years but to be discreet about these intentions.

• • •

Institutions that place a premium on classroom teaching, which deemphasize research productivity, which are far removed (physically and/or psychically) from major university centers, and which expect a quick and heavy load of on-campus and off-campus community service labor can be challenging places to be while simultaneously completing a doctoral dissertation. The young "ABD" (all but dissertation) academic will need to make a realistic and hardboiled assessment of the possibilities of completing her thesis early along the career path. It is not enough for a school to guarantee access to computer or lab resources or major library resources, although these are very important guarantees indeed. Equally important, and harder to weigh, are time and institutional willingness and understanding of the project. What are the expectations of the college regarding summer work? Are there substantial vacations (fall and spring breaks, midwinter holidays) during which real progress can be made? Will the department and/or institution view with favor requests for minimal committee assignments for a few terms while the dissertation is being completed? These are questions that should be asked before the hiring process is complete, rather than after appointment has begun.

This difficulty can be curiously complicated by conflicting institutional expectations. It is not unprecedented, for example, for a college to insist upon the completion of the terminal degree before a review in the second or third year of employment and simultaneously to make this requirement difficult to fulfill for a very busy instructor. Here, as elsewhere, it is sensible to seek the advice of more than one knowledgeable colleague.

◆ ◆ ◆

Faculty development at a small college will have a slightly different connotation than at a large university. Most small colleges focus their faculty development efforts on pedagogical issues. Efforts to introduce new teaching technologies and methodologies will receive significant attention. Funding sources such as the Archibald Bush Foundation have generously supported such teaching-centered faculty development initiatives at small colleges.

On the other hand, support for research equipment, especially in the sciences and at less wealthy institutions, is often very hard to find. Similarly, most small college faculty travel budgets are considerably tighter than at large research universities, where faculty members are often encouraged and funded to participate in multiple professional meetings each year.

Potential faculty members at small colleges should also examine closely the congruence between their sense of what kind of leave program they need and what is offered by the institution. Most colleges do have sabbatical or study leaves, but often the number and arrangement for such leaves is handled more parsimoniously than in major research centers.

◆ ◆ ◆

I have tried to sketch some of the features of academic careers in small colleges with accuracy. I hope the picture that emerges is neither romantically rosy nor forbiddingly bleak. For many of us who have chosen this version of an academic career, it is the quintessence of the collegiate experience: teaching and learning over a broad area, in intense and close intellectual relationships with diverse students and colleagues. If such a culture calls you, you are invited to doff the objectivity of the observing anthropologist and embrace our customs, conventions, and costumes. Small college teaching has never been a more difficult, more rewarding, or more important vocation.

1. What do you see as the central, defining, core mission of this place? Is institutional size relevant to this core purpose? What do you think makes this college distinct from others that may, at first blush, appear similar? Does that mission seem to you to have grown out of the school's history?

2. Do you think that there are other, secondary missions? If so, do they help or hinder the core mission?

3. What do you think is the ideal size for this institution? Why?

4. What seem to be the biggest problems and the greatest achievements the college has made over recent years? What do you think are the major dangers lurking in the next three to five years? the next decade? And what are the greatest opportunities? What is your prophecy for small colleges in general in the coming years?

5. How would you describe the culture of the institution (e.g., intellectually competitive, cooperative, intense, relaxed, friendly, political, etc.)?

6. Any comments regarding financing, student/faculty recruiting, faculty culture, administrative style, physical plant, student life, athletics, liberal learning, curriculum, campus governance, and the like?

7. Why did you decide to come here? Were your expectations accurate? What would you tell someone else considering coming to a similar institution?

8. Is there anything else I should have asked that I did not or that you wish to add?

Interviews were held with the president or chancellor, senior administrators, faculty, students, and trustees.

Throughout *Old Main* I have been using material from my site visits to twelve American colleges. Obviously, no dozen institutions can represent the entire spectrum of small colleges in the nation today, but this group does include a very wide range of missions, history, geography, population, prestige, size, wealth, and the like. Readers will be interested in a bit more information about these schools, both quantitatively and impressionistically. I provide important statistical profile data about each institution in tables A.1 and A.2. This format invites some interesting speculation: there is a remarkable correlation, for example, between size of endowment, tuition rate, first-year retention, and faculty salaries. Wellesley and Grinnell are in the top two slots in all four of these measures.

Following the statistical compilation is a brief narrative description in which I attempt to present some of the less measurable attributes of these institutions, a few idiosyncrasies, my impressions as an open, outside visitor. These descriptions also identify the 238 individuals who were interviewed for this project. In this section I am guided somewhat by the similar section in David Breneman's *Liberal Arts Colleges* (Washington, DC: Brookings Institution, 1994), entitled "The Future" (pp. 116–37). After an exhaustive and detailed economic analysis of liberal arts colleges, Breneman notes that such analyses "miss important intangible factors, such as dedication, commitment, loyalty, sacrifice and belief, which typify and motivate many of those who support these schools. Private colleges have many alumni, friends and employees who believe in them deeply, and an effective president can mobilize enormous support" (137). He then presents a narrative description of some of these factors.

CENTENARY COLLEGE

Occupying a suburban-feeling campus two miles removed from the center of Shreveport, Louisiana, Centenary is actually the oldest institution among my sample, dating its origins to 1825, but the Shreveport facility is just less than a century old: the college moved there from Jackson in 1908.

The college is a self-contained mixture of older and newer buildings in a variety of harmonious architectural styles, emphasizing traditional Georgian red brick structures. Because it is in the midst of the city, the campus is compact, and bounded, although it gives no impression of congestion or crowding.

Centenary has been coeducational since the end of the nineteenth century, primarily an undergraduate liberal arts college with a few preprofessional majors and modest graduate offerings. There is occasional comment on campus about the relationship between these newer programs and the traditional undergraduate liberal arts curriculum. Although there are some commuter students, it is largely residential. The college's historical affiliation with the Methodist Church remains an important characteristic but in a relatively general and nonsectarian fashion: the college prides itself on a tradition of service and ethical cultivation but makes few denominational claims upon its community.

Centenary seems to the visitor a school with a strong and positive regional repute, a school that would very much like to move to a more national stage. At the same time there are some concerns about the level of interest among potential students in the liberal arts and the college's ability to recruit a sufficient quantity of the sort of students it wants.

During my campus visit I met with thirteen faculty members, the provost and the president (Dr. Ken Schwab), three additional members of the senior staff (dean of students, vice president of finance and administration, and athletic director), and four trustees (the college has a very large board—forty-eight members when fully staffed).

Happily, most images of the antebellum old South are gone with the wind, in Shreveport as elsewhere. Still, it would not be easy to confuse Centenary with a small liberal arts college in Maine, either for the lush greenery of the campus or the equally lush cordiality and friendliness of the collegiate atmosphere.

Centenary is somewhat quirky for maintaining an NCAA Division I intercollegiate athletic program. It is the smallest institution in the nation in that category.

Although I describe Centenary College here first because that is its alphabetical place, it would be my observation as well that it comes as close to a "median" institution as would be found among the dozen sample colleges. In most of the quantifiable characteristics noted earlier and in its atmosphere, campus facilities, history, aspirations, and challenges, Cente-

Table A.1 Student Profile

College	Location	Founding Date	No. Undergrad Full-time Students	No. Part-time Students	Percentage		
					White	Retention Rate	Out-of-State
Centenary	Shreveport, LA	1825	888	22	85	75	40
Colby-Sawyer	New London, NH	1837	871	30	95	81	69
College of New Rochelle	New Rochelle, NY	1904	3776	439	29	61	21
George Fox	Newberg, OR	1891	1314	350	90	82	39
Grinnell	Grinnell, IA	1846	1301	37	69	92	86
Minneapolis College of Art and Design	Minneapolis, MN	1886	505	75	80	NA	36
Morehouse	Atlanta, GA	1867	2548	154	2	84	76
Southwestern	Georgetown, TX	1840	1294	26	82	87	8
Warren Wilson	Asheville, NC	1894	773	10	90	64	79
Wellesley	Wellesley, MA	1870	2201	72	48	96	80
Westmont	Santa Barbara, CA	1937	1360	14	87	84	35
University of Wisconsin—Superior	Superior, WI	1893	2003	431	95	66	42
Average			1569	138	77[a]	79	51

Source: U.S. News and World Report, America's Best Colleges, 2003; Barron's Profiles of American Colleges, 25th ed. (Hauppauge, N.Y., 2001).
[a]Excluding Morehouse.

Table A.2 Financial Profile

College	Carnegie Class	Endowment (in Dollars)	Tuition for 2002–3 (in Dollars)	Average Faculty Salary, All Ranks, 2002–3 (in Thousands of Dollars)
Centenary	Master's I	116,124,000	16,450	53.5
Colby-Sawyer	Baccalaureate-General	16,338,000	21,140	50.2
College of New Rochelle	Master's I	16,900,000	12,470 (01–02)	60.3
George Fox	Master's I	16,919,000	18,875	47.2 (2001–2)
Grinnell	Baccalaureate–Liberal Arts	1,114,000,000	23,530	70.5
Minneapolis College of Art and Design	Specialized–Art, Music, Design	37,327,000	21,800	47.7
Morehouse	Baccalaureate–Liberal Arts	101,000,000	13,760	52.4
Southwestern	Baccalaureate	341,000,000	17,570	60.8
Warren Wilson	Master's II	30,718,000	15,848	45.2
Wellesley	Baccalaureate	1,253,385,000	26,702	87.5
Westmont	Baccalaureate	14,838,000	22,256	60.5
University of Wisconsin–Superior	Master's I	8,500,000	3,233[a]	54.8
Average		255,587,400	17,802	52.5

Source: Carnegie Commission (www.carnegiefoundation.org); Yahoo Education (http://education.yahoo.com); http://Petersons.com; U.S. News and World Report; AAUP.
[a]In-state tuition.

nary is the institution among the twelve I would cite as the most characteristic of typical small colleges today.

COLBY-SAWYER COLLEGE

Early in the nineteenth century, the citizens of New London, New Hampshire, created an academy for the schooling of local students. The original
academy building still stands on the archetypical New England town green
of this southern New Hampshire town. The school was renamed for its
first teacher and administrator, Susan Colby, in 1878. Then, in 1928, the
coeducational academy became a women's junior college, under the presidency of H. Leslie Sawyer. In 1943 the college was chartered to offer
the baccalaureate degree, in 1975 it was renamed to recognize President
Sawyer, and in 1989 it returned to coeducation.

Although the college continued to evolve and some notable additions
were made to the physical plant and program, Colby-Sawyer College faced
some severe fiscal challenges in the mid-1980s. Two dramatically successful presidencies led the college to meet and overcome those trials. The first
president, serving from the mid-1980s to the mid-1990s, increased enrollment, renovated facilities, and led a successful capital campaign. Like a
triage physician, her style was not always one that allowed the luxury of
gentleness. From 1996 to the present Colby-Sawyer has been led, equally
successfully but quite differently, by Dr. Anne Ponder, who has continued
the fiscal and physical successes of the prior decade but also has restored
community morale and uplifted campus esprit.

New London is an increasingly gentrifying southern New England
town, in the midst of the charming Sunapee Lake region. The town has attracted retirees and summer residents, giving it a rather urbane feel. The
college campus is on the town's main street, adjacent to the attractive business district.

No longer grappling with issues of basic survival, Colby-Sawyer has, for
the past several years, been reexamining itself and building a vision of
what sort of institution it wishes to become in future decades. The college
has overtly evolved a dual mission of liberal learning and career preparation which seems widely understood and accepted across major campus
and off-campus constituencies.

During my visit to Colby-Sawyer I met with the president, the academic
vice president and dean, three members of the senior leadership group
(the vice presidents for advancement and for student development and the

treasurer), five trustees and former trustees, four faculty members, and four students.

Colby-Sawyer sees itself as an "enabling" institution, one that adds significant value to students during the undergraduate years. The campus exudes a bracing spirit of friendliness and hearty cheerfulness of greater than usual proportions: one senses that there is a realization that today the college is doing well and a collective recollection of a not-too-distant time when well-being was not a given.

GEORGE FOX UNIVERSITY

George Fox University, in the pleasant town of Newberg, Oregon, about an hour's drive west of Portland, belies many of the expectations one might have of a Quaker college. Named for the founder of the Society of Friends and a deeply religious institution, George Fox is nonetheless quite removed from the Earlham/Guilford/Swarthmore orb. (Candor requires me to reveal that I spent a decade as the chief academic officer at another Quaker college, Guilford in Greensboro, North Carolina.) George Fox positions itself strongly in the midst of evangelical Christian colleges. Its threefold admissions brochure, for example, twice describes the institution as "Christ-centered" but does not mention the Society of Friends or Quakerism. In 2000 the trustees approved a ten-point "Statement of Faith" which, for example, affirms that "we believe God inspired the Bible and has given it to us as the uniquely authoritative, written guide for Christian living and thinking. As illumined by the Holy Spirit, the Scriptures are true and reliable." When I spoke to a group of five students, all had searched for a small, Christian college when making their higher education choices; none had examined any other Quaker schools. At the same time, both faculty and administration are quite clear that George Fox University's Christianity is filtered through the historical lens of the Society of Friends: concerns such as social justice and peace occupy a more prominent place in the campus consciousness, they affirm, than they likely would at a non-Quaker Christian college.

As discussed in chapter 7, George Fox has moved beyond its traditional liberal arts programs in Newberg and offers graduate programs, degree completion programs, and seminary degrees in five locations. The Newberg campus retains most of the programs and atmosphere of a traditional, residential, liberal arts Christian college; the majority of the graduate and seminary offerings are at the other venues.

The Newberg campus is, as one might expect in the rural Pacific North-west, very green. It is eclectic in architecture with some stunning modern buildings as well as some handsome older structures, including Minthorn Hall, a wooden two-story academic unit that is one of the original college buildings.

George Fox is, if not an especially Friendly college, a very friendly one. The students and staff on campus seem remarkably open and genuinely eager to be helpful and welcoming. It is also one of the more homogeneous campuses I visited: 61 percent of the students are from Oregon; 90 percent are white.

At Newberg I met with President David Brandt and with the vice presidents for academic affairs and for marketing and advancement, the chief finance officer, five students (mostly majoring in business-related areas), and three faculty members. All the conversations were open, and in every case students, faculty, and administration were eager to talk about the college's religious emphasis as well as its attention to academic and scholarly concerns. The relationship between the liberal arts emphasis and the newer, non-baccalaureate programs came up frequently.

George Fox University gives the impression of an institution that knows it is operating in a very challenging and competitive marketplace and that it does not have enormous resources to throw into the fray. What it does have, which seems to be serving it very well, is a strong sense of niche and of mission. A pervasive belief that the college is devoted to serving a higher cause generates optimism, enthusiasm, and loyalty.

GRINNELL COLLEGE

With an endowment of over $1.1 billion and a student population of about thirteen hundred, Grinnell College is, on a per-student basis, one of America's richest colleges. (You should know that I am a 1964 graduate of Grinnell.) By almost any measure it is also one of the best. It attracts very strong students to its mid-Iowa campus, connects them to an outstanding faculty, and uses its resources to enhance its educational programs and physical facilities in a very wide variety of imaginative and stimulating ways. Grinnell's wealth strikes some as an interesting incongruity, given that the campus has a reputation, not wholly undeserved, for having an activist, generally very liberal, population. Sometimes the social causes espoused on campus seem to contrast with the vast resources available to support them. The college comes by its reputation for social engagement historically: the discipline of political science was arguably invented at Grinnell; the college graduated a number of major figures in Roosevelt's New Deal government; it was an early hotbed of anti-nuclear and anti–Vietnam War activism.

Grinnell, Iowa, is unmistakably a rural midwestern town. It has an aura of prosperity, aided in part by the contribution of the college, but it would never be mistaken for Santa Barbara, California, or Wellesley, Massachusetts. The college campus, on the edge of the downtown area, fronts a U.S. highway. It is a collection of buildings from different eras, many of which are quite handsome, all of which seem to be in very good condition, and few of which seem to have been designed with a particular eye toward blending in with the others: the college has always sought to build structures that speak to their use and their era, and the result is an attractive anthology of very different architectural styles and materials. In recent years the college has also acquired a number of residential properties adjacent to campus, renovated them charmingly, and used them to house offices, centers, and other small collegiate operations.

Grinnell abolished most graduation requirements several decades ago and has not brought most of them back. To some this might seem an invitation to academic irresponsibility. This is an impression immediately dispelled by observing the scholarly assertiveness of the students and the professorial rigor of the faculty.

At Grinnell I met with President Russell Osgood; the vice president for academic affairs and dean of the college; the vice presidents for diversity, for business, and for student services; the director of the art gallery; four faculty members (one of whom, George Drake, might have at different times been in two other sessions, as he served as president of the college and is also a graduate); a trustee; and three students.

Grinnellians know how good the college is; they are very far from complacent. Indeed, there is something of an edge to constituent relations there: at one point a group of faculty members affirmed they really hoped there would develop a worse relationship between the president and the dean! As president, Dr. Drake accurately described the Grinnell faculty as "yeasty."

Although Grinnell can be a home for humor, lightheartedness, and even frivolity, the overwhelming impression given by the college is one of seriousness: the students are serious about studying, the faculty is serious about teaching, the administration is serious about managing. The whole campus community is serious about liberal learning and social engagement.

Although few realize it, Grinnell College has a place in the verbal memory banks of virtually all Americans: it was to the college's first major benefactor, the abolitionist and social reformer J. B. Grinnell, that Horace Greeley said, "Go West, young man."

MINNEAPOLIS COLLEGE OF ART AND DESIGN

Minneapolis College of Art and Design (MCAD) is in many ways the institution among my sample twelve which is farthest from the conventional small liberal arts college. Although there is a general education component to the undergraduate curriculum at MCAD, it is a relatively small part of the program, and nobody attends the institution to acquire a liberal arts baccalaureate. The college's mission is the education of professional artists, and its students and faculty are dedicated with uniform wholeheartedness to that goal.

Nor does MCAD fit into most stereotypes of what a small college should look like. It is in the midst of a major midwestern city, tucked next to the Twin Cities' largest museum of art, the Minneapolis Institute of Arts. The small campus of modern buildings has a very urban look and feel. Inside, too, it is quickly apparent that MCAD is wholly engaged in the visual arts. The campus buildings are filled with studio space, and everywhere one turns there are striking works of visual art.

MCAD offers one bachelor of science degree (visualization), a master in fine arts degree in visual studies, a number of certificate programs and continuing education offerings, but mostly concentrates on work at the bachelor of fine arts level. The range of majors says much about the range of student and faculty interests: advertising design, animation, comic art, drawing, filmmaking, fine arts studio, furniture design, graphic design, illustration, interactive media, painting, photography, printmaking, and sculpture. It is obvious from this list, and from talking to students, faculty, and staff at MCAD, that vocational possibilities as well as aesthetic interests are on the institutional agenda.

Not unexpectedly, a room full of MCAD students is unlikely to be confused with a similar gathering at, say, George Fox University. But the somewhat less conventional appearance of MCAD students should not be taken for any lack of seriousness. Indeed, in many ways the students with whom I met at this college were clearer than average about what they wanted out of the baccalaureate years and about the level of dedicated work required to get them where they were going. There seemed very little of the sometimes charming, sometimes frustrating aimlessness of some undergraduates to be found here. Interestingly, MCAD places a significant emphasis on technology. Students cited as one of the features of the college they liked best the accessibility and state-of-the-art computer facilities.

In 2001–2 the twelve-year president of the college stepped down, and MCAD chose as his successor Michael O'Keefe. President O'Keefe is a physicist by training, has managed a large philanthropic foundation, and was a member of both Minnesota governor Jesse Ventura's cabinet (Human Services) and the University of Minnesota Board of Regents. Obviously, the college was seeking as its CEO an effective public citizen, not a practicing artist.

At MCAD I met with President O'Keefe, with the dean of students, with a large group of students (about twenty), and with a dozen faculty members. In these formal conversations but also listening to discussions in hallways, studios, galleries, and the small campus coffee shop, it is clear that students and faculty members alike are nearly obsessive about their creative work. (On most of my campus visits, I spent a few productive hours lurking—and listening—in the campus café or coffee nook.) The college offers some modest nonartistic recreational outlets—an intramural softball team; trips to local markets, clubs, restaurants—but there is no mistaking that MCAD is focused on teaching art to growing artists.

As one who has spent a lifetime perusing college publications, I have never encountered materials as idiosyncratic and arresting as those produced by MCAD. The 2002–3 catalog, for example, is filled with far more pictures than words—photos, paintings, comics—and includes a substantial "Sketchbook" section of blank and ruled paper. It is also notched at top and bottom to accommodate a rubber band. There are course descriptions, but there is also a "Portfolio" section of student work which is over sixty pages in length. If ever a college bulletin was a work of art, MCAD has produced it.

MOREHOUSE COLLEGE

Morehouse is doubly distinctive as one of the nation's leading historically African American liberal arts colleges and as one of the very few remaining men's colleges. Not surprisingly, these two attributes reinforce and strengthen each other: a deep sense of brotherhood seems to pervade the campus. Indeed, *strength* is a word that often comes to mind in the More-house context. If a strong institution is one that knows what it is and has inspired the loyalty and dedication to survive in the face of any peril, More-house seems to me about as strong as they come.

Morehouse College is located in west Atlanta, not far from the center of the city, in a largely minority neighborhood. It is one of the larger cam-puses I visited, and the impression of its substantial size is strongly re-inforced by the fact that Morehouse is nested among the other institu-tional members of the Atlanta University Center: Clark Atlanta University, the Interdenominational Theological Seminary, Morehouse School of Medicine, Morris Brown College, and Spellman College. There are some shared facilities—most notably, the library. To a visitor the institutions blend together seamlessly, and the resulting impression is of a rather large university community. The area surrounding the college and the center is largely urban residential. It is not affluent.

Morehouse College is justly proud of its tradition of educating leaders for America's black community: the college's connection to Dr. Martin Luther King, a member of the class of 1948, is frequently mentioned and publicly celebrated.

Morehouse, along with two other of my sample colleges, Southwestern and Centenary, is a member of the Associated Colleges of the South, a rel-atively small consortium of institutions, most of which have a national reputation (e.g., Davidson, Trinity, the University of the South, Washing-ton and Lee). This consortium is discussed in chapter 7.

At Morehouse I met with three trustees, all of whom were graduates of the institution and all of whom were leading professionals in the Atlanta community. I met with two student groups of five individuals each, one of them composed of the leadership of the student government association. In one group students were from Ghana, Texas, New York, and California; in the other they hailed from Trinidad, North Carolina, Georgia, and Al-abama. Both student groups emphasized how important it was to them that Morehouse trained leaders. I had an extensive interview with one fac-ulty member (an alumni) and an informal lunch with an additional nine professors. And I had a discussion with President Walter Massey, a physi-cist and former provost of the University of California system and director of the National Science Foundation as well as a graduate of Morehouse. The prominence of Morehouse graduates among the college faculty and leadership is not an accident: it is clearly one result of the powerful bonding that goes on among Morehouse men.

THE COLLEGE OF NEW ROCHELLE

Beginning in the late 1960s and continuing through the next decade, the College of New Rochelle (CNR) in suburban New Rochelle, New York, reinvented itself, in some ways, in order to stay the same. As documented in chapter 7 of the text, CNR was historically a Roman Catholic undergraduate liberal arts college for women. Challenged by the changing roles of Catholic schools, women's colleges, and liberal arts colleges, CNR added graduate programs, a School of Nursing, and a program of continuing education which together have grown to be much larger than the traditional School of Arts and Sciences but which have enabled that school to continue to flourish—as a small, Roman Catholic undergraduate liberal arts college for women.

New Rochelle is some twenty miles north of Manhattan, a pleasant suburban city. The college's New Rochelle campus is located in a residential neighborhood, not far from a small downtown area. The campus is mostly a cluster of harmonious Gothic structures, built of a warm, light-tan stone. At the core of the campus is the nineteenth century Leland Castle, a Gothic Revival residential mansion that dates from the 1850s. The castle has housed a number of the college's operations over the years and continues to be the home for its central administrative offices. Just as Morehouse College looks larger than it actually is, due to the proximity of the other institutions of the Atlanta University Center, CNR looks smaller than its population statistics would suggest because so many of its students actually work in the cluster of peripheral campuses around the New York region and are not housed in New Rochelle. Today more than two-thirds of the overall student population of CNR are students of color; white students are, in fact, the minority of the pupils (interestingly, this is also the case at Wellesley, the other women's college in the group).

CNR takes pride in being the first Catholic women's college in New York, and it is apparent to today's visitor that the school has remained focused on that identity, at least within the School of Arts and Sciences. It is important to CNR students, faculty, and administration that it is a women's institution; it is important that it is Catholic. Most of the students with whom I spoke at CNR made their college choice from among small

Catholic colleges; relatively few of them were seeking specifically a single-sex institution.

At CNR I spoke with the president, Dr. Stephen Sweeny (who came to the college in 1977 as an assistant to the provost, taught educational psychology, and held several administrative positions, including that of chief academic officer); a group of five deans and senior leaders; two student groups (one a first-year Honors seminar class of about a dozen, the other a group of six upperclass students); and a group of eight faculty members (mostly but not exclusively from the School of Arts and Sciences).

Everyone I spoke with at the College of New Rochelle emphasized the quality of individualized attention the college provides, the strong cooperative spirit, and the development of strong, independent women leaders. It is my subjective impression that there remains, even at the dawn of the twenty-first century, a perceptible difference in the overall tone of conversations with women at women's colleges compared to coed institutions. At the College of New Rochelle and at Wellesley, students, women faculty, and administrators seem to this interviewer more comfortably assertive, more confident in disagreeing with others (including male figures of authority), less verbally cautious, and less self-conscious about speaking out. Certainly, women at Grinnell or Westmont and other coed colleges do assert themselves, especially in academic or governance conversations. And certainly those at the women's schools are not without diplomacy. But patterns of social interaction change glacially, and at the women's colleges, it seems to me, women grow more accustomed to diplomacy without delicacy and cultivate a habitual pattern of interacting with others with firmness.

SOUTHWESTERN UNIVERSITY

Like Texas itself, the campus of Southwestern in Georgetown is open, spacious, and winningly attractive. The college is composed almost exclusively of two- and three-story buildings made of a light brownish gray limestone in a simple Romanesque gabled style. While the campus is not without trees, it also features large areas of open lawn, neatly interspersed with sidewalks, fountains, and landscape plantings. Southwestern is located a few blocks from Georgetown's attractive small town center. The campus sense of manicured space is enhanced by the fact that one side of the college is bounded by its golf course. Although Georgetown itself still has much of the feel of a slightly gentrified Texas small town, as President

Jake Schrum remarks, the lights of Austin glow on the horizon, and sub-urbanization seems inevitable.

Of the twelve sample colleges Southwestern has the third largest en-dowment, after Wellesley and Grinnell. It also has the third highest freshman-to-sophomore retention rate and the third highest faculty salary average. Remarkably, it also has the highest percentage of in-state under-graduates—higher, for example, than the University of Wisconsin–Supe-rior, George Fox University, and the College of New Rochelle. For those Texas students, however, admission is highly selective, and the quantita-tive test measures of academic quality are high: SAT cumulative scores are over 1100. It is difficult to tell if Southwestern University is an exception-ally fine regional school or a national level liberal arts college that just hap-pens to attract most of its students from Texas.

My visit to Southwestern included conversations with President Schrum (who has been at the college now three times, having come to Southwestern as a student, then returned as a young faculty member and beginning administrator, and finally coming back again as president); a member of the board of trustees; the associate vice president for university relations and two staff members; nine members of the faculty; ten mem-bers of the senior staff, again including the president; and seven students.

Southwestern's current president follows the long and very successful tenure of his predecessor, Roy B. Shilling Jr. He, and the college, seem to have the opportunity to build on a base of considerable strength. President Schrum holds a master of divinity degree, and it is interesting to observe how Southwestern seems to be reinvigorating, and reinventing, its Meth-odist inheritance for a new millennium. While the college is far less sec-tarian than, say, Westmont or George Fox, the number and range of organ-izations and activities that seem to have an overtly spiritual base is notable. Thus, for example, the college sponsored a major symposium in February 2003 on "Spiritualities of Resistance"; a 2002 issue of the college's alumni and friends magazine featured a lengthy article on the pursuit of environ-mental justice; and Southwestern is investing considerable resources and energy in a new multidimensional liberal arts "Paideia Program," which focuses upon providing all students with an intercultural experience, a leadership experience, a service learning experience, and a collaborative learning experience. Southwestern has defined for itself a statement of "core values," which it widely publicizes on and off campus: "promoting lifelong learning and a passion for intellectual and personal growth; fostering diverse perspectives; being true to one's self and others; respecting the worth and dignity of persons; and encouraging activism in the pursuit of justice and the common good."

WARREN WILSON COLLEGE

Rather like Orwell's barnyard menagerie, all small colleges are unique, but some are more unique than others. Among twelve very different institutions Warren Wilson stands out as especially distinctive. Moreover, its idiosyncrasy is highly self-conscious and seems to be a universal point of pride. The college's most recent view book, for example, proclaims on its cover "Warren Wilson College: we're not for everyone . . . but then, maybe you're not everyone."

Although its mailing address is the small city of Asheville, North Carolina, Warren Wilson is actually located in the smaller community of Swannanoa, in a gorgeous valley nestled in the Craggy Range of the Blue Ridge Mountains. Warren Wilson is visible from the Blue Ridge Parkway, and it is not a difficult hike from the campus to the parkway. The campus itself is a conglomeration of generally small buildings, many of which are, have been, or were designed to appear to have been homes. The campus is hilly, densely wooded, with curving roads and walks. It is surrounded by the fields of the college's farm. Warren Wilson retains a loose affiliation with the Presbyterian Church and also retains a strong sense of its heritage as a farm school.

One of Warren Wilson's more distinctive features is that it does indeed have a farm, and students work it. In fact, every student at the college is given a campus work assignment—for example, custodial, agricultural, clerical, or maintenance—each term. Fifteen hours per week are expected. One might be assigned to the forestry crew or to working as a blacksmith or serving as a student representative to the board of trustees. (The small group of "work colleges"—Warren Wilson, Blackburn, Berea, Deep Springs —is discussed in chap. 3.) Work is one of three points of Warren Wilson's defining "triad." The other two are learning and service. All students are required to accumulate at least one hundred service hours over four years. Two recent additions to the mission are internationalism and environmental awareness. These characteristics are often deliberately synergistic. Thus, as an example, much of the farmwork is done in an environmentally protective manner, using Belgian workhorses for fieldwork; Warren Wilson maintains an organic garden, the student center features a vegetarian café, and several recent buildings, including an eco-dorm, have been designed to be environmentally sensitive. In recent years the college has forged a strong connection with the wilderness expedition program Outward Bound, the regional offices of which are adjacent to campus.

Its location in the mountains of western North Carolina provides the college with other rare programs and qualities. It is home to an annual mountain music festival, the Swannanoa Gathering (President Doug Orr is an accomplished traditional musician and singer). Varsity sports include the traditional offerings of basketball, soccer, cross-country, and swimming but also mountain biking and canoeing/kayaking (all for both men and women), and club sports (which are all coed) include triathlon, climbing, and ultimate Frisbee.

For many years Warren Wilson faculty lived on campus, with housing constituting a substantial portion of their compensation. This is much less the case today, although the system has not yet entirely vanished.

My visit to Warren Wilson included conversations with President Orr; the deans of student life and of work and the academic dean; two members of the student caucus; the current and the incoming chairs of the board of trustees; and a group of about eight faculty members.

If one of the keys to success for small colleges in the coming decades is creating a niche, defining a distinguishing mission, Warren Wilson College is well placed. Its program, emphases, population, and atmosphere are unmistakably its own. And, in a way that commands respect from admirers and detractors of its vision alike, the college practices what it preaches.

WELLESLEY COLLEGE

Wellesley College is usually ranked in the top handful of American liberal arts colleges, commonly the top women's college in the country—for example, in the 2004 *U.S. News and World Report* ratings it is ranked fourth. It is an institution of imposing physical, fiscal, historical, and human resources.

Wellesley's campus is impressive. Located in a bustling and affluent suburb only twelve miles from Boston's downtown, the campus landscape was designed by Frederick Law Olmsted, who created, among other notable American landscapes, that of Central Park in New York and the Biltmore Estate in North Carolina. Set amid lakes, groves, hills, and winding paths are buildings of various styles and eras, with the dominant theme being collegiate Gothic. The older major structures on the campus (including Green Hall, Founders, and Tower Court) are designed and sited to create an impression of authority and educational seriousness. Wellesley shows little of the cozy "cottage" style that characterized some women's colleges; rather, its buildings suggest that here is a major institution that is to be taken seriously.

Among the most impressive structures is the Science Center, originally built in 1927 and with a substantial recent addition. Wellesley notes that it was the second college in the country to have a physics laboratory and that its observatory opened in the nineteenth century.

My interviews at Wellesley included President Diana Chapman Walsh; two students (an American studies and theater major from Atlanta and an economics and German major from Albania); an associate dean and graduate, the vice president for finance and treasurer (also a graduate); the dean of the college and a professor of chemistry (and the faculty director of the Science Center).

Two aspects of student life at Wellesley seem remarkable. The first is that, for a student body of just over two thousand, there are 160 campus organizations (discussed in chap. 3). These groups cover a remarkable range of interests and activities. A random look down the list of R's shows: Real Life (a religious group); Reality Alterations (a role-playing game group); the Recycling Committee; Religious Society of Friends; Republicans; Rugby; and the Russian Club. Wellesley advertises itself as a campus with "an activity for every student," and this does not seem a false claim. Second, and even more impressively, is that Wellesley's student body is now 52 percent "minority." Wellesley has used its national prestige and its international fame to recruit what is surely one of the most diverse student populations of any small, elite college (currently, students come from all fifty states and from over sixty-five foreign nations). When I visited Wellesley, I accompanied an Admissions Office campus tour: at least four languages were being spoken by the dozen or so individuals taking the walk with me.

The campus, student activities, and diverse demographics are some of the features that make Wellesley College interesting and distinctive, but its primary claim to its place among America's small colleges resides with its magnificent academic program. Wellesley's students are academically gifted—average SAT scores in 2002 were 673 Verbal and 673 Math. Seventy-five percent of Wellesley students who apply to medical school and 90 percent who apply to law school are admitted. The college's faculty are equally impressive. They are the best paid, by a significant margin, among my sample institutions, and their teaching load is four courses per year. The faculty members, like the students, are unusually diverse, and class sizes are uniformly small. Wellesley also has the resources to offer courses, departments, and majors in areas not often found in smaller institutions: there are departments of Africana Studies, Japanese, Astronomy, Chinese, Classics, and Russian. There are many interdepartmental majors—for example, in Neuroscience, Cognitive and Linguistic Studies, Astrophysics, and Biological Chemistry. Wellesley offers students even more intellectual opportunities through exchange programs with Babson College, Brandeis University, Spelman College, and Mills College and as a member of the Twelve College Exchange Program with Amherst, Bowdoin, Connecticut College, Dartmouth, Mount Holyoke, Smith, Trinity, Vassar, Wesleyan, Wheaton, and Williams (this group also offers one-semester programs in theater and marine studies).

Bucolic, diverse, imposing, ambitious, scholarly: Wellesley comes by its status as one of America's elite colleges honestly.

WESTMONT COLLEGE

It is a commonly held, and not too carefully examined, belief that to the extent that a collegiate institution advances a sectarian perspective, it veers toward dogma and away from academic freedom. This is a belief that is not without some basis in fact: as a non-Christian, for instance, I would not be eligible for a faculty or administrative appointment at Westmont College. But Westmont College challenges this association very directly and effectively in its printed materials and in conversations with students, faculty, and staff. For example, a recent student recruitment publication is entitled "Five Great Reasons to Choose a Christian College." Reason number 1 is academic freedom:

> Professors and administrators at the world's top colleges and universities hold one concept dear beyond almost any other: the idea of academic freedom. In order to understand the truth and to allow the best ideas to have dominance in society, they say, we must have the freedom to discuss all ideas. To let them rise and fall on their merits. But just try adding a Christian perspective to the discussion in classrooms on secular campuses around the world, and you may find out where the limits to academic free-

dom lie. Most public institutions in this country are less than warmly receptive to faith-based perspectives and contributions in the classroom. Why limit yourself? . . . Westmont's commitment to academic freedom is obvious, not only in courses that demand your best critical thinking, but also through a wide range of opportunities and organizations that explore the world of ideas.

Westmont's mission is overtly Christian—I cite some examples in chapter 3 of the college's bipartite mission as a liberal arts and religious institution. The Christian perspective clearly dominates much of campus life, from the three-times-a-week Chapel-Convocation Series to a range of missionary service opportunities. The publication cited earlier also states, "Westmont professors are also all Christians eager to share their own faith with students." It also maintains a strong, traditional liberal arts curriculum, recruits academically well-qualified students and faculty, and affirms often the value of liberal learning.

Westmont's campus is built around Kerrwood Hall, an opulent 1929 private residence in the southern California Mediterranean style. A cluster of relatively small, more modern buildings is nestled in a heavily wooded rolling campus set in the foothills of Santa Barbara. The college is in a neighborhood of impressive wealth, within a small gem of a coastal city ninety miles north of Los Angeles. The atmosphere at Westmont is impressively open and warmly friendly. An obvious visitor on campus, I was often approached by students, faculty, and staff who asked if they could help me find something and who seemed genuinely welcoming.

At Westmont I had the opportunity to speak with Dr. Stan Gaede, the president and, in a separate conversation, with Dr. David Winter, the past president. Additionally, I met with the vice president for administration, the associate dean for residence life, the provost, three members of the faculty, and five students. I also attended one of the weekly chapel-convocation events, part of Missions Week, and heard a missionary husband and wife discuss their work in Africa. Most of my conversations returned to the liberal arts / Christian dual mission of the college, both because I find this topic an interesting one and because Westmont's people believe that this is an aspect of their institution which is not much understood, nor particularly respected, in the general higher education community.

Another recurring item of conversation involved Westmont's locale and the opportunities and challenges it poses for the college. Westmont's beautiful little campus is bounded by enormously expensive private holdings: it is unlikely the college could grow substantially. This has imposed on Westmont some size restrictions that the college has embraced: its goal is to get better, not larger. A Santa Barbara location also makes it a challenge to recruit faculty members who are not independently wealthy: housing costs are astronomical compared to normal faculty pay scales. The college has been working to develop some subsidized living arrangements to compensate.

Westmont is a strongly evangelical Christian college that offers a rigorous, challenging liberal arts experience. It also challenges some of the comfortable preconceptions of the larger academic community.

THE UNIVERSITY OF WISCONSIN–SUPERIOR

In 2000 the University of Wisconsin (UW)–Superior was designated Wisconsin's public liberal arts college by the University of Wisconsin Board of Regents, and the following year it became a member of the Council of Public Liberal Arts Colleges (COPLAC). This is a distinct evolutionary step for an institution that has been, for most of its history, primarily a teacher training school. In declaring its liberal arts mission, UW-Superior is also joining an increasingly visible, growing niche in the higher education community. There has been focused liberal learning within the public sector of American postsecondary institutions for a very long time, of course —arguably, since the first public institutions were created in the New World (see chap. 2). But deliberately small undergraduate liberal arts colleges in the public sector had been, until about the mid-1980s relatively rare and quite isolated. Since that time, however, several colleges have both sharpened their liberal arts focus and bonded together—for example, the University of North Carolina–Asheville, St. Mary's College of Maryland, New College, Evergreen State University, and my own institution, the University of Minnesota, Morris. Other institutions, such as UW-Superior, Truman State University (formerly Northeastern Missouri State University), and Henderson State in Arkansas, have overtly embraced a new emphasis and moved into this sector.

UW-Superior occupies a good-looking, largely utilitarian red brick campus. Its oldest building is Old Main Hall, a large Gothic-styled structure that combines offices, including those of the senior administration, classrooms, and computer labs. Much of the campus is pleasant lawn-like grounds: it is relatively unwooded and very flat. Superior itself is the smaller sister city of Duluth, Minnesota. Both are historically industrial areas, although much of the industry of the past (including lumbering, mining, and shipping) no longer flourishes. Duluth has developed something of a tourist base, exploiting its harbor and Lake Superior shoreline. Superior has not. UW-Superior sees itself as a college with a strong blue-collar tradition, although it has attracted a growing number of more cosmopolitan students from metropolitan Wisconsin and Minnesota. The college has launched a quite dramatic public relations campaign in, for example, the Minneapolis / St. Paul area, emphasizing its combination of traditional liberal learning and low cost.

As an institution in transition, UW-Superior seems a "work in progress." Many among its students, faculty, and staff embrace the liberal arts college mission enthusiastically. There remain constituents, however, who are skeptical or reluctant to see the college moving in this direction. The current administration has been vigorous in its affirmation of the mission focus.

At UW-Superior I met with Chancellor Julius Erlenbach and Provost David Prior; four faculty members (in history, teacher education, educational administration, and social work); three students (one of whom has written a paper on the history of the college, one a guidebook for student admission tour leaders, and one a faculty child); a group of other administrators, including the dean of students, the university relations director, and the vice chancellor for administration and finance; and with a member of the University of Wisconsin Board of Regents who comes from the Superior region. I also visited with two faculty members I knew from previous connections at another institution.

I end this survey with UW-Superior due to its alphabetical ordering, but it is also appropriate to conclude with this institution because it represents, quietly, a new kind of small college. As noted several times in *Old Main*, it is generally assumed that small colleges are private institutions. But UW-Superior and its COPLAC colleagues are seeking to build a new model for small public American colleges and universities. They are trying to maintain many of the virtues of smallness, including focused, intentional communities with clear universal liberal arts curricular emphases; integration of classroom and out-of-class life; and long-lasting student-faculty relationships. Simultaneously, they aim to offer some of the benefits of public higher education: the accessibility of low-cost public institutions; the focus on service to the region that supports them; and the recruitment of students, especially first-generation college-goers who might otherwise not consider a small college. Freed from some of the challenges of private philanthropic support faced by many nonelite private colleges, the public liberal arts colleges have to learn to survive the rough-and-tumble of the political process and legislative funding in order to sustain their missions.

UW-Superior faces an interesting pair of challenges. On the one hand, like many institutions (and certainly many small, non-flagship public universities), it is beset by fiscal rigors and seems to find itself in a perpetual mode of belt-tightening. But, on the other hand, the college has defined for itself a new identity, a sharpened and refocused mission, and is appealing to a changing clientele. It was my perception that strong academic and administrative leadership is building a consensus that UW-Superior's future is tied to its new liberal arts emphasis and that it is a challenging but bright future.

• • •

These twelve colleges and universities are, obviously, all quite different from one another, and yet they all share many important characteristics. I have tried to emphasize some of these shared attributes throughout *Old Main*—an effort to create an integrated student experience in and out of the classroom, for example, and to cultivate a pervasive and universal spirit of common enterprise throughout the collegiate community.

One attribute that all twelve colleges seem to share, and which I believe characterizes the overwhelming majority of America's small colleges (and a great many of our universities too, of course), is passionate commitment and deep loyalty. Today's small colleges face many challenges, but it may be that their most powerful resource in overcoming today's and tomorrow's obstacles is that depth of attachment. As I visited these twelve colleges, I was re-impressed at each of them by the ways in which their constituents view them as special places. What America's small colleges may often lack today in visibility and in wealth they make up for with love.

Notes

Chapter 1. Introduction

1. This is a difficult figure to pin down: much depends upon who counts and what is counted. In the Carnegie Classification of Institutions of Higher Education, 2000 ed., 606 institutions, or 15.5 percent of all American postsecondary schools, were classified as "Baccalaureate Colleges." The other classes are Doctoral/Research Universities, Master's Colleges and Universities (which includes numerous colleges usually considered "liberal arts colleges"), Associate's Colleges, Specialized Institutions, and Tribal Colleges. Obviously, the actual number of students enrolled at the Baccalaureate institutions is going to be a smaller percentage, since those institutions tend to be significantly smaller. The average enrollment of Doctoral Research Universities is 16,948, that of Baccalaureate Colleges just 1,516. Based on the 1999 data from the National Center for Educational Statistics (NCES), 1.3 million students were enrolled in Baccalaureate Colleges, of an undergraduate national population of 14.8 million, or 9 percent. The smallest figure I have encountered is Steven Koblik's, which also dates from the year 2000: "Today only 4 percent of all American baccalaureate degrees are awarded at [residential liberal arts colleges]" (foreword to *Distinctively American: The Residential Liberal Arts College* (New Brunswick: Transaction Publishers, 2000), xv). Obviously, Koblik's class of concern is slightly different than mine but overlaps with it. David Breneman (*Liberal Arts Colleges: Thriving, Surviving, or Endangered* [Washington, DC: Brookings Institution, 1994]) states that, in 1987, 4.4 percent of U.S. college students were enrolled in small liberal arts colleges. It is therefore possible to estimate that somewhere between 4 and 10 percent of contemporary undergraduate college students attend small colleges.

2. See, for example, George Keller, *Academic Strategy* (Baltimore: Johns Hopkins University Press, 1983).

3. Virginia Lee Burton, *The Little House* (Boston: Houghton Mifflin, 1942).

4. That is, the sorts of changes that Peter Eckel, Madeleine Green, and Barbara Hill call "adjustments," rather than "transformative," in *On Change V* (Washington, DC: American Council on Education, 2001), 6.

5. Community College of the Air Force Web site: www.au.af.mil/au/ccaf/whoweare.html.

6. Breneman, *Liberal Arts Colleges*.

7. Interview, April 2003.

8. Ernest K. Boyer, *College: The Undergraduate Experience in America* (New York: Harper and Row, 1987).

9. Breneman, *Liberal Arts Colleges*. One of Breneman's major points is that the number of focused liberal arts colleges has shrunk.

10. Virginia Smith and Alison Bernstein, *The Impersonal Campus* (San Francisco: Jossey-Bass, 1979), x; my italics.

11. For example, in G. Grant and D. Riesman, *The Perpetual Dream: Reform and Experiment in the American College* (Chicago: University of Chicago Press, 1978).

12. David G. Winter, David C. McClelland, and Abigail J. Stewart, *A New Case for the Liberal Arts* (San Francisco: Jossey-Bass, 1981). See also, even less "new," Sidney S. Letter, ed., *New Prospects for the Small Liberal Arts College* (New York: Teachers College Press, Columbia University, 1968).

13. Boyer, *College*, 146.

14. Winter, McClelland, and Stewart, *New Case*, 20.

15. *National Survey of Student Engagement*, 2002, 7.

16. Office of Institutional Research and Reporting, University of Minnesota, *Students' Perspectives on Their Experiences at the University of Minnesota* (report, November 2001).

17. Howard R. Bowen, *Investment in Learning: The Individual and Social Value of American Higher Education* (1978; rpt., Baltimore: Johns Hopkins University Press, 1997), 248.

Chapter 2. Go West, Young Man

1. Francis Oakley, *Community of Learning* (New York: Oxford University Press, 1992), 145.

2. A. M. Cohen, *The Shaping of American Higher Education* (San Francisco: Jossey-Bass, 1998), 10.

3. These and several other institutional descriptions are taken from Julia Cass-Liepman, ed., *Cass and Birnbaum's Guide to American Colleges*, 17th ed. (New York: HarperCollins, 1996). Bluffton College is a Mennonite institution, founded at the very end of the nineteenth century. It is located in a small town, which is itself only abut 6 percent the size of Ohio State University, less than a two-hour drive away.

4. John D. Pulliam, *History of Education in America*, 4th ed. (Columbus: Merrill, 1987), 36.

5. Arthur Levine, *Handbook on Undergraduate Curriculum* (San Francisco: Jossey-Bass, 1978), 3 ff.; Francis Oakley, *Community*, 25.

6. Richard Hofstadter and Wilson Smith, eds., *American Higher Education: A Documentary History*, 2 vols. (Chicago: University of Chicago Press, 1961), 1:2.

7. Cohen, *American Higher Education*, 62.

8. Donald Tewksbury, *The Founding of American Colleges and Universities before the Civil War* (New York: Teachers College Press, 1932), 28. Other estimates of the mortality of these early-nineteenth-century colleges are not quite this high.

9. David Breneman, *Liberal Arts Colleges: Thriving, Surviving, or Endangered* (Washington, DC: Brookings Institution, 1994).

10. Donald Scott, "Evangelicalism, Revivalism, and the Second Great Awakening," National Humanities Center, Teacher Serve, Web site, www.nhc.rtp.nc.us/tserve/tserve.htm.

11. Tewksbury, *Founding*, 1.

12. Erin J. Brock, *Centenary College of Louisiana* (Charleston, SC: Arcadia Publishing, 2000), 7–33.

13. Alan Jones, *Pioneering: 1846–1996—A Photographic and Documentary History of Grinnell College* (Grinnell, IA: Grinnell College, 1996), 12–20.

14. Anon., *Southwestern: A University's Transformation* (Georgetown, TX: Southwestern University, 1999), 2–4.

15. Irene Harwarth, Mindi Malne, and Elizabeth DeBra, *Women's Colleges in the United States: History, Issues, and Challenges* (Washington, DC: U.S. Government Printing Office, 1997). See the information on small women's colleges in Charlyn Sewell Fisher, "An Analysis of Factors within Institutional Environments That Are Supportive of Women Students in Five Types of Small Colleges in the United States" (Ph.D. diss., Gonzaga University, 2001).

16. Helen Lefkowitz Horowitz, *Alma Mater: Design and Experience in the Women's Colleges from Their Nineteenth-Century Beginnings to the 1930s* (New York: Knopf, 1985).

17. Harwarth, Malne, and DeBra, "Women's Colleges."

18. Encyclopedia Africana Web site, www.africana.com.

19. L. Dean Webb, Arlene Metha, and K. Fordis Jordan, *Foundations of American Education* (New York: Merrill, 1992) 135.

20. Webb, Metha, and Jordan, *Foundations*, 135.

21. Reprinted, in part, in Hofstadter and Smith, *American Higher Education*, 275–91.

22. Burton R. Clark, *The Distinctive College: Antioch, Reed, and Swarthmore* (Chicago: Aldine, 1970), 172.

23. Cohen, *American Higher Education*, 103; my italics.

24. Pulliam, *History*, 109.

25. George A. Baker, *A Handbook on the Community College in America* (Westport, CT: Greenwood Press, 1994), 7–10.

26. Leland L. Medsker, *The Junior College* (New York: McGraw-Hill, 1960), 11.

27. Carnegie Classification 2000 Web site.

28. Breneman, *Liberal Arts Colleges*, 20

29. Hofstadter and Smith, *American Higher Education*, 697–747, esp. 699.

30. Levine, *Handbook on Undergraduate Curriculum*, 28–53.

31. Levine, *Handbook on Undergraduate Curriculum*, 5.

32. Webb, *Foundations*, 147.

33. Cohen, *American Higher Education*, 105.

34. Christopher Jencks and David Riesman, *The Academic Revolution* (Garden City, NY: Doubleday, 1968), 13.

35. Gerald Graff, *Professing Literature: An Institutional History* (Chicago: University of Chicago Press, 1987), 1.

36. Graff, *Professing Literature*, 55.

37. Richard Ohmann, *English in America: A Radical View of the Profession* (New York: Oxford University Press, 1976), 242. See also Wallace Douglas, "Some Questions about the Teaching of Works of Literary Art," *ADE Bulletin* 25 (May 1970): 31–45; and William Riley Parker, "Where Do English Departments Come From?" *College English* 28 (1967): 339–51.

38. Ohmann, *English in America*, 260.

39. Cohen, *American Higher Education*, 187.

40. Breneman, *Liberal Arts Colleges*, 11–15.

41. Cohen, *American Higher Education*, 192.

42. Cohen, *American Higher Education*, 300–301.

43. Levine, *Handbook on Undergraduate Curriculum*, 359–63. Columbia and the University of Chicago initiated at this time similar curricular reforms that were somewhat less in the public spotlight than the Harvard developments.

44. "A Primer on the Associated New American Colleges," Web site, www.anac .vir.org/.

45. Paul Neely, "The Threats to Liberal Arts Colleges," *Daedalus* 129 (Winter 1999): 27 ff. Reprinted in Koblik and Graubard, *Distinctively American;* and online at ELM Expanded Academic ASAP Plus.

46. Cohen, *American Higher Education*.

Chapter 3. Colleges of Character

1. Of course, there are important and perceptible differences between, say, the University of California–Berkeley and Notre Dame. Indeed, the discerning viewer of higher learning can note distinctions between the universities of Michigan and Minnesota, Iowa and Illinois, which go beyond whether one's mascot is a gopher or a wolverine, a Native American chief or a Hawk-eye. Factors such as geography, regional culture, institutional and local history, areas of particular emphasis and distinction, all define major research universities as individual places. Still, there is a very real sense in which, once an institution reaches the size that it may legitimately be called "comprehensive," it might be said to develop an ever-increasing resemblance to every other such place. *Comprehensive,* after all, means "inclusive," and, the more the University of Michigan can include, the more it looks like Minnesota or Texas or Ohio. It is hard to imagine any campus-based collegiate institution of over thirty thousand students without an English Department, for instance, or a German or Physics or Statistics or Geology curriculum. All such universities are going to have a teacher education program, a football team, a swimming pool

and a motor pool, resident and nonresident students, a Human Resources office, parking stickers, internet access, Ph.D. programs, a phone directory, a bookstore selling campus sweatshirts, homecoming, and so on.

But small colleges can never afford to be comprehensive in any meaningful academic way. They have to pick (or accidentally evolve) what programs they will offer—for example, they might have to choose between French and German or between Geology and Physics. They might, or might not, have a remedial skills center or an indoor track or a fitness center or an African American Studies program or a Women's Center or coursework in geography. Small colleges, of necessity, must be highly selective about what they do, for whom, and how. They are far more likely to be instantly and easily perceived as idiosyncratic, unique, even quirky, than are land-grant state universities, large private research universities, or regional comprehensive colleges.

Obviously, there are ways in which small colleges differ from one another which are also partially or wholly applicable to large universities. Both small colleges and large universities, for example, can operate on a variety of academic calendars; their curricula may be more or less prescribed; they may have a long or a short history; they may be secular or sectarian. In this chapter my goal is to compare small colleges to other small colleges, to sketch the range of diversity within this segment of the educational community; it is not to compare small colleges to larger institutions.

2. Stacy Teicher, "Twenty Six Renaissance Men," *Christian Science Monitor*, 19 February 2002; *Chronicle of Higher Education* (September 2002).

3. Council of Public Liberal Arts Colleges, *Prospectus: The Case for Public Liberal Arts Colleges* (n.p., n.d.), 25.

4. Having spent substantial time at both Deep Springs and the College of Charleston, I can offer firsthand testimony that the size differential only begins to describe the flamboyant differences between these two campuses.

5. Loren Pope, *Colleges That Change Lives* (New York: Penguin, 1996), 8.

6. Alfred T. Hill, *The Small College Meets the Challenge* (New York: McGraw-Hill, 1959); Lewis B. Mayhew, *The Smaller Liberal Arts College* (New York: Center for Applied Research in Education, 1962).

7. S. Koblik and S. R. Graubard, eds., *Distinctively American: The Residential Liberal Arts College* (New Brunswick: Transaction Publishers, 2000).

8. Robert Nesbit Hillcoat, "Should and Can the Small American Liberal Arts Colleges Survive?" (Ph.D. diss., Wayne State University, 1982).

9. National Center for Educational Statistics Web site.

10. Howard R. Bowen, *Investment in Learning: The Individual and Social Value of American Higher Education* (San Francisco: Jossey-Bass, 1978), 248.

11. David W. Breneman, *Liberal Arts Colleges: Thriving, Surviving, or Endangered?* (Washington, DC: Brookings Institution), esp. 11–15. This same figure, 212, is used throughout Koblik and Graubard, *Distinctively American*.

12. Carnegie Classification of Institutions of Higher Education, 2000, Web site, www.carnegiefoundation.org/Classification/CIHE2000/Tables.htm.

13. Colby-Sawyer College catalog, 2002–3, 2–3.

14. Grinnell College catalog, 2001–2, 2.

15. Interview, Provost David Prior, University of Wisconsin–Superior, 30 September 2002.

16. Westmont College catalog, 2002–3, 12–19.

17. George Fox University catalog, 2002–3, 9.

18. Chad J. Jolly, "The Relationship between the 'Official' and 'Operative' Identities of a Private Liberal Arts College" (Ph.D. diss., University of Missouri–Kansas City, 2001).

19. Yeshiva University Web site.

20. Burton R. Clark, *The Distinctive College: Antioch, Reed, and Swarthmore* (Chicago: Aldine, 1970), 99, 13–88.

21. Cited in Julia Cass-Liepman, ed., *Cass and Birnbaum's Guide to American Colleges*, 17th ed. (New York: HarperCollins, 1996).

22. Richard Hersch, "Generating Ideals and Transforming Lives: A Contemporary Case for the Residential Liberal Arts College," in Koblick, *Distinctively American*, 180.

23. Ernest J. Pascarella, Patrick T. Terenzini, and Lee M. Wolfle, "Orientation to College," *Journal of Higher Education* 57 (1986): 155–56.

24. George D. Kuh, John H. Schuh, Elizabeth J. Whitt, and Associates, *Involving Colleges* (San Francisco: Jossey-Bass, 1991), 10.

25. Alexander Astin and Calvin Lee, *The Invisible Colleges* (New York: McGraw-Hill, 1972), 99.

26. Ernest J. Pascarella and Patrick T. Terezini, *How College Affects Students* (San Francisco: Jossey-Bass, 1991), 601.

27. Alexander Astin, *What Matters in College: Four Critical Years Revisited* (San Francisco: Jossey-Bass, 1993), 230.

28. National College Athletics Association 2001 Annual Membership Report.

29. See the fascinating discussion of the athletic tradition at Swarthmore in Clark, *Distinctive College*, 171–230.

30. Astin and Lee, *Invisible Colleges*, 47.

31. Fiscal data from Grinnell College and Wellesley College.

32. See, for example, E. F. Cheit, *The New Depression in Higher Education* (New York: McGraw-Hill, 1971).

33. This information is from the catalogs, in order, of Grinnell College, Wellesley College, the College of New Rochelle, Westmont College, Centenary College, Colby-Sawyer College, St. Andrews Presbyterian College, and George Fox University.

34. Alexander Astin, *Achieving Educational Excellence: A Critical Assessment of Priorities and Practices in Higher Education* (San Francisco: Jossey-Bass, 1985), 4.

35. Julia Cass-Liepmann, *Guide to American Colleges*, 680.

36. Astin and Lee, *Invisible Colleges*, 47.

37. Ibid., 52.

38. Grinnell College catalog.

39. Westmont College admissions brochure, "Five Great Reasons to Choose a Christian College," n.d.

40. Mary Ellen Ashcroft, "Risky Business? Teaching Literature at a Christian Liberal Arts College," *American Experiment Quarterly* (Winter 1999–2000): 24.

41. Ashcroft, "Risky Business," 16.

42. Christopher Jencks and David Riesman, *The Academic Revolution* (Garden City, NY: Doubleday, 1968); also see *The Academic Revolution* by Christopher Jencks and David Riesman for a full and thoughtful, if occasionally opinionated, discussion of American Catholic colleges.

43. Donald Tewksbury, *The Founding of American Colleges and Universities before the Civil War* (New York: Teachers College, 1932), 32–33.

44. Clark, *Distinctive College*.

45. Warren Wilson College, campus interviews, February 2003.

46. G. Grant and David Riesman, *The Perpetual Dream: Reform and Experiment in the American College* (Chicago: University of Chicago Press, 1978), 15–178.

Chapter 4. People at Small Colleges

Epigraph: Interview, 10 February 2003.

1. This is not to slight other constituents—alumni, governing boards, parents, philanthropists, and the like. But students, faculty, and staff are the *inhabitants* of colleges in a unique way.

2. Interview with University Relations staff, Southwestern University, 12 February 2003.

3. Statement from the "Conference on the Growing Use of Part-Time and Adjunct Faculty," Washington, DC, 26–27 September 1997.

4. Eugene L. Anderson, *The New Professoriate* (Washington, DC: ACE, 2002), 13. In many cases the part-time employee is the spouse of a full-time faculty member in a two-career family.

5. Interview, April 2003.

6. NCES, figs. 62, 64, and 65.

7. National Study of Postsecondary Faculty, 1999.

8. Ernest Boyer, *College: The Undergraduate Experience in America* (New York: Harper and Row, 1987), 243.

9. NCES, fig. 139.

10. Anderson, *New Professoriate*, 3.

11. Ibid., 6.

12. AAUP Web site, "Part-time and Non-Tenure-Track Faculty," www.aaupnet.org.

13. James Kissane, *Mild Outbursts* (Grinnell, IA: Grinnell College), 1996; James

Axtell, *The Pleasures of Academe: A Celebration and Defense of Higher Education* (Lincoln: University of Nebraska Press), 1998.

14. Howard R. Bowen, *Investment in Learning: The Individual and Social Value of Higher Education* (San Francisco: Jossey-Bass, 1978), 248.

15. See, for example, "The Measured Effects of Higher Education," *Annals of the American Academy of Political and Social Science* (November 1972): 1–20.

16. A. W. Chickering, "Institutional Size and Student Development" (presentation at the Council for the Advancement of Small Colleges annual meeting, 1965); and "Personality Development and the College Experience," with John McCormick, *Research in Higher Education* 1 (1973): 43–70.

17. K. A. Feldman and T. M. Newcomb, *The Impact of College on Students*, 2 vols. (San Francisco: Jossey-Bass, 1969).

18. C. R. Pace, *Evaluating Liberal Education* (Los Angeles: University of California Press, 1974); and *Measuring Outcomes of College: Fifty Years of Findings and Recommendations for the Future* (San Francisco: Jossey-Bass, 1979), 151.

19. D. A. Rock, J. A. Centra, and R. L. Linn, *The Identification and Evaluation of College Effects on Student Achievement* (Princeton: ETS, 1969).

20. Robert H. Knapp and Joseph J. Greenbaum, *The Younger American Scholar: His Collegiate Origins* (Chicago: University of Chicago Press, 1953); Robert H. Knapp and H. B. Goodrich, *Origins of American Scientists* (New York: Russell and Russell, 1952).

21. Knapp and Greenbaum, *Younger American Scholar*, esp. 47.

22. Ibid., 22.

23. Boyer, *College*, 75.

24. Alexander Astin, *Achieving Educational Excellence: A Critical Assessment of Priorities and Practices in Higher Education* (San Francisco: Jossey-Bass, 1985).

25. Russell Kirk, *Decadence and Renewal in the Higher Learning* (South Bend, IN: Gateway Editions, 1975), xv, xvi, 82.

26. This conclusion was expressed, usually hesitantly, at several of my campus interviews (e.g., Southwestern University, where an institutional decision has been made to cease using the word *nurturing* and start using the word *empowering* in recruitment materials) and in conversations with student affairs professionals.

27. Astin, *What Matters in College: Four Critical Years Revisited* (San Francisco: Jossey-Bass, 1993).

28. "How the Liberal Arts College Affects Students," in *Distinctly American*, 83.

29. Wellesley College view book, "Make a Difference," 37.

30. The George Fox University Annual Report, 2000–2001, fig. F-1. Similarly, at George Fox 344 of 345 entering freshmen reported themselves as having a protestant Christian denominational affiliation.

31. Interview, Southwestern University, 12 February 2003.

32. Clark, *Distinctive College*.

33. Deborah Jean Swiss, "The Evolution of a Small College Presidency: Bowdoin College, 1885–1978" (Ph.D. diss., Bowling Green University, 1993).

34. Gary Bonvillian and Robert Murphy, *The Liberal Arts College Adapting to Change* (New York: Garland, 1996).

35. Arthur F. Kirk Jr., "Strategies to Affect the Survival of a Small College: A Case Study" (Ed.D. diss., Columbia University, 1984).

36. Helen Lefkowitz Horowitz, *Alma Mater: Design and Experience in the Women's College from Their Nineteenth-Century Beginnings to the 1930s* (New York: Knopf, 1985).

37. P. F. Kluge, *Alma Mater: A College Homecoming* (Reading, MA: Addison-Wesley, 1993).

38. Roger Kimball, *Tenured Radicals: How Politics Has Corrupted Our Higher Education* (New York: Harper, 1990), 2.

39. Charles Kors and Harvey Silvergate, *The Shadow University: The Betrayal of Liberty on America's Campuses* (New York: Free Press, 1998).

40. Rita Bornstein, *Legitimacy in the Academic Presidency* (Westport, CT: Praeger, 2003).

41. A sampling of studies of the American college presidency, especially at small colleges: F. Stuart Gulley, *The Academic President as Moral Leader* (Macon, GA: Mercer University Press, 2001); James Fisher and James Koch, *Presidential Leadership: Making a Difference* (Westport, CT: Greenwood, 1996); Mary Kay Murphy, *The Advancement President and the Academy: Profiles in Institutional Leadership* (Westport, CT: Greenwood, 1997); Robert Birnbaum, *How Academic Leadership Works: Understanding Success and Failure in the College Presidency* (San Francisco: Jossey-Bass, 1992); Ann Sontz, *The American College President, 1636–1989: A Critical Review and Bibliography* (Westport, CT: Greenwood, 1991); Francis Oakley, *Leadership Challenges of a College Presidency* (Lewiston, NY: Edwin Mellin Press, 2002); Joseph Crowley, *No Equal in the World: An Interpretation of the Academic Presidency* (Las Vegas: University of Nevada Press, 1995); Peter Sammartino, *The President of a Small College* (Rutherford, NJ: Fairleigh Dickinson College Press, Associated University Presses, 1954); Duane Dagley, ed., *Courage in Mission: Presidential Leadership in the Church-Related College* (Washington, DC: CASE, 1988); James Fisher, *The Power of the Presidency* (New York: ACE, Macmillan, 1984); Lyman A. Glenny et al., *Presidents Confront Reality: From Edifice Complex to the University without Walls* (San Francisco: Jossey-Bass, 1976).

42. Erin J. Brock, *Centenary College of Louisiana* (Charleston, SC: Arcadia, 2000), 45–46.

43. Wellesley College Web site, college president's page, www.wellesley.edu/PublicAffairs/President/president.html.

44. John Scholte Nollen, *Grinnell College* (Iowa City: State Historical Society of Iowa, 1953), 103 ff.

45. Nollen, *Grinnell College,* 107.

46. Rita Bornstein, *Legitimacy in the Academic Presidency* (Westport, CT: Praeger, 2003).

47. Bornstein, *Legitimacy in the Academic Presidency*, 13–14.

48. *Newsweek*, 5 January 2004, 78.

Chapter 5. Colleges of Community

Epigraphs: Interview, Morehouse College, 16 January 2003; Cardinal J. H. Newman, *The Idea of a University* (London: Longmans, Green, 1852), 146–48.

1. Campus visit, February 2003.

2. Zelda Gamson and Associates, *Liberating Education* (San Francisco: Jossey-Bass, 1984), 31.

3. Loren Pope, *Colleges That Change Lives* (New York: Penguin, 1996), 3.

4. Interview, April 2003.

5. Douglas A. Heath, *Growing Up in College: Liberal Education and Maturity* (San Francisco: Jossey-Bass, 1968), 241.

6. Alan E. Bayer, "Faculty Composition, Institutional Structure, and Students' College Environment," *Journal of Higher Education* 46, no. 5 (September–October 1975): 549–65.

7. Humphrey Doerman and Henry Drewry, *Stand and Prosper* (Princeton, NJ: Princeton University Press, 2001), 236.

8. National Center for Education Statistics (NCES), *2000 Digest of Educational Statistics* Web site, www.nces.gov. See also Association of American Colleges and Universities (AAC&U), *American Pluralism and the College Curriculum: Higher Education in a Diverse Democracy* (Washington, DC: AAC&U, 1995).

9. AAC&U, *American Pluralism*, xi.

10. *The Compact Edition of the Oxford English Dictionary* (Oxford: Clarendon Press, 1971), 702. A dictionary of sociology (*Iverson's WebRef Sociological Dictionary*) notes that community is "the most ambiguous word used by sociologists!"

11. Gamson, *Liberating Education*, 170.

12. Morehouse College catalog, 2002–3, 75, 64, 95.

13. Bratton, *Southwestern*, 27–28.

14. Martin Van Der Werf, "Money and Management: Mount Senario's Final Act," *Chronicle of Higher Education*, 14 June 2002, www.chronicle.com.

15. Colby-Sawyer College catalog, 2001–2, 2–5.

16. *Wellesley Bulletin*, 92, no. 1 (September 2002): 4.

17. Robert D. Putnam, *Bowling Alone* (New York: Simon and Schuster, 2000).

18. Putnam, *Bowling Alone*, 405. Roger Barker and Paul Gump, in *Big School, Small School: High School Size and Student Behavior* (Stanford: Stanford University Press, 1964), similarly make the case that the qualities inherent in small high schools support characteristics that have been associated with effective high schools.

19. Howard R. Bowen, *Investment in Learning: The Individual and Social Value of American Higher Education* (San Francisco: Jossey-Bass, 1978), 142–57.

20. Bowen, *Investment in Learning*, 143.

21. See, for example, G. Gallop, *Attitudes of College Students on Political, Social, and Economic Issues* (Princeton: Gallup Poll, 1975), Daniel Yankelovich, *The New Morality* (New York: McGraw-Hill, 1974).

22. Campbell, Converse, Miller, and Stokes, *The American Voter* (New York: Wiley, 1960).

23. Yankelovich, *New Morality*, 120–21.

24. Bowen, *Investment in Learning*, 248.

25. David G. Winter, David C. McClelland, and Abigale J. Stewart, *A New Case for the Liberal Arts: Assessing Institutional Goals and Student Development* (San Francisco: Jossey-Bass, 1981), 90–95.

26. Winter, McClelland, and Stewart, *New Case for the Liberal Arts*, 116–17.

27. D. A. Heath, *Growing Up in College: Liberal Education and Maturity* (San Francisco: Jossey-Bass, 1968).

28. This information about student participation opportunities is gleaned from the Wellesley College Web site, www.wellesley.com; the 2002 "Wellesley facts" brochure; and the 2002 Wellesley College view book.

29. Burton R. Clark, *The Distinctive College: Antioch, Reed, and Swarthmore* (Chicago: Aldine, 1970), 257.

30. Campus visit, March 2003.

31. Gamson, *Liberating Education*, 107.

32. Campus visit, December 2002.

33. Michael McPherson and Morton Owen Shapiro, "The Future Economic Challenges for the Liberal Arts Colleges," in *Distinctively American: The Residential Liberal Arts College*, ed. S. Koblik and S. R. Graubard (New Brunswick: Transaction Publishers, 2000), 71.

34. Ernest J. Pascarella, "Student-Faculty Informal Contact and College Outcomes," *Review of Educational Research* 50 (Winter 1980): 571.

35. Arthur Chickering and J. McCormick, "Personality Development and the College Experience," *Research in Higher Education* 1 (1973): 64.

36. Arthur W. Chickering and Zelda Gamson, "Seven Principles for Good Practice in Undergraduate Education," *Wingspread Journal* 9, no. 2 (June 1987): 1.

37. Eva T. H. Brann, "The American College as *the* Place for Liberal Learning," in Koblik, *Distinctively American*, 168.

38. Interview, April 2003.

39. Interview, 12 February 2003.

40. Interviews, Centenary College and Southwestern University, 10 and 12 February 2003.

41. Comment recorded during a conversation with a faculty member at Morehouse College, Atlanta, January 2003.

42. Richard Ekman, telephone interview, 21 January 2003.

43. William G. Perry Jr., *Forms of Intellectual and Ethical Development in the College Years: A Scheme* (New York: Holt, Rinehart and Winston, 1970), 213.

44. Francis Oakley, *Community of Learning* (New York: Oxford University Press, 1992), 152.

Chapter 6. The Integrated Campus

1. Francis Oakley, *Community of Learning* (New York: Oxford University Press, 1992), 171.

2. Jerry Gaff in conversation with the author, February 2003.

3. Zelda Gamson and Associates, *Liberating Education* (San Francisco: Jossey-Bass, 1984), 40.

4. Gamson, *Liberating Education*, 125–26.

5. Carnegie Foundation for the Advancement of Teaching, *Missions of the College Curriculum: A Contemporary Review with Suggestions* (San Francisco: Jossey-Bass, 1977).

6. See G. W. Hazzard, "Knowledge Integration in Undergraduate Liberal Learning," *Forum for Liberal Education* 2 (1979): 1–3.

7. Ernest Boyer, *Scholarship Reconsidered: Priorities of the Professoriate* (Princeton: Carnegie Foundation for the Advancement of Teaching, 1990), 54–55.

8. See, for example, Alexander Astin, "How the Liberal Arts College Affects Students," in *Distinctively American: The Residential Liberal Arts College*, ed. S. Koblik and S. R. Graubard (New Brunswick: Transaction Publishers, 2000), 77–100; Arthur W. Chickering and Zelda Gamson, "Seven Principles for Good Practice in Undergraduate Education," *Wingspread Journal* 9, no. 2 (June 1987); Richard Hersh, "Generating Ideals and Transforming Lives," in Koblik, *Distinctively American*, 173–94.

9. Interview during site visit, 10 February 2003, Centenary College.

10. Opening Convocation, Denison University, August 2001.

11. Richard Hersh, "Generating Ideals and Transforming Life: A Contemporary Case for the Residential Liberal Arts College," in Koblik, *Distinctively American*, 180.

12. Parker J. Palmer, *The Courage to Teach* (San Francisco: Jossey-Bass, 1998), 2, 167–68.

13. Campus visit, February 2003.

14. Virginia B. Smith and Alison R. Bernstein, *The Impersonal Campus* (San Francisco: Jossey-Bass, 1979), 17.

15. Centenary College view book, "Centenary: More than a College," 2002, 15.

16. Morehouse College view book, 2002, 13.

17. Wellesley College view book, 2002, 25–27.

18. Warren Wilson College view book, 2002, 25.

19. Martha Nussbaum, *Cultivating Humanity: A Classical Defense of Reform in Liberal Education* (Cambridge: Harvard University Press, 1997). This book won the Grawemeyer Award.

20. Geoffrey Canada, "The Currents of Democracy: The Role of Small Liberal Arts Colleges," in Koblik, *Distinctively American,* 121–22.

21. NSEE Annual Report, spring 2002, administration of the NSSE, by the Indiana University Center for Postsecondary Research and Planning, George D. Kuh, director, 35.

22. Richard Ekman, phone interview, 21 January 2003.

23. University of Minnesota, Office of Planning and Analysis; University of Minnesota, Morris, Office of Institutional Research, 2002–3.

24. Interview, April 2003.

25. Interview at Southwestern University, 12 February 2003.

26. Hersh, "Generating Ideals," 180.

27. See, for example, the exhaustive studies of student "involvement" in Alexander Astin, *What Matters in College: "Four Critical Years" Revisited* (San Francisco: Jossey-Bass, 1993).

28. This material is all from the "College Student Report" of the spring 2002 administration of the NSSE.

29. "How the Liberal Arts College Affects Students," in *Distinctly American,* 77–100, 83.

30. D. G. Winter, D. C. McClelland, and A. J. Stewart, *A New Case for the Liberal Arts* (San Francisco: Jossey-Bass, 1981), esp. 146.

31. *The Compact Edition of the Oxford English Dictionary* (Oxford: Clarendon Press, 1971), 1455.

32. Cardinal J. H. Newman, *The Idea of a University* (Garden City, NY: Image Books, 1959), 145.

Chapter 7. Blurring the Boundaries

Epigraph: Derek Bok, *Higher Learning* (Cambridge: Harvard University Press, 1986), 69.

1. The material about the College of New Rochelle is drawn from the campus visit; the college's Web site, www.cnr.edu; and the college's history, James T. Schleifer, *The College of New Rochelle: An Extraordinary Story* (Virginia Beach: Donning Co., 1994).

2. Deborah W. Thomas, "The Founding of the College of New Rochelle," fact sheet, 2.

3. Site visit and printed materials from George Fox University, esp. the *George Fox University Annual Report: 2000–2001;* and Ralph K. Beebe, *A Heritage to Honor, a Future to Fulfill* (Newberg, OR: Barclay Press, 1991).

4. Saint Leo College Web site, www.saintleo.edu.

5. Information about these consortia comes primarily from two sources. I deliberately visited three members of one consortium, the Associated Colleges of the South (ACS)—Morehouse, Centenary, and Southwestern—and tried to learn how constituents at those three schools view the ACS. Similarly, at other institutions I

learned about specific consortial relations at those colleges. And I visited on the Internet the home pages of the Associated Colleges of the South, the Five College Consortium, the Great Lakes College Association, the Greater Greensboro Consortium, and the Associated Colleges of the Midwest.

6. Virginia Smith and Alison Bernstein, *The Impersonal Campus* (San Francisco: Jossey-Bass, 1979), 28.

7. Centenary College of Louisiana catalog, 2002–3.

8. University of Wisconsin–Superior catalog, 2002–4.

9. Westmont College catalog, 2002–3.

10. NSEE Annual Report, 2002, 35. One assumes these percentages will continue to rise sharply.

11. National Study of Postsecondary Faculty, 1999.

12. Diane Balestri, "Stability and Transformation: Information Technology in Liberal Arts Colleges," in *Distinctively American*, 293.

13. See, for example, Eva Brann, "The American College Is *the* Place for Liberal Learning," in *Distinctively American*, 151–71.

14. Paul Neely, "The Threats to Liberal Arts Colleges," *Daedalus* 129 (Winter 1999): 27 ff. Reprinted in Koblik and Graubard, *Distinctively American;* and online at ELM Expanded Academic ASAP Plus.

15. Neely, "Threats to Liberal Arts Colleges."

16. Joan Digby, *Peterson's Guide to Honors Programs* (Princeton, NJ: Peterson's, 1977).

17. Samuel Schuman, *Beginning in Honors,* 3d ed. (Radford, VA: National Collegiate Honors Council Handbook, 1995).

18. Large university claims of small college qualities, especially in publications designed for student admissions work, closely parallel the claims of small colleges to university diversity and comprehensiveness. Not surprisingly, each is seeking to attract students who see the virtues of both intimacy and breadth.

19. Digby, *Honors Programs,* 340.

20. Calhoun Honors College, Clemson University, Web site, http://virtual.clemson.edu/groups/CUHONORS/.

21. Digby, *Honors Programs,* 379.

22. Ibid., 376.

23. Alexander Meiklejohn, *The Experimental College,* intro. Roland L. Guyotte (1932; rpt., Madison: University of Wisconsin Press, 2001); hereafter cited in the text.

24. Miami University Web site, www.miami.muohio.edu/.

25. Karen Kellogg, "Learning Communities. ERIC Digest," *ERIC Digests,* ED43-512 (Washington, DC: ERIC Clearinghouse on Higher Education, 1999).

26. This and the subsequent information about "learning communities" is taken from the home pages of the institutions described.

27. University of Missouri Web site, www.missouri.edu/.

28. University of Michigan Web site, www.umich.edu/: University Library and Living/Learning Communities.

29. Interview, April 2003.

30. The concluding phrase was suggested by a reader of this manuscript.

Chapter 8. Small College Futures

Epigraph: Frank Aydelotte on becoming president at Swarthmore College, 1921; cited in B. R. Clark, *The Distinctive College* (Chicago: Aldine, 1970), 186.

1. In discussion with the author, February 2003.

2. These and all the following comments regarding constituent hopes and fears are drawn from the campus site visits I conducted for *Old Main*.

3. Campus visit, March 2003.

4. Campus visit.

5. *MLA Newsletter* (Spring 2003).

6. I must note that to me both seemed geographical regions of great interest and charm.

7. Preparing Future Faculty (PFF) national office Web site, www.preparing-faculty.org/.

8. Conversation with Jerry Gaff, director of the PFF program, February 2003.

9. Joseph A Kershaw, in *The Very Small College* (New York: Ford Foundation, 1976), concludes that smaller institutions, while facing rather different fiscal challenges than larger ones, do not, in fact, suffer from "economies of scale."

10. For an illuminating discussion, see Gordon C. Winston, "'Grow' the College? Why Bigger May Be Far from Better," Williams Project on the Economics of Higher Education, DP-60 (October 2001).

11. C. D. Spangler, Asheville, NC, 1992, quoted in the campus newspaper, the *Blue Banner.*

12. Bill Bryson, *The Lost Continent: Travels in Small-Town America* (New York: HarperCollins, 1989).

13. Arthur Vidich and Joseph Bensman, *Small Town in Mass Society* (Princeton, NJ: Princeton University Press, 1958); hereafter cited in the text.

14. E. F. Schumacher, *Small Is Beautiful* (London: Blond and Briggs, 1973); hereafter cited in the text.

15. Wendell Berry, *The Unsettling of America: Culture and Agriculture* (San Francisco: Sierra Club Books, 1977); hereafter cited in the text.

16. Sarah Susanka, *The Not So Big House* (Newtown, CT: Taunton Press, 1998); hereafter cited in the text.

Epilogue

1. An earlier version of this chapter was included in the second edition of A. Leigh Deneef and Craufurd D. Goodwin, *The Academic's Handbook* (Durham:

Duke University Press, 1955), 17–28. Reprinted with permission of Duke University Press.

2. For example, "Coming out of Iowa you're not going to get a job at a research university," says [a new Ph.D. holder], who will happily take a job at [a small college in the Northwest] this fall. "You realize *you're going to have to work your way toward those positions*" (*Chronicle of Higher Education,* 27 July 1994, A16).

Index